Charles Lee Raper

**The Church and Private Schools of North Carolina**

A historical study

Charles Lee Raper

**The Church and Private Schools of North Carolina**
*A historical study*

ISBN/EAN: 9783337003661

Printed in Europe, USA, Canada, Australia, Japan

Cover: Foto ©Lupo / pixelio.de

More available books at **www.hansebooks.com**

# The Church and Private Schools of North Carolina

## A HISTORICAL STUDY

### BY CHARLES LEE RAPER

Published through the kindness of President Dred Peacock. All books referred to are in the library of Greensboro Female College.

# The Church and Private Schools
# of North Carolina

---

## A HISTORICAL STUDY

### BY CHARLES LEE RAPER

GREENSBORO, N. C.:
JOS. J. STONE, BOOK AND JOB PRINTER.
1898.

# CONTENTS.

| | |
|---|---|
| Adams, James | 22 |
| Archibald, Robert | 59 |
| Arndt, Gottfried | 61–62 |
| Asheville Female College | 200–202 |
| The Baptist Female University | 247 |
| Beuthahn | 63 |
| Bingham School | 76–84 |
| Caldwell Institute | 104–106 |
| Caldwell's Log College | 37–44 |
| Carolina Female College | 118–119 |
| Caswell Academy | 75 |
| Catawba College | 226–228 |
| Charlotte Female Institute | 124–125 |
| The Chowan Baptist Female Institute | 219–220 |
| Claremout College | 240 |
| Clio's Nursery and Science Hall | 52–56 |
| Cokesbury School and Early Methodism | 63–67 |
| Crowfield | 35–37 |
| Church of England, First Schools | 21–24 |
| Davenport College | 231–234 |
| Davidson College | 147–166 |
| Earl, Daniel | 24 |
| Edenton Academy | 29–31 |
| Edgeworth Female Seminary | 108–114 |
| The Eighteenth Century Schools | 9–71 |
| Elizabeth College | 246–245 |
| Elon College | 242–245 |
| The Episcopal Theological School | 102–103 |
| The Fayetteville Female Seminary | 120–121 |
| Floral College | 118 |
| German Schools | 60–63 |
| General View, 18th Century | 9–21 |
| Greensboro Female College | 202–219 |
| Greensboro High School | 106–108 |
| Griffin, Charles | 21–23 |
| Guilford College | 166–174 |
| Hico Academy | 75 |
| Horner School | 224–226 |
| Horner and Graves | 128–129 |

| | |
|---|---|
| Some Incorporated Schools | 67-71 |
| Innes Academy | 23-24 |
| Introduction | 3-8 |
| Judson College | 127-128 |
| Kerr, David | 59-60 |
| Lenoir College | 245-246 |
| Littleton Female College | 240-241 |
| Louisburg Female College | 234-235 |
| Lutheran Schools | 60-63 |
| Mashburn | 23 |
| Moir, James | 23 |
| Mount Amoena Female Seminary | 237 |
| Newbern Academy | 24-29 |
| North Carolina College | 230-231 |
| Oak Ridge Institute | 222-224 |
| Oxford Female Seminary | 220-222 |
| Henry Patillo's Schools | 50-52 |
| Peace Institute | 238-240 |
| The Early Presbyterian Schools | 31-35 |
| Queen's Museum | 44-50 |
| Robinson, John | 73-74 |
| Rutherford College | 235-236 |
| Salem Female Academy | 84-102 |
| St. Mary's College | 241-242 |
| St. Mary's School | 198-200 |
| Statesville Female College | 235 |
| Thomasville Female College | 125-127 |
| Trinity College | 174-198 |
| Wake Forest College | 132-147 |
| Wallis, James | 72-73 |
| Warrenton Female College | 114-116 |
| Warrenton Female Collegiate Institute | 116-117 |
| Wayne Female College | 121 |
| Weaverville College | 228-230 |
| Wesleyan Female College | 119-120 |
| Wilson Collegiate Institute | 130 |
| Wilson, John McKamie | 74-75 |
| Yadkin College | 121 |
| Zion Parnassus | 56-58 |

# INTRODUCTION.

To the student of history North Carolina presents many phases and contrasts. It is a queer State, and one often hard to understand. Many classes and distinctions have marked her life. There has been much of politics—often too much. There has been some real industry, though it has sometimes been misguided. There has been intellectual and social culture, but this has been very limited. Indeed it is a State of a number of separate forces, all having something in common, but held together by no very strong ties. The opposition to royal rule and creed early in our existence divorced Church and State; and they have thus remained throughout our history. The country was settled by many different peoples and under various conditions; religious, economic, social and other causes gradually filled up the fertile spots. The English, with a deep love for country aristocracy, with clear distinctions of social classes, with ideas of religion and civil rule of their own, settled and made their mark upon the north-eastern part; the Quakers, of simple and economic, free and peaceful dispositions, opposed to social distinctions, the north-eastern and middle; the Scotch-Irish, of restless and independent natures, made daring and intensely patriotic by the conflicts in their own countries, the south-eastern, along the Cape Fear, and the section of which Charlotte is now the center; the Moravians, peace-loving and energetic, that which is Forsyth county; the Lutherans and Germans, thrifty and prosperous farmers, opposed to city life and crowded conditions, on both sides of the Catawba and between this and the Yadkin; the French Huguenots as far north as Hillsboro and south as the Pedee river; the Swiss and Palatines at the junction of the Neuse and Trent. All these made their distinct markings upon each section and have shown their life in their various institutions, especially their churches and schools.

The State has never been united on any one great question—on any one idea. Planted as separate elements and under various conditions and faiths, the State is but an aggregation of many distinct forces, all in the main having the same end in view, but endeavoring to attain this in different ways and by different methods. This has been and is especially true in matters pertaining to education. Though the State University has existed more than one hundred years and done her part well, yet the majority of men, and all the women until 1892, have received their education from church and private enterprises; and these have failed to reach hundreds and thousands. For the last forty years or so a public school system has been experimented with; and for the past fifteen or twenty years a good many towns have levied a special tax and had graded schools for nine months in the year. Still many, very many, of the white population cannot read and write. There are now almost as many illiterate whites in this State as in all the other of the original thirteen put together. It is within very recent times that changes in public thought and sentiment on this line have taken place; and a good deal of this is due to the worthy efforts of Dr. Charles D.

McIver, President of the State Normal and Industrial College, and Dr. E. A. Alderman, President of the University of North Carolina. While there is an Agricultural and Mechanical College for the whites at Raleigh, an Agricultural and Mechanical College for the negroes and a Normal and Industrial College for white girls at Greensboro, and several schools of a similar nature for negroes at other points, none of them are old enough to belong properly to history. One State, many church and private schools, and a very poor public system, have fought the battle with ignorance; and fought it nobly, but still there is a great deal to do.

The writer does not want to be misunderstood on this point; and does not say these words from a lack of patriotism and true appreciation of his State's history. He has studied very carefully into the real life of its people. He has seen many phases commendable and great; others far below what they might be. There are latent forces in great abundance, but there has been a decided failure to cultivate them. There is strength of character and intellect as vigorous by nature as any state can supply, but it has rarely been moved to its best. The many and great deeds of valor during the Civil War have demonstrated to the world that many of our people have the stuff of which heroes are made. We are quiet and conservative, yet strong and true; and we have done far more in our life than most people give us credit for. Still we have not done by any means up to the extent of our abilities and opportunities; and in the way of deep interest and enthusiasm in education we have perhaps done least.

As a rule the history of the State has never been written, at any rate with much fullness and accuracy. For the most part the standard histories are only political treatise, and ignore the social, religious and intellectual development. With one or two exceptions it is to the church histories, and in many cases these are very meager, that one must go for information on the early schools: Foote's Sketches and Caruther's Life of Caldwell for the Presbyterian; Reichel's History for the Moravian; Bernheim for the Lutheran and German Reformed; Cheshire for the Episcopal; Weeks for the Quakers. On the educational history anything like a full and comprehensive work has never appeared. The only works of any kind on this line are those of Dr. Kemp P. Battle, who has written a short sketch of the University and is now engaged in writing a full history of the same, and Dr. Charles L. Smith, who, in 1888, published through the Bureau of Education, of Washington, the History of Education of North Carolina. Both of these are excellent works as far as they go; the first does not touch the church and private schools at all and the latter very meagerly. So that the forces which have had more to do in the growth and shape of our institutions of society than all others have yet to be searched out and written.

That there is a need for investigation on this line is very apparent. The whole field is full of interest and demands attention. Much of the history of the State is passing away; and soon its recovery will be impossible. Some of the present conflicts are due for the most part to a lack of knowledge and appreciation of our educational history. Much difficulty, however, is met with in obtaining sufficient material; in some cases a large part of the history is lost and its recovery is doubtful. The writer has been collecting material from every obtainable source; and in the case of many of the schools his collection is fairly complete. He has written hundreds of letters to parties directly or indirectly concerned; and shall use in this sketch many of their replies, after they have been compared and condensed. He has at his disposal about twelve hundred different titles on North Carolina, besides a large collection of catalogues, reports and clippings; also has the originals or copies of many of the historical sketches of the schools. Due acknowledgement will be given in the proper place to all the authorities used and to those who have given assistance. The writer would be ungrateful indeed if he did not mention in this connection the kind appreciation and aid of Dr. Dred Peacock, President of the Greensboro Female College, whose collection on North Carolina history for the College Library is about the largest and most complete in existence. In the investigation facts alone have been searched for; and in the writing the plain truth will be the aim. Some statements will perhaps displease, but no ill-will is embodied in them. Some mistakes will doubtless be made, but they will be due to wrong information given. Some rash conclusions may be drawn; the writer's inexperience is his apology.

Before bringing this introduction to a close a few more points are especially worthy of notice. During the early development the Church and School went hand in hand. Wherever there was established a church in most cases a school was annexed. This is notably true with the Presbyterians, and to a large extent with the Lutherans, Germans and Churchmen. As a rule the one who preached for the congregation was also their teacher, and there are a good many instances where the preacher was wanting and the teacher became the "lay-reader" for the churches in his section. The two have all the time been of mutual relation and assistance to each other; the growth of one has been the growth of the other. Their combined influence has been deeply felt in every phase of life. Really, one does not at all understand and appreciate North Carolina history until he has gone to the depths of the church and private institutions of learning. Often peculiar and characteristic ideas in politics and society are found; and in many cases these are due to some teacher or school. Thomas Cooper and Francis Lieber, in South Carolina College, shaped the public thought of the whole State and much of the South for a quarter of a century prior to the Civil War. Thomas Jefferson and the Universiy of Virginia have made a deep mark upon the intellectual, political and religious life of the whole South. In North Carolina the University and other leading schools have played equally as conspicuous a part. In the early period Dr. David Caldwell was the controlling force in the middle section for well nigh sixty years; and he gained entrance into the minds of men through his "log-college" as well as by means of his pulpit. Dr. Braxton Craven, who was the guiding star of Trinity College for about forty years, stamped his great force upon many a one now prominent in religious, literary and political life. The same is true of Dr. Nereus Mendenhall, who moulded and shaped to a large extent the institution now known as Guilford College; and equally true of some leader in every school in the State. Much of the best of our life has been and is in them; much of the history of the State has been made by them. But in reviewing the subject there is much of sadness as well as hope and promise. There has been lack of appreciation and sympathy on almost every hand. Many heroic characters have toiled and spent their lives for the minds of their fellow-men, still have died in want. Strong minds have dwelt among us and great opportunities for intellectual culture have been opened, but few have said "yes."

## CHAPTER I.—THE 18TH CENTURY SCHOOLS.

### GENERAL VIEW.

Some general statements were made in the introductory chapter about these earlier schools. It is the intention to give here the fullest possible account: their origin, growth, relation to church, society and civil government. In the investigation the fact comes out that the State took very little interest and part in these schools. It did practically nothing till the University was projected; and this was at the close of the century, it being chartered December the 11th, 1789, and opened in February, 1795. At this time there was not a single public school; nor did any public system come about for a long time thereafter. In most cases the schools were taught by the preacher of the congregation. The professional teacher was a rarity indeed; and where one is found he was under the church's auspices, and in many ways assisted his section in matters religious. In the whole history of the State the Church and School have gone hand in hand, and each has always been of assistance to the other. These schools were by no means numerous; and ignorance was the common thing among most of the settlers and their children. During the proprietary government (1663-1729) there are on record but two or three little schools, which will be considered later; and from this till the beginning of the nineteenth century the school history is very meager.

Many different interpretations of these facts and conditions have been made. Some have said that the State was first peopled by political and religious refugees, by cut-throats, irreligious and worthless characters. Others have been more favorable in their explanations. To say the least, the character of the early settlers has been and is yet a doubtful question. Williamson, in speaking of the Province up to about the year 1775, says that education was entirely neglected by the settlers as a whole, but that many of the inhabitants were well educated and that some sent their children to the schools in England.[1] Martin, whose history very meagerly covers the period from the settlement to almost the beginning of the War of the Revolution, says that there were only two schools in the whole Province—Edenton and Newbern—and that religion was at a low ebb indeed; that very few ministers of any denomination could be found.[2] The same author, in speaking of the population of about 1703, gives a still more unfavorable view. He makes them as almost total strangers to any religious principles or public worship; declares them to be loose, licentious characters, and persons who regard the fundamental principles of religion with ridicule. He says that they were of various nations and sects; "Scotch Presbyterians, Dutch Lutherans, French Calvinists, Irish Catholics, English Churchmen, Quakers, and Dissenters; Emigrants from Bermuda and the West Indies, which from their late settlements, could not be places remarkable for the education of young people in Christianity and morality."[3] Bancroft says (and Dr. Chas. L. Smith also quotes this on page 130 in his "History of Education in North Carolina"): "Here was a colony of men from civilized life, scattered among forests, hermits with wives and children, resting in the bosom of nature in perfect harmony with the wilderness of their gentle clime. With absolute freedom of conscience, benevolent reason was the simple rule of their conduct."[4] The same

---
1. Williamson's History of North Carolina, Vol. II., p. 82.
2. Martin's History of North Carolina, Vol. II., p. 395.
3. Ibid, Vol. 1, p. 218.
4. Bancroft's United States, Vol. II., p. 154.

historian makes the statement in another place that the first settlers took affairs very easy and had little industry—that they were hunters and tillers of the soil at their leisure; untroubled by external wars; unpolished, but of the highest personal freedom.[1] Many of the wealthy planters had tutors for their children. Others sent them away to colleges: those along the Cape Fear to Harvard; those on the northeast to England.[2] Hawks, who is the most accurate and exhaustive, but whose works cover only from the settlement to the end of the proprietary government (1729), says that among the higher classes there was much learning and that the officers of State had fine education and culture; and cites as illustrations Gale, Little, Moseley, Swan and Lawson.[3] In another place he says that there were many bad men, and a few good ones, (especially among the Quakers).[4] The same eminent author gives copies of several original manuscripts bearing on the subject of religion and culture among the English settlers. He gives a letter from Rev. James Adams to the Secretary of the Society for Propagating the Gospel, dated 18th of September, 1708. This letter is about to this effect: that there were in general three kinds of people in the province: many members of the Church of England who had truth and religion; some Quakers; most of the population made up of the ignorant and of those who neither knew nor professed religion at all; that the Quakers, though they were few in number (about the seventh part), still had great influence in government by the assistance of Governor Archdale, and that they with the Presbyterians who sided with them would soon become strong enough to bear down and break up the Church of

---

1. Bancroft's History of United States, (1879), Vol. II., p. 202.
2. Wheeler's Reminiscences, p. 257.
3. Hawks' History of North Carolina, Vol. II., p. 369.
4. Ibid, Vol. II., p. 338.

England.¹ Wheeler gives the Province a good deal of intelligence and brings up as examples, in addition to the above named, Hyde, Porter, Lillington, Harvey, Sanderson, Pollock, Lowe and others.²

After looking very carefully and extensively into the subject, the writer thinks that the early settlers did in part their duty as to education. It must be confessed that they were negligent, as they are to-day, and that they did not come up to the fullest development that was within their reach. Many points are worthy of consideration in this connection; and from this consideration comes a more favorable view. For a long time the Province was settled only very sparsely—in the fertile spots along the rivers;³ and these settlements were as a rule far apart.⁴ There were few means of communication; and these were poor and tedious. Anything like a common intercourse was for quite a while almost impossible. Life was for a long time individual and separate. There was nothing to stimulate general intelligence and culture. Wild and rugged nature had to be subdued; food for the body was of far greater importance than that of the mind. The soil, the climate, and sometimes the hostility of the Indians, were all against education.⁵ Though the first settlers often had fine training and culture, they were compelled to spend their lives in more active and heroic measures than in literature and teaching. The entire population in 1728, when the Province went back to the Crown, was not more than ten thousand;⁶ and by 1752 it had increased only to about fifty thousand.⁷ Town-building never has taken much hold on this State. There was not a single one

---

1. Hawks' History of North Carolina, Vol. II., pp. 299-300.
2. Wheeler's Reminiscences, p. 259.
3. Colonial Records, Vol. IV., p. 605.
4. Wheeler's Reminiscences, pp. 258-259.
5. Colonial Records, Vol. II., Prefatory Notes.
6. Weeks' Libraries and Literature, p.173; Martin says that there were about 13,000.
7. Weeks' Libraries and Literature, p. 173; Martin, Vol. II., p. 59, gives only 45,000.

until 1704. Bath was built 1704, Newbern 1710, Edenton 1714, Beaufort 1723, Brunswick 1725, Wilmington 1734, Hillsboro 1759, Fayetteville (at first called Campbelltown, afterwards Cross Creek) 1762, Charlotte and Salisbury about 1758.[1] None of these had as many as one thousand inhabitants in 1750. There were scarcely any good sea-ports; and in consequence commerce was almost unknown. Manufacturing was not known at all; and even corn and wheat mills were very scarce.[2]

However, about the middle of the eighteenth century things began to take on a new phase. While in 1752 the population was hardly fifty thousand, yet in 1790 there were more than three hundred and ninety-three thousand. From about 1750 to 1770 there was a great flow in this direction; also a general awakening on educational matters. The Scotch-Irish Presbyterians came in great numbers; and with them came deeper and more practical ideas of religion and culture. Before or as early as 1740 they had begun their settlements along the Eno, Haw and Catawba rivers.[3] In 1736 sixty-four thousand acres of land were secured in Duplin county by Henry McCulloch for settlers from Ulster, Ireland. These were descendants of the Scottish folks whom James I. had influenced to move to Ireland. Ulster saw Scotch and Irish blood mixed together; and after awhile sent this new life forth in search of new lands and homes. A good number came to this State. They have had much to do in the political and industrial, social and intellectual growth. From 1730 to 1740 also came the Scottish Highlanders. They settled the lower Cape Fear. These increased many fold after the fatal battle of Culloden Moor in 1746. The counties of Bladen, Cumberland, Robeson,

---

1. These dates are taken from the standard histories.
2. Colonial Records, Vol. II., Prefatory Notes.
3. Moore's History of North Carolina, Vol. I., p. 64.

Moore, Richmond, Harnett, and some parts of Chatham and Anson, were peopled by these. About 1750 great numbers of the Scotch-Irish from Ulster came to Charleston, South Carolina, and Lancaster county, Pennsylvania. Those in the South soon moved toward the North; while those who at first settled in Pennsylvania came down the Blue Ridge to North Carolina. Here they met and settled permanently.[1] The present counties of Union, Mecklenburg, Gaston, Cabarrus, Lincoln, Rowan, Catawba, Iredell, and Guilford, all bear many of the marks of their life. More churches were built up, and these assumed more energy. Schools became their right arm; patriotism was stirred, quickened and promulgated. The Battle of the Regulators, May 16th, 1771, and the Meklenburg Declaration of Independence of May 20th, 1775, are some of the manifestations of the life of these peoples.[2] The Moravians came about the same time; and their influence upon a large part of Forsyth and Davidson counties has been very strong. Peace, industry, simplicity, virtue and prosperity have been their works; churches and schools have been vital points in their life.[3] In 1751 they purchased about one hundred thousand (98,985) acres of land between the Dan and Yadkin, and named it Wacovia after an estate of Count Zinzendorff in Austria. Upon this tract they built six towns: Bethabara (Old Town), Bethany, Salem, Friedberg, Friedland and Hope. As a rule when the town lot was laid off, in the middle was reserved a place for a church.[4] These people had first settled in Georgia as early as 1735; and they settled there upon the condition that they would not have to take up arms and fight.

---

1. Rev. Jethro Rumple, D.D., in Home Magazine, Mar. 1881; also points taken from his History of Rowan county.
2. Foote's Sketches and Caruther's Life of Caldwell bring out these points in different places.
3. Martin's History of North Carolina, Vol. I., Appendix, p. xxiv.
4. Ibid, Vol. I., Appendix, pp. xxxiii-xxxvii.

This promise to them having been broken, they moved to Pennsylvania about 1739 or 1740 and settled Bethlehem and Nazareth. From there they came to North Carolina for a freer and milder clime.[1] With them, as well as with the Scotch-Irish who came from Pennsylvania, came new ideas of religion, society, schools and state government. Many Germans besides the Moravians came about the same time. They began coming in 1750 and kept it up till about 1775. These Germans, from whom came the Lutheran and German Reformed Churches, first settled in Pennsylvania. Land was hard to get in that State, while Lord Cartaret's in North Carolina was very cheap. Church freedom was also limited there, while here there was perfect liberty of worship.[2] So that much of the middle part of this State was filled up by these "Pennsylvania Dutch," a very industrious, economic, thrifty folk.[3] They scattered for the most part along either side of the Catawba and Yadkin rivers. Alamance, Guilford, Davidson, Rowan, Cabarrus, Stanley, Iredell, Catawba and Lincoln counties owe very much of their condition and life to them.[4] These people are worthy of great consideration; they have formed a distinct and strong element in our life and history. They have been simple, honest farmers; and have always been opposed to living in towns and crowded conditions, and especially to church interference, particularly on the part of the Church of England.[5] The Germans who settled in the western part showed themselves very different on this point to the Swiss and German Palatines who settled near Newbern; these were soon absorbed in matters religious by those about them.

---

1. Bernheim's German Settlements and Lutheran Church in the Carolinas, p.155.
2. Williamson's History of North Carolina, Vol. II., p. 71.
3. Bernheim's German Settlements and Lutheran Church in the Carolinas, p. 153.
4. Ibid, p. 148.
5. Ibid, p. 176.

On the other hand those in the west have always kept their own forms of worship.[1] For a long time they spoke no other than their own language; they read the German Bible and devotional books.[2] They have cared little for intellectual development until recently; tenacious to the creed and customs of their fathers, they kept themselves apart from the ways of the world and out of politics.[3] Cleanliness, order, comfort and prosperity have always been their characteristics. Their churches have been as a rule in the country, and for a long time they were poorly supplied with preachers and teachers. While these people have not had so much to do with the educational interests in a positive way, their example has had great influence; and it is for this reason that they have been spoken of somewhat at length.

The Quakers need mentioning more fully. They have at all times in our history constituted a very distinct part. They are like the Germans in many ways—in thrift and frugality, in energy and opposition to tyranny and war; also like them in their tenacity to creed. They have been a quiet and peace loving element; bold and aggressive against the established Church—the leader in religious liberty during the first half of the eighteenth century, as the Presbyterian was the latter half.[4] They were at first in Perquimans and Pasquotank. About 1703 they went southwest; and by 1760 are found in Hyde, Beaufort, Craven, Carteret, Jones, Bladen, Lenoir, Northampton, Hertford, Bertie and Halifax counties.[5] From the middle of the century to about 1783 came a new element from New Jersey, Pennsylvania and

---
1. Bernheim, p. 179.
2. Ibid, p. 154.
3. Ibid, pp. 185-186.
4. Weeks' Southern Quakers and Slavery, p. 145.
5. Ibid, pp. 86-88.

Nantucket's Island.[1] They settled in the middle part of the State—Guilford, Alamance, Chatham, Randolph and Surry. Their purpose of coming was in the main economic.[2] They came at about the same time as the Scotch-Irish and Germans and for the same reasons. While they have not been such a large portion of our population, however, by their systematic and earnest life and decided views on matters religious and educational, they have had great influence in shaping the State's sentiment and growth.

The writer has now given a general view of the first settlement; and has traced the filling up of the different sections. In the main he has left the reader to draw his own conclusions about the character and condition of the early history as a whole. In this connection it is well to give some points more in favor of our early life than were given in the first part of this sketch. Wheeler says on page 30 of his Historical Sketches: "No freer country was ever organized by man. Freedom of conscience, security from taxation except by their own consent, were their first objects. The emigrant was exempted from taxation for a year; every emigrant received a bounty of land. These simple laws suited a simple people, who were as free as the air of their mountains; and when oppressed were as rough as the billows of the ocean. They submitted to no unjust laws, they bowed the knee to no earthly monarch." Another historian says that our people were bent upon following their own views in civil government and religion[3]; and that they have been slow to change their convictions and have been very loyal to what they held as truth.[4] There was some religion, but it was local and not widely

---

1. Weeks' Quakers and Slavery, p. 96.
2. Ibid, p. 96.
3. Moore's History of North Carolina, Vol. I., Introduction, p. xiv.
4. Ibid, Vol. I., Introduction, p. xv.

felt. There was some learning; it was among the few. There was some of wealth and comfort; it was confined to the indolent gentleman. There were some collections of books, but these were private. There have been a good many churches and a few schools, but affairs have been too different and scattered to be deeply moved by them. Sea-coasts, lowlands, rivers, valleys, hills and mountains; Churchmen, Quakers, Presbyterians, Germans, Moravians, Lutherans, Baptists and Methodists (the latter two not being of great force until the 19th century)—all have had their distinct influences upon our history, especially for the first century and a half. We then came very little in contact with the outside world; there was nothing to stir us up or polish us. We became negligent, indifferent and in many ways rude; we had not reached the industrial stage in development—agriculture and hunting were our means of support. The Colonists were not so ignorant as they were unappreciative of the benefits of literature. They had some books as early as 1680. In 1705 the circulating library, which Rev. Thomas Bray, D. D., a representative of the Society for Propagating the Gospel, had given the Colony in 1700, was established at Bath. It was intended for the clergy and was made up of religious books for the most part.[1] The collection was worth about one hundred pounds.[2] Rev. James Adams, another representative of the Society for Propagating the Gospel, left his library, valued at about ten pounds,[3] in Currituck[4] in 1710. According to Dr. S. B. Weeks, there was one more library—perhaps two—in the beginning of the century. He thinks that Urmstone about 1708 had one

---

1. Colonial Records, Vol. II, p. 119; and Weeks' Libraries and Literature, pp. 177-179.
2. Ibid, Vol. II, p. 130.
3. Ibid, Vol. II, p. 75.
4. Ibid, Vol. I, p. 858.
3 and 4 are also given by Weeks in his Libraries and Literature, pp. 185-186.

more library—perhaps two—in the beginning of the century. He thinks that Urmstone about 1708 had one of some size and value, and that it doubtless followed him around in his work; also that there was possibly one belonging to Rainsford in 1712.[1] In the Cape Fear section there were no books until after the middle of the century. About 1755 the St. James Parish received some Bibles, prayer-books and such like from the Society.[2] This Society for Propagating the Gospel ended its existence in 1776. During its life it had had a great influence in teaching the young colony; and its influence was as much educational as religious. Dr. Weeks thinks that it sent to North Carolina as many as six hundred bound volumes and about two hundred pounds worth of tracts.[3]

In 1720 Edward Moseley, the greatest man in the Province for fifty years,[4] gave tenpounds to the Society for buying books, but it seems that they were never bought. In 1723 he gave also seventy-six volumes for a public library to be kept at Edenton,[5] which was for a long time the center of culture. His own private collection was large for that time, amounting to about four hundred volumes.[6] The Johnston library, which is now owned by Mr. John G. Wood, of "Hayes," about one-half a mile from Edenton, goes back to times as early as the Moseley collection.[7] There are evidences of the existence of several other private libraries in the eastern half of the State: Col. James Innes, at Point Pleasant, near Wilmington, in 1759, bequeathed his library to a free school;[8] John Hodgson, speaker of the

---
1. Weeks' Libraries and Literature, pp. 185-186.
2. Ibid, pp. 186-187, giving as his authority, Burr, Sketch of St. James Parish, Wilmington, pp. 18-22.
3. Weeks' Libraries and Literature, p. 187.
4. Ibid, p. 193.
5. Ibid, p. 189.
6. Ibid, p. 196.
7. Ibid, p. 198.
8. Waddell's A Colonial Officer and His Times, pp. 53-54.

house of commons in 1739 and 1741; James Iredell, a Justice of the Supreme Court of the United States in 1790—a citizen of Chowan county; William Hooper, the signer, who lived in Wilmington; Joseph R. Gautier, in Bladen, a member of the house of commons in 1791, gave his valuable collection to the University;[1] Willie Jones, who died in 1801, a citizen of Halifax county, had a fine and large one; and John Burgwyn, who died about the same time at the "Hermitage," near Wilmington.[2] There were doubtless more. Edenton, Newbern and Wilmington, in the eastern half of the State, were centers of culture; and if the whole truth were known, many more evidences of early training and education in and around these places would come to light. Dr. Weeks, whose statements the writer always finds true, says: "I think it accurate to say that the political leaders of the Colony of North Carolina at the time of the Revolution were better acquainted with the literature of their times than the leaders of political North Carolina are to-day with either contemporary English or American literature."[3] This was said in connection with the English life and culture as found in the eastern part. When a view is taken of the western, with Salisbury, Charlotte and Fayetteville as centers, as much may justly be said. These places were dominated by the Scotch-Irish and Scotch elements; and give many evidences of education, culture and religion. They had both libraries and schools. These libraries were in almost every case private: Waighstill Avery, who settled in Charlotte in 1769; Rev. David Caldwell, D. D., who began his "log college" three miles northwest of Greensboro about 1767; Rev. James Hall, D. D.,

---

1. Battle's Address on the History of Raleigh, p. 17.
2. Weeks' Libraries and Literature, pp. 206-208; a good many of the points on the libraries have been taken from him; Wheeler has also been consulted.
3. Weeks' Libraries and Literature, p. 200.

who was another pioneer of religion and education, located in Iredell; Rev. John Barr, of Rowan; Rev. Lewis Fenilleteau Wilson, of Iredell; Rev. Henry Patillo, of Orange; Gen. Joseph Graham, of Lincoln; and Rev. Samuel Eusebius McCorkle, D. D., at Thyatira.[1] There were a few public or circulating libraries after the Revolution: Mecklenburg,[2] Iredell,[3] Thyatira, founded by Rev. John Barr;[4] Centre Benevolent Society of Mecklenburg and Rowan.[5] These libraries have been spoken of to a greater extent than a sketch of this nature and length will perhaps justify. The intention is to give that which will most clearly present the educational conditions. These libraries have been of great influence in making such conditions; and the conditions have made and called for the schools.

### THE FIRST SCHOOLS—CHURCH OF ENGLAND.

The first report of any schools in the Province is from Dr. John Blair, a missionary to the Colony in 1704. From his reports we find that the first churches had lay-readers to supply them with sermons.[6] These lay-readers were teachers in almost every case. While the Scotch-Irish Presbyterians have given more teachers to the State than any other church—more than all the others together during the eighteenth century—still the first assistance to intellectual life was given by the Church of England.[7] The first teacher was Charles Griffin, who came from the West Indies to Pasquotank about 1705.[8] His school was very prosperous for a short

---
1. Weeks' Libraries and Literature, pp. 214-216; Caruther's Life of Caldwell, Foote's Sketches and Wheeler.
2. Foote's Sketches, pp. 248-249.
3. Ibid, p. 330.
4. Weeks' Libraries and Literature, p. 221.
5. Ibid, p. 221.
6. Colonial Records, Vol. I, p. 601.
7. Brickell's Natural History, p. 35.
8. Cheshire's Sketches of Church History in North Carolina; Paper by Rev. R. B. Drane, pp. 163-164.

while, and was patronized by all classes and churches. At first his character and behavoir were so fine that even the Quakers sent to him.[1] He taught in Pasquotank till about 1708. In Hawks' History, Vol. II, pp. 299-300, is given a copy of an original manuscript letter from Rev. William Gordon to the Secretary of the Society for Propagating the Gospel, dated May 13, 1709. In this, after giving some account of the different precincts of the north-eastern part, (Chowan, Perquimans, Pasquotank, Currituck and Bath), Mr. Gordon says: "The next precinct is Pasquotank, where as yet there is no church built; the Quakers are here very numerous; the roads are, I think, the worst in the county; but it is closer settled than others, and better peopled in proportion to its bigness. In their way of living they have much the advantage of the rest, being more industrious, careful and cleanly; but above all I was surprised to see with what order, decency and seriousness they performed the public worship, considering how ignorant the people are in other parishes. This we owe to the care of one Mr. Griffin, who came here from some part of the West Indies, and has for three years past lived amongst them, being appointed reader by their vestry, whose diligent and devout example has improved them so far beyond their neighbors, and by his discreet behavior has gained such good character and esteem that the Quakers themselves send their children to his school, though he has prayers twice a day at least, and obliges them to their responses, and all the other decencies of behavior as well as others." In 1708 Rev. James Adams moved to Pasquotank and took charge of the school,[2] and Mr. Griffin went to the precinct and Parish of Chowan. Here he became lay-reader of the church and clerk of

---

1. Colonial Records, Vol. I., p. 714.
2. Ibid, Vol. I, p. 714.

the vestry; also opened a school. He was selected for the above duties at the suggestion of Mr. Gordon and received for his work for the church and vestry twenty pounds a year.[1] It seems that his school here did not succeed very well. From the records of that time, one would suppose that he became a Quaker and sinner;[2] his school here lasted but a short while at any rate. Of Mr. Adams' school in Pasquotank nothing is known. In 1712 a Mr. Mashburn had a little school at Sarum, on the border of North Carolina and Virginia. The Indians also attended this school.[3] Rev. G. Rainsford, a missionary to the Province, says of the school, writing July 25, 1712, that the teacher was well deserving of encouragement and that he should be given a salary; that the pupils under his care could read and write, and had the principles of the christian religion; that the Bible had been one of his text books.[4]

These schools of Griffin, Adams and Mashburn are the only ones under the proprietors of which there is any record. One would judge that they cared nothing for schools or churches, but only for taxes. For some time after the Province went back to the Crown local schools were unknown. The wealthy planters sent their sons to England or Harvard, or had tutors in their own homes. The next school is found in New Hanover. Rev. James Moir, a representative of the Society for Propagating the Gospel, at Brunswick, in 1745, used the down stairs of his house for a chapel and school-room.[5]

In 1759 Col. James Innes died at Wilmington. By his will, which was made in 1754 and proved before

---

1. Colonial Records, Vol. I, p. 681.
2. Ibid, Vol. I, p. 721.
3. Ibid, Vol. I, p. 859. Dr. Charles L. Smith gives his name as Washburn (p. 17, History of Education in North Carolina), but he must be mistaken; Weeks and Drane both give it as Mashburn.
4. Colonial Records, Vol. I, p. 859; also quoted by Smith (p. 17) and Drane (p. 165).
5. Colonial Records, Vol. IV, p. 755; also Drane—Church History, p. 166.

Gov. Dobbs at Newbern in 1759, his plantation, Point Pleasant, near Wilmington, his large personal estate, his library and one hundred pounds sterling were given for the use of a school. This was the first gift for educational purposes in the State. The trustees were: "The Colonel of the New Hanover regiment, the parson of Wilmington Church, and the vestry for the time being, or a majority of them." Not very much was recovered from his property for school purposes, as the houses were burned. However, by an act of the Legislature of 1783 the Innes Academy was started on foot; and it was kept up for some time by private subscriptions.[1] About 1763 a school for the higher education of the youth was kept at Bandon, about fifteen miles above Edenton on the Chowan river, by Rev. Daniel Earl and his daughter, Miss Nancy. The course included Latin, Greek, English branches and Mathematics. Mr. Earl was at the same time rector of St. Paul's Parish of Chowan; and his school had quite a good deal of influence in promoting correct principles of religion.[2]

### NEWBERN ACADEMY.

In 1764 the school idea took hold of Newbern, and provisions were at once made for opening one there. This school has been claimed as a State institution by some; by others it has been considered as purely a church enterprise. The truth seems to be that it has some of both in its history, but that for the most part it was a church or private school. The first mention of this is an act by the Assembly of 1764, by which a school building was to be erected on the church property by

---

1. See Waddell's A Colonial Officer and His Times, pp. 53-54. This is given by Weeks in his Libraries and Literature, p. 206. Drane also gives it, but states that the gift was made in 1754. The will was made in 1754, but not proved till 1759.
2. Drane—Church History, pp. 168-169.

private subscription.[1] Mr. Drane quotes from a letter of Rev. James Reed to the Society for Propagating the Gospel, dated June, 1764: "We have now a prospect of a very flourishing school in the town of New Berne. In December last Mr. Tomlinson came here . . . . . and, on the first of January, he opened a school in this town and immediately got as many scholars as he could instruct; and many more have lately offered than he could possibly take, to do them justice. He has therefore wrote to his friends in England to send him an assistant."[2] The next year the people of Newbern petitioned Governor Tryon to get the Society to give Mr. Tomlinson a salary for teaching their children useful knowledge and the principles of the Church of England.[3] The Society made the grant, and gave him ten pounds that year and fifteen for the next.[4] Mr. Drane thinks that this fifteen pounds became a regular annual stipend. A new building was doubtless completed by 1766. At this time the school was in a very prosperous condition. The preamble to the act of the Assembly says: "Whereas, a number of well disposed persons, taking into consideration the great necessity of having a school established, whereby the rising generation may be brought up and instructed in the principles of the Christian Religion and fitted for the several offices and purposes of life, have, at a great expense, erected and built, in the town of New Berne, a convenient house for the purpose aforesaid; and being desirous that the same may be established by law on a permanent footing, so as to answer the good purposes of the said persons intended, therefore trustees were to be elected to whom a charter should be given."[5]

---

1. Drane—Church History, p. 169.
2. Colonial Records, Vol. VI, p. 1048.
3. Drane—Church History, pp. 169-170.
4. Ibid, p. 170.
5. Ibid, p. 170.

A provision was made for a tax on rum, in order to raise twenty pounds a year for the master and his assistant. In return for this money the teacher admitted ten poor children free of tuition, upon the advice of the trustees. It was required that the master be a member of the Church of England, as well as be licensed by the Governor.[1] This school was begun as a private and church affair; and so it remained. The provision, by which the institution received a penny a gallon for all the rum imported and in return gave free tuition to ten poor children, was but a trade and did not take it from the hands of the Church. The Trustees, appointed in 1764, were: Rev. James Reed, rector of the Parish, John Williams, Joseph Leech, Thomas Clifford Howe, Thomas Haslen, Richard Cogdell and Richard Fenner.[2] The ground for the school purposes was taken from the church yard. Rev. James Reed was the chief mover in all this educational movement and work; his name stands at the head of the original trustees; and also at the head of the thirty-nine leading citizens who petitioned Governor Tryon to secure an annual stipend for the teacher, Mr. Tomlinson. It was he who obtained and collected the subscriptions.[3] The building was forty-five feet long and thirty wide. Mr. Tomlinson, who began work in this new house about 1766, taught to the satisfaction and benefit of his fellowmen for several years. According to statements of both Governor Tryon and Mr. Reed, he was the only person of his profession who had good repute and could run a school successfully in the colony; he was also a good collector of tuition bills. In 1765 he had thirty pupils, from whom he received twenty shillings by the quarter in proclama-

---

1. Drane—Church History. p. 170.
2. Sketches of Church History in North Carolina, note by the Editor, Rt. Rev J. B. Cheshire, Jr., D. D., p. 172.
3. Ibid, p. 173.

tion money. This was increased by the grant from the Society. In 1766 he was given twelve pounds for acting as lay-reader during the absence of Mr. Reed.[1] The income from the rum tax turned out to be more than was ever expected. In 1768 it brought to the trustees something like sixty pounds. There was also another source of income. The two half lots from the church yard, which belonged to the school, were leased for twenty-one years and the money from them went annually to the school fund. The first board of trustees was under the influence of Mr. Reed and the Church. When the new one came in, which was not long after the real beginning of the institution, they, to a large extent, cut themselves loose from the Church's jurisdiction; and in consequence some difficulties soon arose.[2] However, the school still continued as a church institution; and its prosperity for some time was rather marked. The first assistant, as far as there is any record, was Mr. James McCartney. He served from the beginning of the year 1767 till May 1768. In the Academy building were held the Assemblies of 1768, '69, '70 and '71. For the first year twenty pounds were given for its use; and afterwards the amount was increased to forty. In 1772 the Trustees had some trouble with Mr. Tomlinson and dismissed him. Mr. Reed took his part and defended him strongly; and in his defense said that he had been a great teacher in every respect. Mr. Tomlinson, however, was not reinstated and moved to Rhode Island. His leaving was with much regret on the part of the Society, at least, as they gave him a farewell gift of fifteen pounds.[3] He seems to have been the first professional teacher in North Carolina. His influence upon a large section of the country around Newbern was great.

---
1. Church History, note by the Editor, p. 174,
2. Ibid, pp. 174-175.
3. Ibid, p. 176.

From the time he left till about 1792 it is difficult to say who taught, or whether any one. It seems rather probable that Dr. Solomon Halling, who was born in Pennsylvania and was a physician by profession, was teaching in the Academy in 1792, when he was ordained deacon. He was a man of great force, and served with much acceptance the Church in Newbern until his removal to Wilmington in 1795. Whether he was also teacher from 1792 to 1795 we have no records. Among the subscribers to Francis Xavier Martin's Private Statutes of North Carolina, published in 1795, the name of Thomas Pitt Irving, A. M., Principal of Newbern Academy, is found. How long he had been principal before this is unknown. During his term the old building of Mr. Reed's was burned;[1] so also was Tryon's Palace, which was used as the school house after the destruction of the Academy. He does not seem to have had much force. He remained in charge of the Church until 1813; whether he was teacher in the Academy so long we cannot say. It is very probable that there was no school for some time after the burning of the Tryon Palace. Dr. Vass, in his History of the Presbyterian Church in Newbern, says on page 75 that the present brick building was erected in 1806. The writer finds no record of any school between this time and the burning of the Palace. He also states that Gaston, Badger, Stanley, Spaight, Hawks, and many others equally as great, were educated in the older building. This brings the eighteenth century part to a close. However, as the history of the school is in the main continuous, the nineteenth century part will also be given in this connection. Rev. George Strebeck took charge of both the pulpit and the school-room in 1813. He had as an assistant in 1814 Mr. John Phillips. They

---

1. Cheshire—Church History, Decay and Revival, p. 258.

both left about 1815. In 1816 Rev. Jehu Curtis Clay took charge of both the school and Church.[1] Rev. Edward B. Freeman, D. D., was principal 1818-1819. He filled the same place some years before, but the writer has not been able to find out when or how long. He was followed by Mr. Fredrick Freeman. The school was then in a very flourishing condition, there being almost two hundred pupils. He was succeeded by Mr. Robert G. Moore; and he in turn gave place to Mr. William B. Wadsworth, who held it for several years. So far as can be ascertained he gave up the work about 1834. Mr. Edward Hughes was then principal for some time. Messrs. Mayhew, Gordon and Bryant guided the institution to the beginning of the Civil War. Mr. Gordon was principal for about two years; the other two were in control for quite a while each, and both succeeded well.[2]

### EDENTON ACADEMY.

Edenton came right along with Newbern in educational ideals and works. As early as 1770 two lots had been bought and a house built. During this year the school was chartered, according to which the teacher was to be a Churchman.[3] The money for the building was obtained by private subscription. Joseph Blount, Joseph Hewes, Robert Hardy, Thomas Jones, George Blair, Richard Brownrigg and Samuel Johnston were the first trustees. These were all Churchmen, members of St. Paul's Parish. The school in this place was very much like the one in Newbern, though it never received any money from the State Government. The teacher and minister sometimes

---

1. Cheshire—Church History, Decay and Revival, p. 259.
2. Letter from Col. John D. Whitford, of Newbern.
3. Drane—Church History, p. 171.

interchanged their work here. The requirement that the teacher had to be a Churchman was not carried out. Messrs. Pettigrew and Freeman were Presbyterian preachers when they took charge; and Mr. Avery, another teacher, was a member of the Congregation Church.[1] As the eighteenth and nineteenth century parts of the history of this school are so closely connected, they will be considered together, as in the case of the one at Newbern. Mr. Pettigrew, at first a Presbyterian preacher, had charge in 1773; and it seems that he continued principal till his death in 1808. Then Rev. Jonathan Otis Freeman, a brother of Bishop Freeman, took charge. During the year 1809 the Trustees paid him six hundred dollars for his services in the Academy and four hundred "for delivering lectures to the students on the Sabbath." He was a man of fine ability and culture; and had great influence upon his community. In 1811 he turned over both the Church and Academy to Rev. Fredrick W. Hatch, of Maryland. He received the same salary for the first year. At the end of 1811 he gave up the school-room to Mr. John Avery, though he continued as preacher till 1815. Mr. Avery became lay-reader in 1815, and soon afterward turned his entire attention to the ministry.[2] He was a native of Massachusetts; went to Williams' College, afterwards to Yale, where he graduated in 1812. Though a son of a Congregation deacon, he became a Churchman soon after he took charge of the Academy. He was ordained deacon in 1817 and priest in 1818; and continued as rector of St. Paul's Church, of Edenton, until 1835. He was a man of fine learning, and commanded the respect of all.[3]

Both the Newbern and Edenton academies had much

---

1. Drane—Church History, note by the Editor, p. 179.
2. Cheshire—Church History, Decay and Revival, p. 256.
3. Ibid, p. 257.

to do in the political, social, intellectual and religious development of the eastern part of the State; they were the sources of life and light for a long while. The early history of the State was to a large extent in the hands of the men of the east; and these had come in contact with such centers. Bishop Cheshire says, in his note to Drane's paper on the Colonial Parishes and Church Schools: "If the roll of the pupils of these two academies could be recovered, and if the story of their influence upon the public men of North Carolina from 1790-1835 could be fully told, it would probably be found that only the University of the State has had a greater effect in our history than these two Colonial Schools."[1]

### THE EARLY PRESBYTERIAN SCHOOLS.

As has already been mentioned, these schools played a very important part in the early culture and life of the State. The Presbyterians were leaders of intellectual and religious growth during the latter half of the eighteenth century. They introduced a new life principle, and gave vigor and enthusiasm to many sections, especially in those along the Cape Fear river and in Guilford, Alamance, Orange, Rowan, Cabarrus, Mecklenburg and Iredell counties. They were a restless and energetic people, and taught and loved patriotism. Many of the first conflicts between the inhabitants of the Province and the royal Governors took place among them.[2] They have been more thoroughly devoted to education than any other denomination. It has meant life as well as light to them; it has made them independent and patriotic, strong and noble. They were really our first teachers, and during the latter half of the eighteenth

---
1. Church History, p. 179.
2. See Foote's Sketches and Caruther's Life of Caldwell.

century they were well nigh our only ones. While the Church of England furnished some, still taking the whole Colony into consideration, it was the Presbyterian who preached, and governed the school-room. In almost every case when a church was organized a school soon became a permanent fixture; and the preacher was the teacher.[1] As proof of the above assertion Sugar Creek, Poplar Tent, Centre, Bethany, Buffalo, Thyatira, Grove, Wilmington and the churches of Henry Patillo in Orange and Granville counties, all had schools taught by the pastor.[2]

In these schools as well as in the churches the college of New Jersey (or Nassau Hall, now called Princeton College) had great influence. Look over the roll of most of the great characters of this State during the last century, and one will find a very large number of them graduates or students of this famous institution; it was the never failing source of life and light to this dark Colony. Dr. Charles L. Smith gives three full pages to its influence;[3] and much more could be written. In this sketch, however, only the principal names will be mentioned. Rev. Hugh McAden, of the class of 1753, a native of Pennsylvania, came here in 1755 and became the real founder of the Presbyterian Church in this State and much of the South.[4] Alexander Martin, a Colonel in the Revolutionary War, Governor in 1782 and again in 1789, Senator in United States Senate from 1793 to 1799, was educated there.[5] Rev. Alexander McWhorter, a native of New Jersey, who came to Charlotte as president of Liberty Hall Academy in 1780, was of the class

---

1. See Foote's Sketches for these general statements about the Presbyterian Schools.
2. Foote's Sketches, p. 513.
3. Smith's History of Education in North Carolina, pp. 23-26.
4. Foote's Sketches, pp. 158-160.
5. Smith's History of Education, p. 24; Wheeler's Historical Sketches, Vol. II, pp. 181-182.

of 1757.[1] Rev. Joseph Alexander, the preacher and teacher of Sugar Creek for some time after 1766 and the promoter of Queen's Museum, was of the class of 1760.[2] Rev. David Caldwell, the great preacher and teacher of Guilford county, was of the class of 1761.[3] Ephraim Brevard, M. D., and Waightstill Avery, Esq., the first the great and leading spirit of the Mecklenburg Declaration of Independence and the second a promoter of education and culture, were of the classes of 1768 and 1766.[4] Isaac Alexander, M. D., at one time president of Liberty Hall Academy, of the class of 1772;[5] Rev. James Hall, of Clio's Nursery, 1774; William R. Davie and Nathaniel Alexander, Governors of the State 1798 and 1805,[6] of the class of 1776; Rev. Joseph Caldwell, D. D., president of the University of North Carolina from 1797-1812 and 1816-1835, of the class of 1791;[7] Judge William Gaston, perhaps our most illustrious jurist, of the class of 1796.[8] These are but a few of the many strong characters in our early history who were educated there.

In this connection the efforts of the New York and Pennsylvania Synods should be mentioned. The first churches and schools in most of the Colony were due to their worthy missionary works. Many Presbyterians had come to North Carolina before they began to consider this as missionary territory. Among those who first came there were very few who had fine education or culture. The Synods of the North saw their opportunity and sent to this and others of the Southern Colonies enthusiastic and learned preachers and teachers; and it

---
1. Foote's Sketches, p. 514.
2. Ibid, p. 513; Smith, p. 24.
3. Caruther's Life of Caldwell, p. 19.
4. Foote's Sketches, p. 515; Smith, p. 24.
5. Foote's Sketches, p. 322.
6. Wheeler's Historical Sketches, Vol. I, p. 98.
7. Foote's Sketches, p. 538.
8. Wheeler's Historical Sketches, Vol. II, p. 114.

was this new element that gave such life to the middle part of North Carolina.¹

When we come to decide upon the oldest of these schools much uncertainty and difficulty are met with. The fact seems to be that several of them were begun about the same time. Foote, on page 513 of his Sketches, says that the one within the bounds of the Sugar Creek congregation seems to be the oldest. Rev. Alexander Craighead was pastor from Sept. 2, 1757 to March, 1766.² Rev. Joseph Alexander, a relative of the McKnitt Alexanders, was his successor. He was licensed by New Castle Presbytery in 1767, and during October of the same year he accepted the call to Sugar Creek.³ He seems to have been a very fine scholar, a graduate of the class of 1760 at Nassau Hall. Foote says that he in connection with a Mr. Benedict taught a classical school of high excellence.⁴ How long this school was kept here there is no record; nor could it have begun sooner than 1768. Mr. Alexander went from Sugar Creek to Bullock's Creek, South Carolina, and remained there a long time as preacher and teacher; and had the reputation of being a great teacher. Rev. Samuel C. Caldwell, son of Dr. David Caldwell, of Guilford, became pastor of Sugar Creek and Hopewell early in 1792;⁵ and there is no record of another pastor between him and Mr. Alexander. So that it is rather probable that the school here was run for some time after its beginning. As this school could not have begun earlier than 1768, Foote is mistaken in supposing it the first of the Presbyterian

---
1. See Foote and Caruthers for these general statements.
2. Foote's Sketches, pp. 186-192.
3. Ibid, pp. 193-194.
4. Ibid, p. 194.
5. Ibid, p. 194.

schools. He himself says that Rev. James Tate established a classical school in Wilmington in 1760,[1] the first ever opened in that town. He taught here for eighteen years, and educated and influenced many of the young men of New Hanover who took such an active part against the British in the War of the Revolution. His principles were so strong and his patriotism for his adopted country so true, being an Irishman, that he left here during the Revolution and went to Hawfields, Orange county. While he taught for his living, he also preached for many of his faith through New Hanover and the surrounding counties. He was a very striking personality and had great influence wherever he went.[2]

### CROWFIELD.

During the same year (1760) another school was begun in Centre congregation; and many claim this as the first. This congregation was very large at first, filled a broad area from the Yadkin to the Catawba. It had within its bounds many of the greatest men of our early history—the Brevards, Osbornes and Davidsons.[3] Rev. James McRee, D. D., a graduate of Nassau Hall, of the class of 1775, was its pastor from 1798 to about 1828. Davidson College was built and still has its location in this charge. The name of the school was Crowfield. Rev. Jethro Rumple in his History of Rowan County, in speaking of Rev. Alexander Craighead establishing Thyatira, Fourth Creek and Centre churches, says that there were "oldfield" schools in these charges as early as 1758; and that by 1760 there was a classical school at Belle Mont, the old manor of Col. Alexander Osborne, by the name of

---
1. Foote's Sketches, p. 178.
2. Ibid. p. 178.
3. Ibid, pp. 433-434.

Crowfield Academy.[1] This school was about two and one-half miles north-east of the present site of Davidson College, in the lower end of Iredell county, at the head waters of Rocky river and within the bounds of Centre church.[2] It continued for twenty years, until the British invasion in 1780 broke it up.[3] Some of the most learned men of the time conducted this school: Rev. David Kerr, a graduate of the Dublin University, who was later a Professor in the University of North Carolina; Dr. Charles Caldwell, who afterwards became a Professor in a medical school in Philadelphia.[4] Dr. David Caldwell is said to have taught here a short while before he began his work in Guilford.[5] The statement, however, is not well established.

Many great characters were educated here; its influence was deep and wide. Students came even from the West Indies.[6] Mr. Leazer says: "Here in this institution were moulded the minds of some of the bravest spirits and strongest men of that or any day and generation, the men who made glorious history and gave original direction to the civil and ecclesiastical policy of the embryo nation. Here were educated Dr. McRee, the scholarly divine; Dr. James Hall, the learned and military parson; Dr. McCorkle one of the foremost educators the country has ever produced; Col. Adlai Osborne, the wise counsellor and able defender of the people's rights; Dr. Ephraim Brevard, the heaven-inspired author of the Historic Declaration, and probably Hugh Lawson White, a prominent candidate for the

---

1. History of Rowan County, p. 82.
2. Rev. E. F. Rockwell, D. D., in North Carolina Journal of Education, July,1859, pp. 204-206.
3. Foote's Sketches, p. 484.
4. Address to the Alumni of Davidson College by Hon. A. Leazer, June, 1887, Semi-Centenary Addresses, p. 5.
5. Rumple's History of Rowan County, p. 84.
6. Address by Leazer, p. 6.

Presidency of the United States in 1836."[1] These assertions will perhaps be considered too high praise. Admitting that there may be some of flattery in them, still there is very much of truth. The writer finds that Dr. Rumple, in his History of Rowan County, page 84, fully approves of such statements; also that Dr. Rockwell, Journal of Education, July, 1859, gives equally as strong praise, and to the number given adds: Dr. Alexander Osborne, Dr. William Houston, Professor in Nassau Hall, Adam Springs, E. J. Osborne, Dr. Charles Harris, Rev. James McKnight, Rev. Josiah Lewis, and John Carrigan. Foote gives the name of another principal of this school, Mr. McEwin.[2]

### CALDWELL'S LOG COLLEGE.

The next school in order of time was Caldwell's "Log College," which began in 1766 or 1767, about the same time as the one in Sugar Creek Congregation. In order of importance and length of duration it is by all odds the first; in fact, Dr. David Caldwell has no equal in the whole educational and religious history of the State. He lived in active and heroic times; he moulded and shaped much of North Carolina for sixty years. His life and character are so striking that a rather extensive sketch of him as a preacher and teacher will be given here. However, the writer has been unable to find anything absolutely original on the subject. Most of the points given are taken from Foote's Sketches, Caruthers' Life of Caldwell, Wheeler's Historical Sketches and Reminiscences. The writer has talked with Hon. D. F. Caldwell, of Greensboro, his oldest living descendant, and has obtained from him confirmation of most of the

---
1. Address by Leazer, p. 6.
2. Foote's Sketches, p. 434.

statements made in this connection. Dr. Smith also has given a rather extended view of him; and he has used the same authorities as have been consulted for this sketch.

Dr. Caldwell was born in Lancaster county, Pennsylvania, March the 22nd, 1725. His parents were in fairly good circumstances and were of spotless character.[1] While in his teens he was bound to a house carpenter, for whom he worked till he was twenty-one years of age. He had received the mere rudiments of an English education while a boy, but was twenty-five before he began in deep earnestness to educate himself up to the best of that time.[2] He determined now to make every sacrifice necessary to educate himself for the ministry; and too he had high hope of Christ in his heart. Very little is known of his disposition and talents till he had made up his mind to go to Nassau Hall. While his father had enough means to send him, still he of his own accord made the proposition to his brothers, that, if they would supply him with the necessary money with which to go through college, he would give up any further claim to a share in the estate.[3] He seems to have received his preparation from Rev. Robert Smith, the father of John. B. Smith, President of Hampden-Sidney College, of Virginia, and of Rev. Samuel Stanhope Smith, D. D., President of Princeton College,[4] in the eastern part of his native State; and he taught school a year or so before going to college. It is not known as to when he entered Nassau Hall, but he received his A. B. degree in 1761;[5] and with great earnestness and perseverance had he pursued his studies. Though he was thirty-six years

---
1. Caruthers' Life of Caldwell, p. 10-11.
2. Ibid. p. 14-15.
3. Ibid, p. 18.
4. Foote's Sketches, p. 232.
5. Caruthers' Life of Caldwell, p. 19.

of age when he graduated, he felt no shame—he had done his best. After his graduation, he taught for one year at Cape May, and in connection with teaching he kept up his theological studies. At the end of the year he went back to Princeton and became an assistant in the department of languages during the absence of the regular Professor; and at the same time he spent most of his force in his studies for the ministry.[1] He was ordained and licensed by the Presbytery of New Brunswick during the year 1762. He was given supply work in this Presbytery's territory 1763 and 1764.

On the 16th of May, 1765, he was appointed by the Presbytery to labor one year at least as a missionary in North Carolina. From the fact that at the same meeting he received a call from Buffalo and Alamance settlements in North Carolina it is rather probable that he had visited here as early as 1764. On the 6th of July, 1765, he was set apart for the ministry and was dismissed to join the Presbytery of Hanover in Virginia. He doubtless came to North Carolina as early as he could get off after this meeting.[2] At any rate, he seems to have been located in Guilford (then a part of Rowan) county by 1766. He settled about three miles north-west of Greensboro, among friends who had emigrated from Pennsylvania a few years before. Soon after his coming he married a daughter of Rev. Alexander Craighead, of Mecklenburg county, who once lived in his native section in Pennsyvania. His installation as pastor of Buffalo and Alamance churches took place March 3rd, 1768.[3] He now began one of the longest ministries on record and a career that has few equals among any people. He came and settled permanently among the very

---
1. Caruthers' Life of Caldwell, p. 20.
2. Ibid, p. 22.
3. Ibid, p. 23.

first ; and remained longer than almost any one of them. He had these two churches for the remaining part of his long life ; and nobly did he serve them. They were quite a distance apart and at the beginning were rather poor. The whole colony was in bad financial circumstances ; the French War had left a heavy debt, and trade was restricted by the unjust laws made by the Royal Governors.[1] At first they promised their pastor but two hundred dollars ; and this was to be paid in grain if the people chose. He at once saw that he could not support a family on this and bought a farm of about two hundred and fifty acres, near Buffalo church. Upon this tract of land he raised most of his provisions.

Very soon after his installation as pastor he began his famous school at his own log home. He kept this up with only two or three interruptions until old age told heavily on him ;[2] and it was here that he really performed his great life work. Not long afterwards he turned his attention to the study and practice of medicine. In the wilderness around him he saw the great need of an educated physician. He acquired a fair knowledge of medicine, and practiced it in connection with his ministerial duties for several years, until his fourth son was prepared to do his work.[3] He was a conspicuous figure in the War of the Regulators, which terminated in the battle of Alamance, May 16th, 1771 ; not as a soldier, but as an arbiter and promoter of peace. Many of his members, especially of Alamance church, belonged to the Regulators.[4] Some think that he himself had preached and worked for their principles and cause. It is more probable that he gave his influence to reconcile both sides. Dr. Caruthers, on page 142 of his Life of

---

1. Caruthers' Life of Caldwell, p. 29.
2. Ibid. p. 29.
3. Ibid, p. 42.
4. Ibid, pp. 148-154.

Caldwell, says: "If my information be correct, Dr. Caldwell was favorable to the cause of the Regulators, but not to some of their means." He was without a doubt a true American; and took a very active part in behalf of the War of the Revolution. He was a member of the Convention which met in Halifax, Nov. 12th, 1776, in which our Bill of Rights and State Constitution were formed and adopted;[1] was also a member of the Convention of 1778 to consider the Constitution of the United States. He had shown himself of so much worth to the cause of Independence, that when the British made their cruel invasion of middle North Carolina, in the early part of 1781, they offered a reward for him. It is even said that his character was well known to Cornwallis before he reached the boundary of the Colony;[2] also that the offered reward was two hundred pounds, but that no betrayer for this great amount of money could be found within his congregations.[3] He was never obtained by the British, though the army of Cornwallis encamped on his premises, occupied his house, consumed all of his provisions, and burned his large library and valuable manuscripts and papers.[4]

Though his home, which was near the scene of the Battle of Guilford Court House, March 15th, 1781, and the whole surrounding country were pillaged by the ruthless soldiers of Cornwallis, still prosperity soon afterward began to come back; and Dr. Caldwell again worked with the hearts and minds of his fellowmen. He taught and fought against the great flood of French infidelity which was then reaching the far away State of North Carolina. When the University of this State was established he was offered the Presidency, but in conse-

---
1. Caruthers' Life of Caldwell, p. 189-190.
2. Ibid, p. 209.
3. Ibid, p. 210.
4. Ibid, pp. 218-224.

quence of his age and his love for his churches, he preferred to spend the remaining part of his life among those for whom he had toiled for more than a quarter of a century.[1] Though he would not accept their offer, they made him a D. D. in 1810.[2] He continued to preach to his churches until about 1820; and when his end on earth came, August 25th, 1824,[3] he had spent well nigh sixty years in the service of the ministry to his fellowmen. During the most of which time he had been their teacher as well as their preacher. He was stout and enduring, affectionate to family and friends, diligent and conscientious in teaching intellectual and spiritual truths, patriotic and learned.

When we consider his school and its influence a great deal may well be said. He was a thorough scholar and had great tact in managing boys. He knew the correct theories of life and education and had a wonderful faculty of imparting instruction.[4] His mode of discipline was very peculiar to himself and very effective. He did not use the rod, nor is there any record of his ever having expelled a single student. His scholarship and character commanded their utmost respect. His disposition was of such a unique kind that he would give rebukes and corrections never to be forgotten; and such rebukes never won the ill-will of the pupil toward him. His countenance and manners, calmness and humor, won their hearts.[5] He knew how to inspire deep thoughts and great deeds in the boy. This was a school without a single parallel in North Carolina. The only school like it in the Thirteen States that the writer knows of was the famous academy at Willington, Abbeville county,

---

1. Caruthers' Life of Caldwell, p. 265.
2. General Catalogue of the University, p. 238.
3. Caruthers' Life of Caldwell, p. 268.
4. Ibid, p. 80.
5. Ibid, pp. 81-82.

South Carolina, run by Dr. Moses Waddel.[1] Think of such a character in a log school house, a doubled storied one with a chimney in the middle, which was built in his own yard, pouring out his deep life to about fifty boys or young men in those early times of darkness, and this too year after year for a long while. His pupils numbered from fifty to sixty—a large number indeed for such times and conditions.[2]

He soon won such a reputation that students came to his school from every State south of the Potomac. It is the opinion of every one who knew him, that he influenced more men to take high stands in the public professions than any other man of his times in the Southern States.[3] Many pupils of his became famous as statesmen, lawyers, jurists, physicians and preachers. Some prepared for Princeton or Chapel Hill, after it was established; many of those who became most distinguished in the various vocations received their only education under his guidance. Five of them became Governors of different States; a great many more members of Congress. John M. Morehead, one of the State's greatest Governors and citizens; Judges Murphy and McCoy, two of our most eminent jurists; and Rev. Samuel E. McCorkle, D. D., Rev. John Mathews, D. D., and Rev. John Anderson, D. D., great among divines—these are a few of his illustrious students. To have passed through the course at his school with his approbation was a passport throughout the whole South.[4] Dr. Caruthers says on page 31 of his Life of Caldwell: "Probably no man in the Southern States has had a more. enviable reputation as a teacher, or was more beloved by his pupils; and no man, with the same number of scholars, ever had so few

---

1. See Meriwether's History of Higher Education in South Carolina, pp. 37-44.
2. Caruthers' Life of Caldwell, p. 31.
3. Caruthers' Life of Caldwell, p. 30.
4. Ibid, pp. 30-31.

occurences of an unpleasant kind while they were under his care, or saw less to regret in their subsequent conduct." His pupils, without a single exception, whatsoever their abilities or attainments, regarded him through life with the greatest veneration as an instructor, and cherished his memory as a christian man with the deepest and truest affection. Many of them are said to have shed tears at the mention of his name, or when passing by the church in which he preached to them so long and well, and the graveyard in which his remains lie buried.[1]

His school was in every way the right arm of the church.[2] While the whole country is much and deeply indebted to it for the general spread of knowledge and culture, literature and science, still the Presbyterian Church especially owes much of its very existence and growth to this heroic character,[3] who in almost a wilderness kept a beacon light brightly burning for more than thirty years. A great preacher, a true pastor and patriot; a greater teacher and guide of the youth.

### QUEEN'S MUSEUM.

The next school in order of time was Queen's Museum at Charlotte. It was intended to be on the most extensive scale of any institution in the country, and, had its plans been carried out, would have equalled the University.[4] It began, as has already been mentioned, about 1767. It was the outgrowth of the little classical school run by Rev. Joseph Alexander and a Mr. Benedict, within the bounds of Sugar Creek congregation.[5] The school was in an intelligent and prosperous community;

---

1. Caruthers' Life of Caldwell, p. 36.
2. Ibid, p. 39.
3. Ibid, p. 40.
4. Ibid, p. 194.
5. Foote's Sketches, p. 513.

and to keep up with the demands of such a people vigorous efforts were made to raise it to the rank of a college.[1] On December 5th, 1770, it was chartered as Queen's Museum by the Colonial Legislature, which met at Newbern.[2] This charter was set aside by the King and his council. The charter was afterwards amended and passed the second time, but only to be annuled again by the King. Royalty too well recognized that such an institution would be the producing force of democratic ideas and principles.[3] The school went on, however, without a charter. The great majority of the people living in this section, between the Yadkin and Catawba rivers, were Presbyterians. They used their combined influence to secure a charter.[4] The King and his Governors were of the Church of England, and had no desire or intention of seeing a strongly organized force of another church growing up in their own bounds, especially when that church was the Presbyterian, their opponent by nature and principle. The hall was used for political debates and literary clubs previous to the Revolution; and the debates of that historic convention which formulated the Mecklenburg Declaration of Independence also took place here.[5] This was indeed the center of the "hornets' nest of the Revolution."

It seems that students were here at work from the time of its first charter till the British invasion of Charlotte in 1780. Foote gives a copy of an original diploma:

"The Moderator and Members of Union Society in Queen's Museum, Charlotte, to all whom these presents

---

1. Foote's Sketches, p. 513.
2. Davis's Second Revisal.
3. Foote's Sketches, p. 513.
4. Caruthers' Life of Caldwell, pp. 192-193.
5. Foote's Sketches, p. 514; Vass's Eastern North Carolina, p. 46.

may come, with Peace and Safety. Be it hereby certified that we have bestowed upon James McEwen this Diploma in testimony of his having been a member of our Society, and of his having through the whole time of our connection together deported himself in such a manner as to merit our full approbation, both as a faithful assistant in school, and a regular, useful member of Society.

"Of the above let our names under-written be a witness.

"Given in Union Society, at the stated meeting in the Hall of Queen's Museum, Charlotte, on Friday, 27th of September, in the year of our Lord one thousand, seven hundred and seventy-six." This diploma was signed by Jno. Kerr, Moderator, Handy Harris, Clerk, William Humphrey, Thos. Henderson and Francis Cummins, members.[1]

The name was changed to Liberty Hall Academy, perhaps during the year 1775;[2] and under this name it received a charter. It did not receive any funds from the State and was entirely under the control of the Presbyterian Church.[3] During April, 1777, an act was passed by which the following were made trustees: Isaac Alexander, M. D., President; Col. Thomas Polk, Col. Thomas Neal, Abraham Alexander, Waightstill Avery, Ephraim Brevard, M. D., Adlai Osborne, John McKnitt Alexander, Rev. David Caldwell, Rev. James Hall, Rev. James Edmunds, Rev. John Simpson, Rev. Thomas Rees, Rev. Thomas McCaule, and Rev. Samuel McCorkle.[4] Dr. Isaac Alexander, Rev. Thomas McCaule and Dr. Ephraim Brevard were made a committee to frame a system of laws for the government of the Academy.

1. Foote's Sketches, p. 514.
2. Wheeler's Reminiscences, p. 230; also quoted by Dr. Smith.
3. Foote's Sketches, p. 515.
4. Ibid, p. 515; Caruthers' Life of Caldwell, p. 103.

The first meeting of the whole body of trustees was held on January 3rd, 1778. At this meeting it was determined to buy lots from Col. Thomas Polk at the price of nine hundred and twenty pounds. On these lots were already some buildings. This meeting appointed commissioners to make improvements, especially to build a suitable frame house for a dining room. They fixed the salary of the President at one hundred and ninety-five pounds. This was to be increased in proportion as provisions increased in price. Their regulations about boarding were fine. In April, 1778, the laws formed by the special committee appointed for the purpose were adopted by the whole board. The course of studies was in the main the same as was later formulated by the trustees of the University of the State. The trustees had no power to give degrees, but only certificates of studies and improvements.

After they had the institution set on foot as a college, they began to look out for a President.[1] The fame of Dr. Alexander McWhorter, of New Jersey, had reached the leading characters of North Carolina; and too he had visited the churches here in 1764-1765.[2] His name was the first choice in this meeting of April, 1778. He could not accept their offer and request. His affairs at home were too much deranged in consequence of the War of the Revolution and also of his absence on that missionary tour of independence, through the Southern States, which he made at the request of the Continental Congress. Mr. Robert Brownfield then accepted the office for one year, at the end of which Dr. Ephraim Brevard and Rev. Samuel E. McCorkle, D. D., were sent North to make overtures the second time to Dr. McWhorter.

---
1. See manuscript of Adlai Osborne in the Library of the University of North Carolina; quoted by Caruthers in his Life of Caldwell, pp. 193-194; the points of which are given by Foote, Sketches, pp. 514-515.
2. Foote's Sketches, p. 514.

This time he accepted. He at once settled up his affairs in his native State and moved to Charlotte. He was ready to take charge of the institution, when the whole affair was suspended on account of the coming invasion of the British. This was done February 15th, 1780; and the school was never resumed again.[1]

When the forces of Cornwallis were in Charlotte Liberty Hall Academy was used as a hospital and was badly injured. This school occupied the ground upon which the dwelling house of Mr. Julius Alexander was afterwards erected.[2] When peace came the idea of having a college here any longer was given up; and past hopes were turned over to Mount Zion College at Winnsborough, South Carolina, over which the great Rev. Thomas H. McCaule, D. D., once the pastor of Centre, presided. To this or to Princeton College the Presbyterian boys went for their higher training until the University of North Carolina was opened.[3] Foote says that Mr. Thomas Henderson used the Academy for a High School, which he carried on with great credit and influence for several years.[4] He also gives a copy of a certificate of scholarship granted by the trustees of the old academy:

"STATE OF NORTH CAROLINA, }
MECKLENBURG COUNTY. }

"This is to certify that Mr. John Graham hath been a student in the Academy of Liberty Hall in the State and County above mentioned, the space of four years preceding the date hereof, that his whole deportment during his residence there was perfectly regular; that he prosecuted his studies with diligence, and made such acquisitions both in the languages and scientific learning

---

1. Manuscript of Adlai Osborne.
2. Footes' Sketches, p. 516.
3. Ibid, p. 517.
4. Ibid, p. 517.

as gave entire satisfaction to his teacher. And he is hereby recommended to the friendly notice and regard of all lovers of Religion and Literature wherever he comes. In testimony of which this is given at Liberty Hall, this 22d of November, 1778, and signed by Isaac V. Alexander, President, Ephraim Brevard and Abraham Alexander, Trustees."[1]

Of this school Dr. Caruther's says on pages 194-195 of his Life of Caldwell: "The history of Liberty Hall Academy is interesting to the friends of literature as a bold and vigorous effort made for its promotion at that early day, and under the most discouraging circumstances; and it is especially interesting to Presbyterians as being one in a series of efforts made by the people in that region to establish a literary institution, not only of a high order, but on Christian principles, and under Christian influence. Before and after its incorporation, the Presbytery of Orange exercised a degree of supervision over Liberty Hall, as they probably would have done over Queen's College, if it had gone into operation; but precisely on what grounds and to what extent does not appear. For this purpose the Presbytery met, during its existence, much oftener in Charlotte and Sugar Creek than in any other part of their bounds; they appointed committees to examine the students; and they co-operated with the trustees in procuring the services of Dr. McWhorter. They sometimes held part of their sessions in one of these places, and the remainder in the other. Thus, having met in Charlotte, October 1, 1776, they adjourned in the evening to Sugar Creek, where they transacted the rest of their business; and among other things they appointed Messrs. Caldwell and Rees to examine the school in Charlotte. It ap-

---

[1]. Footes' Sketches, p. 516.

pears to have been an object of their constant and anxious solicitude; and their whole influence was exerted for its promotion; nor was its failure owing to any neglect or want of zeal on their part; but to the causes which were beyond their control." This quotation may seem rather too long in this connection. It, however, shows clearly how much interest the Church took in the enterprise and of what value they regarded such an institution in their midst. It has also been quoted to show that the Presbyterians have always stood square by all their affairs, especially in their educational undertakings.

### REV. HENRY PATILLO'S SCHOOLS.

Rev. Henry Patillo is among the greatest of the early teachers in this State. He seems to have been teaching at the same time as Dr. Caldwell in Guilford and Dr. Alexander at Charlotte; and perhaps began this work earlier than either of the two. Dr. Caruthers states that he was teaching classical schools in Orange and Granville counties at the same time as Caldwell, but says that nothing is known of their location or success.[1] According to Foote he went to reside with Rev. Samuel Davies in Hanover in 1751. There he pursued his studies under this learned divine; and was supported partly by the kindness of friends and partly by teaching a little school.[2] He was ordained in 1757. At a meeting of the Presbytery at Hico, October 2nd, 1765, a call came from Hawfields, Eno and Little River, for his services. He accepted the call and moved among these churches; and there or somewhere else in Orange and Granville counties spent about thirty-five years of his life.[3] Dur-

---

1. Life of Caldwell, p. 30.
2. Footes' Sketches, pp. 215-216.
3. Ibid, p. 217.

ing this time he preached and taught. His influence seems to have been very strong and wholesome upon a large territory. He was a great student of books and men. He had received his classical and theological training under Davies; and continued to spend a good deal of his time in close study during life. His scholarship was extensive and deep. The degree of Master of Arts was conferred on him *causa honoris* by Hampden-Sydney College, of Virginia, in 1787.[1] During this year he published, through the press in Wilmington, a volume of sermons. He also prepared a Geography for Youth by way of Question and Answer. Foote says of this work, that it was doubtless superior to any printed work of the kind in those times.[2] On the same page he states that for twelve years he had a classical school in Granville county; and that a part of this time it was at a place occupied by Mr. M. J. Hunt a few years prior to 1846, and part of the time at Williamsburgh.[3]

A school by the name of Granville Hall was incorporated in 1779. This was located in Granville county, exactly where the writer has not been able to find out. According to Martin's Collection of Private Acts, page 93, the following were made trustees: Governor Richard Caswell, Abner Nash, speaker of the senate, Thomas Benbury, speaker of the house of commons, John Penn, Rev. George Micklejohn, Rev. Henry Patillo, Thomas Person, Edmund Taylor, John Taylor, Memucan Hunt, Philemon Hawkins, Jr., Howell Lewis, Robert Lewis, Charles Rush Eaton, John Young, and Samuel Smith. They were given instructions to purchase five hundred acres of land, and to erect suitable buildings.[4] Mr. Patillo taught in this school for some time, but probably

---

1. Foote's Sketches, p. 222; Dr. Smith gives the date as 1789.
2. Ibid, p. 222.
3. Ibid, p. 222.
4. Given also by Smith, p. 87.

was not the first teacher. According to Foote, page 218, he did not move to Nutbrush and Grassy Creek, in Granville, till 1780; and it is likely that he was not connected with the school in their bounds before he became the pastor. However, it is rather certain that he taught in this school a large part of the twelve years of his teaching in Granville county. Considering the prominence of many of the trustees, one would be led to believe that this was another famous institution.

He lived among the Regulators, and many of their meetings were within his bounds; Hillsboro was for some time the Capital of the State and the center of the meetings of the Regulators.[1] Still he, like Dr. David Caldwell, gave his life to educate them and to make them true and loyal citizens. He, nevertheless, took quite a good deal of interest in politics. In 1775 he was a delegate from Bute county (now Warren and Franklin) to the first Provincial Congress of North Carolina, August 20th, 1775, in Hillsboro. He was selected by the convention to read prayers every morning, and Rev. Charles Edward Taylor every evening. Mr. Patillo was made chairman of the Congress in a committee of the whole, when the plan of the General Confederation of the United Colonies was considered.[2]

### CLIO'S NURSERY AND SCIENCE HALL.

The founder of these schools was Rev. James Hall, D. D., one of the most conspicuous and useful characters in the early history of the State. He was great alike in his churches and schools; and moulded and shaped the minds and characters of many prominent men. His influence was so great, that he deserves more than a mere passing notice. He was born in Pennsylvania, August 22d, 1744, of Scotch-Irish parents. His family came

---

1. Martin, Williamson, Wheeler, Caruthers and Moore.
2. Foote's Sketches, pp. 217–218.

to North Carolina when he was but eight years of age.[1] They settled in the upper part of Rowan county, which is now Iredell. His home was within the bounds of his congregation, which he served during his whole career of thirty-eight years.[2] In this secluded forest he grew up under the kind and pious care of his parents, and became imbued with the missionary spirit, and the desire to give his life to truth and Christ. He was twenty-six before he began a study of the classics. However, when only seventeen he became deeply interested in Geometry and other branches of mathematics, and this with the exact sciences were through life his favored subjects.[3] He took his college education at Princeton, where he was graduated with A. B. degree in 1774, at the age of thirty-one. Dr. Witherspoon was then president, and he was so much pleased with young Hall that he offered him a position as teacher of mathematics. The offer was not taken. Mr. Hall had already determined to give his life to the benefit and advancement of his adopted Colony, North Carolina. He was licensed to preach by the Presbytery of Orange about 1776.[4] On the 8th of April, 1778, he was installed as pastor of Fourth Creek, Concord and Bethany. These united congregations extended from South Yadkin to the Catawba, and even beyond these rivers. He served these until 1790, when he was relieved of all except Bethany. With this he continued till his death, July 25th, 1826.[5]

His activity during the Revolution was very great. By nature and education he was strongly in favor of American Independence; and he gave his mind and body to this cause. He met with his fellow-citizens in

---

1. Foote's Sketches, pp. 315–316.
2. Ibid. p. 316.
3. Ibid. p. 316.
4. Ibid. pp. 322–323.
5. Ibid. p. 324.

political discussions; he gave them his spirit and enthusiasm, and increased their love of liberty many fold. He was indeed the military parson of North Carolina. When Cornwallis was plundering and devastating South Carolina, he enthused his flock so deeply that a company of cavalry was at once organized. They by common consent demanded him for their leader. He, though strongly opposed to leading them in battle, still accepted the command. He gave great courage to his countrymen, and served them well as leader and chaplain.[1]

When the war was over and his country had won its freedom, he went back to his real work—preaching and teaching. He found everything in a deplorable condition; morality and religious zeal had declined in his congregation. He went to the work with such enthusiasm and consecration that his people soon became deeply interested in religious and intellectual affairs.[2] He was great as a preacher, and equally great as a teacher.[3] It seems that he set on foot Clio's Nursery very early after he was installed as pastor. Foote says in this connection that Humphrey Hunter had a certificate, stating that he was a pupil of this school from August, 1778, to October, 1779.[4] The institution was located on Snow Creek, in the bounds of Bethany congregation. He superintended this with great care. In it many men, who afterwards became leaders in society, church and politics, were trained. Among these were: Rev. Richard King, of Tennessee, of the greatest ability of any man educated in the western part of the state during the early history; Dr. Waddel, of South Carolina; Judges Laurie, Harris and Smith.[5]

At the same time he opened at his own home The

---

1. Foote's Sketches, pp. 324-325.
2. Ibid. p. 327.
3. Ibid. p. 330.
4. Ibid. p. 330.
5. Ibid. p. 330.

Science Hall. Of this he was the sole teacher. He purchased several philosophical apparatus, and made this school the best in scientific advantages in the State. The institution was kept up for many years, and with great success and usefulness. Andrew Pickens, Israel Pickens, Governor of Alabama, Hon. Joseph Pearson, Judge Williams, of Tennessee, are a few of the many men who received their scientific training in this school.[1] His influence in leading men into the ministry was very strong. He had such great talents and ability of instructing others, such deep piety and soundness of theology, that his home also became the meeting place of the prophets. From this home school or Science Hall came many prominent divines: Revs. Robert Hall, James McEwin and Daniel Thatcher; Francis Cummins, D. D., and John Brown, D. D., of Georgia; James Blythe, D. D., of Kentucky; J. M. Wilson, D. D., of Rocky River; Revs. George McWhorter, James Adams, Thomas Price, James McIlheney, Thomas Neely, Andrew Flinn, D. D., of South Carolina; John Robinson, D. D., of Poplar Tent; Rev. J. Andrews, of Ohio; Revs. John and James Bowman, and Thomas Hall, of Tennessee; Rev. Joseph D. Kilpatrick and William Barr, D. D. In addition to his work as a pastor and teacher in this school, he did much for the intellectual welfare of his congregation by establishing a circulating library among them, and by organizing and encouraging debating societies.[2] He also had a class of young people in Grammar, which met every Saturday. For their use he wrote a system of grammar. At first manuscript copies were circulated among the class, but afterwards the book was published, and it seems that it had an extensive circulation.[3] His work was deeply appreciated far and

---

1. Foote's Sketches, p. 330.
2. Ibid, p. 330.
3. Ibid, p. 330.

wide. He also received many honors during his long life, among which was the degree of D. D. from his alma mater, Nassau Hall,[1] and from the University of North Carolina in 1810.[2]

## ZION PARNASSUS.

This is another one of the great Presbyterian academies, which had such vast influence on middle and western North Carolina during the eighteenth century. It was organized by Rev. Samuel E. McCorkle, D. D., about 1785.[3] He, like Dr. Hall, played a conspicuous part, and deserves much at the hands of the writer of the church and educational history of the State. He was born in Lancaster county, near Harris's Ferry, Pennsylvania, August 23d, 1746. When only ten years of age his parents came to North Carolina and settled in the western part of Rowan county, within the bounds of Thyatira congregation. While very young he was placed in an English school and acquired knowledge so rapidly that soon after coming to this State he was employed in a free school. His classical training for college was received under the guidance of Dr. David Caldwell, in Guilford. From here he went to Princeton, where he was graduated with the A. B. degree in 1772.[4] He received license to preach from the Presbytery of New York in 1774. After this he spent two years in Virginia, before he began his ministerial life in North Carolina. He was ordained pastor of Thyatira congregation by the Hanover Presbytery, August 2d, 1777. This was the scene of his great energies till his death, June 21st, 1811.[5] He strove hard to improve his charge in divine and

---
1. Foote's Sketches, p. 335.
2. General Catalogue of University of North Carolina, p. 288.
3. Foote's Sketches, p. 357.
4. Ibid, p. 351.
5. Ibid. p. 354.

human knowledge. He had great native ability, and improved and increased this many fold by close study. He was a striking and leading character in a large section; and his influence came as much from his school as from his pulpit.

His school was on the road from Statesville to Salisbury; it was at his home, which was not more than nine miles from Salisbury. It was begun as a classical institution, but he soon opened in connection with it a department for preparing teachers. This was a new feature; and its results seem to have been good. He gave great assistance in the way of free tuition to poor yet worthy young men; also helped numbers to buy books. His discipline was of a higher order than was usual; he cared to have nobody as students unless they had good talents and a strong desire to work.[1] Foote says that there were seven graduates in the first class at the University of North Carolina, and that six of these had been pupils of this great teacher.[2] So great was his reputation for sound scholarship and strong influence in teaching young men that he was offered the first Professorship in the University of the State. This was the Chair of Moral and Political Philosophy and History; and it gave the occupant the power of a presiding office. He, however, did not accept the office and honor; he preferred to spend his life as a pastor and instructor of the youth of his congregation.[3] Foote says on page 358 of his Sketches: "His students were, in after life, found on the bench, in the Chair of State, and forty-five of them in the pulpit." Hon. A. Leazer says: "The school of Dr. Samuel E. McCorkle . . . . could have flourished only among a broad-minded, public-spirited people, devoted to true learning. Here the sturdy youth of that

---
1. Foote's Sketches, p. 357.
2. Ibid, p. 358.
3. Ibid, p. 358.

day found thorough training in Theology, elaborate learning in the Ancient Classics, profound studies in Mathematics, a less extended course in the Natural Sciences, and even then, one hundred years ago, this great pioneer and philosopher taught the art of teaching, but didn't call it pedagogics. Dr. McCorkle's school was called Zion-Parnassus, indicating his idea of learning— the combination of religion and polite literature."[1] It seems that he kept up this school till his death. After that it went down for a while, and was afterwards re-opened in Salisbury. Dr. Smith thinks this has been continued with a few intermissions to the present, as the Salisbury High School.[2]

### SOME OTHER PRESBYTERIAN SCHOOLS.

There were several other schools run by Presbyterians than those already mentioned. However, in most cases very little can be found out about them. Foote says on page 179 of his Sketches that Rev. William Bingham came from Ireland to Wilmington, and began a classical school there about 1785; and in his teaching he was very successful. From here he removed to Pittsboro, Chatham county, and established the real Bingham School, which has been so famous in the cause of secondary education. The date of his leaving Wilmington was about 1793.[3] He also preached in Wilmington and the surrounding country.[4] He continued at Pittsboro till 1801, when he became Professor of Latin and Greek in the University of the State. He resigned this place in 1805 and re-opened his school in Orange county.[5] The

---

1. Semi Centenary Addresses, 1887, p. 7.
2. History of Education in North Carolina, p. 89.
3. Wheeler's Reminiscences, p. 336.
4. Foote's Sketches, p. 179.
5. General Catalogue of University of North Carolina, p. 79.

further history belongs to the nineteenth century and will be considered later.

Rev. Robert Archibald, a graduate of Princeton in the class of 1772, became pastor of Rocky River and Poplar Tent churches about 1778.[1] Soon after being installed as preacher, he began a classical school at Poplar Tent, Cabarrus county. It seems that he continued at this work for some time, and that he had great influence in his community.[2] Rev. James Wallis was pastor of New Providence from 1792 till 1819. He established an academy at Providence about 1792; and kept a classical school in it for many years. He was not so poor that he had to teach for a living, but taught for the sake of his countrymen, and especially of his congregation. His success was great. He was for some years a member of the trustees of the University of the State, and had great influence generally.[3] This, as well as the school at Poplar Tent, was kept up for a long time during the nineteenth century.

Rev. David Kerr, a graduate of Trinity College, Dublin, came from Ireland to become the first regular pastor of the church in Fayetteville. He was among the best preachers in the Presbytery of Orange and one of the finest scholars of his times. He began his regular preaching in the Courthouse in 1791. He taught school at the same time. The trustees paid him a salary of four hundred dollars for teaching and the same amount for preaching.[4] He was Professor of Latin and Greek in the State University 1794–1796.[5] Dr. Smith[6] and others think that Fayetteville has had an academy during most

---

1. Foote's Sketches, p. 482.
2. Ibid, p. 482.
3. Ibid, pp. 247-250.
4. Ibid, p. 490.
5. General Catalogue of University of North Carolina, p. 79.
6. History of Education, p. 39.

of its history since the one organized by Mr. Kerr.

### LUTHERAN AND GERMAN SCHOOLS.

These people, as has already been said, did not take a very live interest in intellectual pursuits and attainments. They belonged to the agricultural stage. In consequence of their lack of schools and teachers they did not grow rapidly, nor have they ever had a very strong influence over the State as a whole. However, they have been a pure and noble people; and have formed a good element of our common citizenship—the middle classes. Most of the schools that they did have were run by the churches. They had few preachers as well as teachers. Rev. G. D. Bernheim, on page 154 of his History of the German Settlements and Lutheran Church in North and South Carolina, says: "Inasmuch as these settlers located themselves so gradually, besides being divided into two denominations, it was some time before they were sufficiently numerous to have a pastor located and permanently settled among them; sermons and prayers were usually read on Sunday by their German school teacher, and whenever they were permitted to enjoy the regular administration of the preached word and sacraments, which was seldom, it was afforded them by some self-appointed missionary, whilst their school-teacher usually buried their dead with an appropriate ceremony from the liturgy, and, in case of urgent necessity, baptized their children." They have been very slow to make changes; their progress has been very conservative. However, they have avoided many of the vices and immoralities into which others have gotten so deeply. They had parochial schools whenever a teacher could be obtained. In these schools the catechism and other departments of rudimentary knowledge were taught. The Bible was, as a rule, the text-book in reading.[1] They had most of their religious services in the German language, and this was for some time the only language taught in their schools. They at first strongly opposed the introduction of the English language; and this custom made them more exclusive and retarded their growth in the way of churches and schools.[2]

Their settlements in middle North Carolina were made in the main by emigrants from Pennsylvania, who came from 1750 to 1770.[3] Perhaps the first church organized in this State by the Germans and Lutherans was at Salisbury. The movement was begun in 1768,[4] and by 1772[5] they were wanting a preacher and a teacher. Their church known by the name of Hickory Church was the first of any denomination in Salisbury. When the congregation, at first composed of both Germans and Lutherans, was organized there was no preacher to lead them in the ways of Christ; and in order to supply this want they were compelled to send to Europe. During the time of the organization of this church in Salisbury, there were a few other congregations in Rowan and in that part of Mecklenburg, which is now Cabarrus county. In 1772 Christopher Rintelmann, of Organ Church in Rowan county, and Christopher Layrle, of St. John's Church in Mecklenburg, were sent to Europe for the purpose of securing ministers and teachers. They applied to the Consistory Council of Hanover, Germany.[6] They brought back with them Rev. Adolph Nussman as pastor and Mr. Gottfried Arndt as teacher. They arrived in North Carolina in 1773.[7]

---

1. Bernheim, p. 187.
2. Ibid, p. 188.
3. Ibid, p. 258.
4. Ibid, p. 241.
5. Ibid, p. 256.
6. Ibid, p. 256.
7. Ibid, p. 257.

Mr. Nussman at once became the pastor of Hickory Church in Salisbury. He remained here but a year; then removed to Dutch Creek Church, now known as St. John's Lutheran Church, in Cabarrus county.[1] During his pastorate some dissension arose between the two denominations. The Lutherans withdrew and built Organ Church; and the German Reformed organized Grace Church.[2] After Mr. Nussman left Salisbury the newly organized congregation known as Organ Church asked Mr. Arndt, who had been their teacher for a year, to become their pastor. He was sent to be ordained to the office of the ministry in 1773. He served them in the capacity of preacher and pastor till 1786, when he went to Lincoln county, along the Catawba river. He was the real founder of the Lutheran Church on the western side of the Catawba, and was one of the strongest forces in his whole church. When at Salisbury he had influenced all the territory of Davie, Iredell and Davidson counties.[3] The writer has not been able to find out for certain whether Mr. Arndt continued to teach after his ordination in 1775 or not, though he rather thinks he did.

There is some record of other school-teachers among these denominations in other counties, though very little except the names in a few cases has been found out. The first church edifice of the Dutch Buffalo congregation (aftewards St. John's Lutheran Church) in Mecklenburg was used for the double purpose of sanctuary and school-house.[4] Whether Mr. Nussman was also the teacher at any time during his pastorate cannot be found out. At any rate, he was not during the first part. According to the record of this Church Mr. Friesland

---

1. Bernheim, p. 242.
2. Ibid, p. 245.
3. Ibid, p. 246.
4. Ibid, p. 261.

became their teacher almost at the same time that Mr. Nussman was ordained pastor.[1] In accordance with the Constitution adopted by this Church about 1780, the pastor and teacher were to be supported by the members; and the members had to bind themselves to a definite amount of salary before the services of either minister or teacher could be secured. Bernheim, in referring to this, says, on page 252 of his history: "A portion of the school-teacher's salary consisted in the use of a certain amount of good land, which the members were to cultivate for him, and also to gather the grain, hay, &c., into his barn, when the proper time arrived." Mr. Nussman, while pastor of St. John's Lutheran, made many journeys into Davidson, Guilford, Orange, Stokes and Forsyth counties;[2] and as a result a good many churches were established within this large territory. It is also very probable that schools were begun in several of these communities. According to Caruthers, a Rev. Mr. Beuthahn, of the German Reformed Church, organized some congregations in Guilford and Orange. He also taught a German school in the southeastern part of Guilford. This was his principal means of support.[3] As to how long he taught here there is no record. He began teaching about the time that Mr. Nussman made his missionary journeys.

#### EARLY METHODISM AND COKESBURY SCHOOL.

The people called Methodists were few in North Carolina until after the Revolution. In 1773 no regularly organized church was in existence in America. At this time there were only one thousand, one hundred and sixty members of the society, and ten preachers. None

---
1. Bernheim, p. 259.
2. Ibid, p. 260.
3. Ibid, p. 262.

of these were from North Carolina.¹ However, by 1785 there were eighteen thousand members, of which number about four thousand were from this State; and to supply this whole flock there were one hundred and four ministers.² It is claimed that the work was divided into fifty-two circuits, of which twelve were in North Carolina.³ In the minutes for 1793 fifty-one thousand, four hundred and sixteen whites, and sixteen thousand, two hundred and twenty-seven negroes, were reported; and to lead this flock there were two hundred and sixty-nine preachers.⁴ In this rapid growth North Carolina had its share.

The first Methodist preacher to reach this State was Rev. Joseph Pilmoor. He made a preaching tour from Norfolk, Virginia, through eastern North and South Carolina, as far south as Savannah, Georgia; and this journey was made during the year 1772. He, however, did not organize a society here; Rev. Robert Williams has the honor of organizing the first society within the bounds of our State.⁵ His regular field of work was in Virginia, but he came across the boundary line occasionally, and preached and organized societies along the Roanoke river.⁶ The first circuit in this State was not formed until three years later. At the Baltimore Conference, May 21st, 1776, the North Carolina Circuit was set apart; and Revs. Edward Drumgoole, Francis Poythress and Isham Tatum were ordained as preachers of the charge.⁷ At the same time six hundred and eighty-three members were reported from this circuit.⁸ In the

---

1. Minutes of the General Conferences, Vol. I., p. 5.
2. Ibid, Vol. I., p. 24.
3. Centennial of Methodism in North Carolina, pp. 58–59.
4. Minutes of the General Conferences, Vol. I., pp. 51–52.
5. Moore's Pioneers of Methodism in North Carolina and Virginia, p. 44; R. H. Willis-Thesis at Trinity College, June, 1893.
6. Centennial of Methodism in North Carolina, p. 48.
7. Ibid. p. IX,; Minutes of the General Conferences, Vol. I., p. 7.
8. Minutes of the General Conferences, Vol. I., p. 7.

minutes for the same year Pittsylvania Circuit, with one hundred members, is found. This circuit was partly in Virginia and partly in North Carolina. It was by Rev. Isaac Rollins, preacher of this charge, that Methodism was first preached in the western part of this State.[1] From 1776 to 1781 the Yadkin section was included in Pittsylvania Circuit.[2] In 1781 Yadkin is reported with twenty-one members;[3] and in 1782 Yadkin and Pittsylvania were reported together with four hundred and ninety-one members.[4] At this same conference three preachers were reported from Yadkin: Revs. John Cooper, Enoch Matson and George Kimble.[5] It may seem that more has been spoken of Yadkin than its importance deserves. However, it has been given to show under what conditions Cokesbury school had its beginning and history.

Bishop Asbury, the great organizer of the church, came to North Carolina during the year 1780. He travelled and preached through Halifax, Warren, Franklin, Wake, Granville, Chatham, Orange and Cumberland counties.[6] He says that he found the people for the most part ignorant and hard to influence by his preaching. However, he saw some evidences of real true life among a few of them.[7] When he made another journey in 1794, he found a good many changes; there had been considerable growth in the number and strength of the preachers and members. This time he visited the western part of the State. In his Journal (1852), Vol. II., on page 224, is found, under the date Wednesday, April 2d, 1794, this entry: "Came to E.'s meeting-

---

1. Centennial of Methodism in North Carolina, p. 54.
2. Ibid.
3. Minutes of the General Conferences, Vol. I., p. 13.
4. Ibid, p. 16.
5. Ibid, p. 15.
6. Moore's Pioneers of Methodism in North Carolina and Virginia, p. 24-29.
7. Asbury's Journal (1852), Vol. I., p. 376.

house, near Hunting Creek, in Surry county: here I met with some old disciples from Maryland, Delaware, and Virginia, who have known me for these twenty-two years. Our meeting was attended with mutual pleasure; my soul enjoyed much sweetness with these people. There has been some trouble amongst them, but I know God is with them. I was secretly led to treat on sanctification at W.'s; and if the Lord will help me, I am resolved to speak more on this blessed doctrine. After preaching, I came to Cokesbury school, at Hardy Jones; it is twenty feet square, two stories high, well set out with doors and windows; this house is not too large, as some others are; it stands on a beautiful eminence, and overlooks the lowlands, and river Yadkin."

Cokesbury school in North Carolina was named after Cokesbury College at Abingdon, Maryland. Maryland was the real cradle of Methodism in America; and the first Methodist college in the world was Cokesbury. This was begun in 1784, and continued till 1796 with one short interruption. The name was made in honor of the first two bishops—Coke and Asbury.[1] This little school in North Carolina was begun about 1793. It is the oldest Methodist institution in the State, and the second oldest in the world. According to Asbury, who made another visit to this section in 1799, the school was of a short life. On page 427 of his Journal (1852), Vol. II., under the date of October 12th, 1799, he says that the academical school-house was used for a house of God. The first teacher—perhaps only one—was Rev. James Parks. It seems that he was appointed by the Conference to work here as early as 1793. In the minutes of 1794 he is assigned to Cokesbury School.[2] He married the daughter of Hardy Jones; and as was the

---

1. Steiner's History of Education in Maryland, pp. 229-245.
2. Minutes of the General Conferences, p. 56.

custom of that time when ministers married located there. Mr. Parks seems to have been a good preacher.[1] What success came to him in the school-room the writer can not say; nor has he any idea of what the course of studies was. Rev. W. L. Grissom, who had pastoral work on the Mocksville Circuit, in this section, 1889 and 1890, and who took the time to look up the history and exact location of this school, tells the writer that Rev. M. H. Moore once had in his possession a Greek Grammar with writing on the fly leaf as follows: "Cokesbury School, Rowan county, North Carolina." To this was added a name and date. From this and a few other evidences, one might judge that it was a classical school in which Greek, Latin and Mathematics were taught. The school was located in what was then a part of Rowan county, but now Davie; Davie was not formed until 1836.[2] Asbury says, as has been quoted, that it was at the home of Hardy Jones. Mr. Grissom has looked up the old home-place of Hardy Jones, and says that there is within a hundred yards an eminence, from which can be had a fine view of the Yadkin river and its lowlands. His description corresponds exactly with Asbury's; and he obtained from the oldest citizens of that section direct testimony as to where Hardy Jones lived. The place now belongs to the family of Mr. W. A. Bailey.[3]

### SOME INCORPORATED SCHOOLS.

Very little more than the names, location and date of incorporation of these is known. The writer has endeavored to make the list fairly complete: Smith's Academy, Edenton, Chowan county, 1782; Morgan Academy, Burke county, 1783; Davidson Academy,

---
1. Grissom's History of Methodism in Davie County, p. 12.
2. Wheeler's Historical Sketches, Vol. II., p. 137.
3. Grissom's History of Methodism in Davie County, pp. 11-12.

Davidson county, 1785; Kinston Academy, Dobbs county, 1785; Grove Academy, Duplin county, 1785; Warrenton Academy, Warren county, 1786; Franklin Academy, Franklin county, 1786; Pitt Academy, Martinborough, Pitt county, 1786; Pittsborough Academy, Chatham county, 1786; Richmond Academy, Richmond county, 1788; Currituck Seminary, Currituck county, 1789; Onslow Academy, Onslow county, 1791; Lumberton Academy, Robeson county, 1791; Stokes Seminary, Wadesborough, Anson county, 1791; Tarborough Academy, Edgecombe county, 1793; Murfreesborough Academy, Hertford county, 1794; Stokes Seminary, Henderson, Montgomery county, 1797; Raft Swamp Seminary, Robeson county, 1797; Bladen Academy, Elizabeth, Bladen county, 1797; Salisbury Seminary, Rowan county, 1798; Smithville Academy, Brunswick county, 1798; Unity Meeting-House Academy, Randolph county, 1798; Adams Creek Academy, Craven county, 1798; Fayetteville Seminary, Cumberland county, 1799; William Peasley Academy, Moore county, 1799.[1]

From the number of academies in operation during the latter part of the eighteenth century, one would judge that there was a more general awakening on educational matters than had ever taken place in the State. As was stated in the early part of this sketch, by the close of the century North Carolina had about four hundred thousand inhabitants. Though the tyranny of the royal rule and the War of the Revolution had hindered growth at all times, still this State had, upon the whole, made steady progress from 1750 to 1800. The University began its career in 1795; and along with this were

---

[1]. Martin's Collection of Private Acts (1804), Vol. I., p. 405 for 1785, pp. 428–429 for 1786, p. 455 for 1788; Vol. II., p. 42 for 1791, p. 51 for 1793, p. 69 for 1794, p. 102 for 1796, p. 112 for 1797, p. 181 for 1798, p. 147 for 1799. A large number of these are given by Dr. Smith.

a number of excellent academies, the most of which have been described or named, to fight ignorance. Rev. W. Winterbotham, who published a four volume work on "A View of the United States of America" in 1796, says: "There is a very good academy at Warrenton; another at Williamsborough, in Granville, and three or four others in the State of considerable note."[1] He made this statement in connection with a description of the University.

Foote, in speaking of the conditions under which President Joseph Caldwell, of the University, had to struggle, when he began his work with that infant institution in 1796, says: "There were in operation in the State, particularly in the upper part of it, some academies of high merit and established reputation. The embryo University, without apparatus and without a competent number of teachers to perform the labors of the University, could, after all the patronage of the State, offer little to draw students from these established, well known schools, to come to Chapel Hill. . . . . . There was the school of David Caldwell, in Guilford, in active operation, sending out its pupils to be divines, physicians and lawyers, and ultimately professors in institutions and judges of the courts; the public were not sure that Joseph Caldwell could equal, much less excell him. And there was the academy of Dr. McCorkle, one of the Board of Trustees, a man of literature and reading, kept in the bounds of Thyatira congregation, near to Salisbury. And a little further on was the school of Rev. Mr. Wallis, at Providence, twelve miles from Charlotte, a man of logical mind, connected with a vehement spirit, afterwards a member of the Board of Trustees. And next the school in Bethany, Iredell county, under the direction of the well known servant

---

1. Winterbotham's A View of the United States of America, Vol. III., p. 214.

of God, the Rev. Capt. James Hall, D. D., the soldier of the Revolution, and the leading domestic missionary of the South. Next, the school at Rocky river, from which many excellent men came. . . . . To these add the public schools of Charlotte, Mecklenburg, which occupied the place of Liberty Hall and Queen's Museum; the academy in Duplin, which has been more or less flourishing; Science Hall, near Hillsborough; Warrenton Academy, under Mr. George, who, with Bingham and Kerr, were graduates of Trinity College, Dublin; Granville Hall, and the academies in Edenton, Newbern and Onslow."[1]

However, there was a great amount of ignorance still. It has been estimated that from 1750 to 1775 hardly one-third of the inhabitants of the State could even read; and that many of this number who could read could not write their own names with legibility. From 1775 to 1800 about one-half of the people obtained what was then called a fair English education—"to read, write and cipher as far as the rule of three."[2] There had been a good many fine academies, but these could not reach very many; and these had as a rule educated members of the churches under whose influence they existed. Those who did not belong to these churches were left out of the consideration of educational affairs. Of necessity the Church had too much to do for her own members to spend any time with those outside her bounds. Those were days of teaching among their own flocks, not a time of missionary activity among the unbelievers about them. On the other hand, those who did not belong to the churches, for the most part, cared little for the culture and advantages of an education. These academies,

---
1. Foote's Sketches, p. 543.
2. University Magazine, Nov. 1860, p. 222—The County of Caswell in 1810 by Bartlett Yancy, first published in Raleigh Star, August, 1810. This is also given by Dr. Smith.

individual and separated as they were, made education exclusive and confined to the few. There was consequently a great need for a school to unify these and to reach the class outside of the church, hence the founding of the University. However, upon the whole North Carolina had done a great deal during the eighteenth century. It had begun at the beginning of the century with almost nothing but a wild soil; it had very few inhabitants then, but at the end almost a half million; institutions, both political and educational, were born and partly matured. It gave over to the nineteenth century a good heritage for those times and in such a new country. Most of the causes that have shaped our social, political, religious and intellectual forms to the present time, originated in the century that has preceded ours. Many North Carolinians were ignorant, unappreciative and slow then; and many are still, at the close of the nineteen century, in the same condition.

CHAPTER II.—SCHOOLS FROM 1800 TO 1835.

### SEVERAL ACADEMIES.

With the birth of the University the famous classical schools of North Carolina began their decline. However, many of these were kept up for many years during the first part of this century; and some still exist, though they have had for the most part a few interruptions. Among those already treated that had part of their life in this period are: Granville Hall, which began the last year of the eighteenth century; Caldwell's School in Guilford, kept up till old age told too heavily upon him, perhaps for more than fifteen years after this century came in; Clio's Nursery and Science Hall, run till about 1835, when it gave place to Davidson College; Zion-Parnassus was in operation by Dr. McCorkle till 1811, and with a few intermissions it has been kept up till the present in the Salisbury High School; the academies of Newbern and Edenton, which still exist; Liberty Hall, run as an academy for many years after the War of the Revolution by Dr. Henderson; Bingham School, the oldest and most famous high school in the State; and a good many of those merely named under some incorporated school.

Rev. James Wallis has only been mentioned; and deserves a further consideration. His school in New Providence congregation was noted for many years, and it belongs almost altogether to this period. He was born in Sugar Creek in 1762; was educated at Liberty Hall and at Mount Zion College at Winnsborough, South Carolina. In 1792 he was ordained pastor of the New

Providence charge,[1] and remained here till his death in 1819.[2] He lived about twelve miles south of Charlotte on one of the roads leading to Camden,[3] and here he taught his school. According to Foote he was very successful in his teaching as well as in his ministry; he was a trustee of the University for some time. He did not need to teach for a living, but from the duty he owed his charge and his fellow-men. He seems to have kept up this school almost till his death, and it was run for several years afterwards by different teachers.[4]

Rev. John Robinson had another noted school about the same time as Mr. Wallis. He was born in 1768, near Charlotte;[5] was educated by Mr. Archibald of Poplar Tent, and took his A. B. degree from Mount Zion College.[6] His influence was great in religious and intellectual growth. Foote says on page 446 of his Sketches that the University conferred the D. D. degree upon him. The writer finds that A. M. was conferred in 1810, when the same degree was granted to Revs. James Wallis and John McKamie Wilson; also that D. D. was conferred upon Revs. John Robertson (the same as John Robinson) and John McKamie Wilson in 1829.[7] He was ordained in 1793, and was assigned the field first occupied by Rev. Hugh McAden. In 1800 he moved to Fayetteville and became the resident minister of that church. The salary was so small and the youth so ignorant that he opened a classical school. He found the duties of both preacher and teacher too heavy, and in 1801 went to Poplar Tent, not far from Charlotte. He was with this church for about four years, and was their

---

1. Foote's Sketches, p. 217.
2. Ibid, p. 250.
3. Ibid, pp. 244.
4. Ibid, p. 250.
5. Ibid, p. 445.
6. Ibid, p. 446.
7. General Catalogue of University of North Carolina, p. 238.

teacher also. In 1896, he went back to Fayetteville again to teach and preach for three more years; and again in 1818 came back to Poplar Tent to spend the remaining part of his life, which ended in 1843.[1] He was very successful as a teacher in both places, especially at Poplar Tent. It is stated by Foote that many leading men were educated under him there. His force, precision and kindness made a deep mark. In addition to his own school, he made every effort to promote sacred learning. He took a very active part in the building and organizing of Davidson College, and was chosen one of the Board of Trustees for several years.[2]

Rev. John McKamie Wilson (also written MaKemie) was another great educational power, especially among the Presbyterians, during the first quarter of this century. He was born six miles from Charlotte, within the bounds of Sugar Creek congregation, 1769;[3] educated at Liberty Hall and at Hampden-Sydney College, Virginia. He was given his first work in Burke county, where he remained from 1795 to 1801. At this time he came to Rocky River, where he spent his life.[4] In 1812 he opened an academy about four miles from his home. He taught in this till 1824. His school was very prosperous. A large number of his pupils entered public life. It is stated by Foote that twenty.five became preachers: Revs. James Morrison, N. R. Morgan, Thomas Alexander, John Silliman, John M. Erwin, Robert King, James B. Stafford, R. H. Morrison, Elam J. Morrison, Hugh Wilson, Samuel L. Watson, Thomas Davis, Cyrus Johnston, Henry N. Pharr, J. LeRoy Davies, William B. Davies, C. LeRoy Boyd, James Stafford, Alexander

1. Foote's Sketches, p. 447.
2. Ibid, p. 450.
3. Ibid, p. 476.
4. Ibid, pp. 478–479.

[TO BE CONTINUED.]

E. Wilson, James E. Morrison, Robert Hall, John M. Wilson, Dion C. Pharr, William N. Morrison, A. R. Pharr.[1]

The Caswell Academy, near the court-house of the county by the same name, was opened for students in 1803. The first teachers were Rev. Hugh Shaw and Mr. Bartlett Yancy. During the two years which they taught there were about sixty pupils. From 1805 to 1808 it did not succeed very well. In 1808 Mr. John W. Caldwell, the son of Dr. David Caldwell, of Guilford, took charge, and for some time it was prosperous under his guidance. Hico Academy was another school in Caswell county, and was in operation about the same time. It was located near the Red House, and was run for two or three years by Mr. Shaw, who was one of the first teachers in the Caswell Academy.[2]

During this time many schools were in operation throughout the State. Many of the counties, like Caswell just mentioned, had one or more. But for the most part these schools did not become especially noted, except in their own localities. Those of more than mere local importance have already been considered, except Bingham among male academies and Salem Female Academy among the higher institutions for girls. These have played a unique and interesting part in our educational history. Next to the University of the State they have had the longest careers; and really Bingham began about two years before the State institution was opened. In their different spheres they both have had great influence upon the intellectual and moral growth of the whole of North Carolina and of much of the South.

---

1. Foote's Sketches, p. 485.
2. University Magazine, Nov. 1860, p. 222—paper by Bartlett Yancy, first published in the Raleigh Star, August, 1810.

## BINGHAM SCHOOL.

A few statements were made about the early history of this school under the eighteenth century institutions. As has been stated, the first principal was Rev. William Bingham. He was a Scotch-Irish Presbyterian; and was a man of fine ability and culture, having graduated at Glasgow University with high honors.[1] His family became involved in the efforts for Irish independence; and his uncle with several more of his relatives were executed by the British soldiers. He in company with a brother came to America in 1788. Though he at first landed at New Castle, Delaware, he soon came to Wilmington, North Carolina.[2] His work as a teacher in Wilmington, Pittsboro and the University, has already been mentioned. About 1806 he began his school at Hillsboro, in Orange county. In a very short while it was removed to Mt. Repose, about five miles from Mebaneville. Here for almost twenty years he instructed the youth as few others have instructed them.[3] Long before his death he had won a great name for himself as a scholar and teacher and for his school as a place where true manhood was developed and cultured.

Upon his death in 1825, his oldest son, William James Bingham, became principal. He was the second and greatest of all the principals. He took his A. B. degree at the University of North Carolina in 1825, and won the first honors.[4] At the time of the death of his father, he was studying law under Judge Murphy. He at once took charge of the school. Though he at first did not intend to run it long, still was at its head till 1863. He was born in 1802 and died in 1866. His services to this

---

1. North Carolina Presbyterian, Dec. 24, 1896, data furnished by his descendants.
2. Facts furnished by Maj. Robert Bingham; Our Living and Our Dead, Vol. II., pp. 371–372.
3. Catalogue, 1874; Our Living and Our Dead, Vol. II., p. 372.
4. General Catalogue of the University of North Carolina, p. 95.

State and the whole South were many and great. In 1827 he moved the school from Mt. Repose to Hillsboro; and in 1844 from Hillsboro to Oaks, Orange county, about ten miles from the North Carolina Railroad. He lived in a time that gave remarkable opportunities in his line; and he added remarkable ability. When he began teaching was rather in disrepute, but he raised it to a high and honorable calling. He increased tuition fees from twenty to one hundred and fifty dollars per year.[1] He limited his number to thirty students; and one or two years his school had such a reputation all over the whole country, that he had to refuse admission to three hundred applicants each year.

Walter P. Williamson, Editor of *The Tarboro Southerner*, on page 372 of Vol. II. of Our Living and Our Dead, says: "His success was pre-eminent; and his reputation, though less brilliant than that of some of his cotemporaries, was more extensive than that of any one of the men of his day, and while he was a stern and rigid disciplinarian, I may say truly, though upon the testimony of others, that his pupils loved him like a father, and trusted him as a tender and sympathetic friend. I venture to say he was the means of putting more teachers upon the rostrum, more professional men into the various professions, more preachers in the pulpit and more missionaries into the field than any ten other men in the State."

In 1857 his two sons, William and Robert, came in with him. They had just graduated from the University of the State with fine distinction.[2] They increased the facilities to a large extent; and under them the number of students was limited to sixty. Their method of instruction was of the very highest grade. The father still

---

1. Our Living and Our Dead, Vol. II., p. 372.
2. North Carolina Presbyterian, Dec. 24, 1896.

had all the beginning classes; and the sons did the upper and advanced work. They worked with boys upon the principle that the best teaching and training is needed for the youngest.[1] Their system of examination was very rigid; and by this means all of the unworthy were thrown out and those of better talent and industry took their places. It was the custom before the war to give written examinations, which required in several cases about ten hours to answer. Those were days when this school stood unequalled in the State and the whole South. For a good many years two-thirds of the first honor graduates of the University were prepared at Bingham.[2] The first class that left them under the new name of William Bingham and Sons was composed of five. Of these four took first honors at the University; and the fifth took second honors. There were more than eighty members of this class at the University; and besides the four from Bingham but one took first honors, and he was from Horner's, whose founder was James Horner, a pupil of William J. Bingham.

Just before the Civil War, they built a fine and commodious academy building at Oaks, and were getting in shape for a more enlarged field of work and usefulness. As soon as the war came Robert gave up the school to his aged father and his elder brother, William. From beginning to end he was a gallant and brave soldier.[3] He raised a company and went to the front at the beginning; and he was one of Gen. Lee's seven thousand, five hundred men at Appomatox Court House. However, the school went right on during the war, in spite of the general demoralization, the depreciation of money and the demands upon the teachers and pupils for police

---
1. Our Living and Our Dead, Vol. II., p. 873.
2. Ibid, Vol. II., p. 873.
3. Ibid, p. 874.

work.¹ After 1863 the father practically retired from the principalship; and William then took charge of the management, though in reality he did not become nominal principal until 1865.² William J. Bingham died February 19th, 1866; and his death removed one of the most striking personalties and unique teachers this State has ever produced.

William Bingham, the third principal, was born 1835, and died February 18th, 1873. He took his A. B. from the University in 1856.³ He was of very delicate health, hence did not do active service in the field of war, though he was made a Colonel of the Confederate States Army. He was equally great as a teacher, public speaker and author of text books. His Latin texts have received the greatest praise. They at one time were used in every State in the Union, especially in the South and West; they were perhaps used more extensively than the works of any other Southern author.⁴ His first book was a Latin Grammar, a rather small and elementary work; and at the end of the preface is found: "Oaks, N. C., May 10, 1863." This was published at Greensboro, North Carolina, by Sterling, Campbell and Albright, a firm which published most of the North Carolina books during the war times. During December, 1863, a Cæsar came from his hands, written at the same place. On October 30th, 1866, he sent forth from Mebaneville a revised and enlarged edition of his Latin Grammar. This was revised the third time by Prof. W. Gordon McCabe, now of Richmond, Virginia. In 1868 a revised Cæsar came out.⁵ He was also the author of an English Grammar and Exercise. The school was moved from

---
1. Our Living and Our Dead, Vol. II., p. 375.
2. General Catalogue of University of North Carolina, p. 95.
3. Ibid, p. 95.
4. Our Living and Our Dead, Vol. II., p. 380.
5. See Books in Greensboro Female College Library.

Oaks to Mebaneville in 1865, where it remained till its removal to Asheville in 1891.[1] It was placed under military control about the year 1865; and so it has remained. The principal was given the title and rank of a Colonel by the State.

At his death in 1873 his brother, Robert, became the fourth principal; and he still guides the institution. He was born in 1838; took his A. B. degree from the University in 1857, and later his A. M. In his class were Judge A. C. Avery, of Burke, Hon. B. F. Grady, of Duplin, Hon. John W. Graham, of Orange, Col. Thos. S. Kenan, of Raleigh, and others equally distinguished.[2] As has been mentioned, he took an active part during the Civil War, with the rank of Captain in the Southern States Army.[3] His administration of twenty-four years has been wise and progressive. He has endeavored to maintain the high standard of scholarship set by his predecessors; and in addition to this he has increased the patronage to a considerable extent. The faculty for the year 1874-1875 consisted of Major Robert Bingham, William Bingham Lynch, Captain T. L. Norwood and W. G. Quakenbush.[4]

Major Lynch deserves some further notice than a mere mention. He was a grandson of the first William Bingham. He took his A. B., with first honors, from the University in 1859, and became a Lieutenant of the Confederate States Army.[5] He was Professor of Greek in Davidson College 1860-1864; and teacher and co-principal of Bingham School 1864-1879. While professor at Davidson, he took his A. M. at the University in 1862. After leaving Bingham he ran a military school

---

1. Catalogue, 1891. p. 1.
2. North Carolina Presbyterian, Dec. 24, 1896.
3. General Catalogue of the University of North Carolina, p. 95.
4. Catalogue, 1874. p. 1.
5. General Catalogue of University of North Carolina, p. 166.

at High Point until 1883. From here he went to Lake Mary, Florida.[1]

They gave fine instruction, and they charged for it. The expenses for session of twenty weeks in 1874 were: tuition $62.50; board $82.50; books and washing $15.00. Their course of studies at the same time was extensive for academical work. English and Commercial: first year—Spelling, Reading, Writing, English Grammar, Composition, Geography, History and Arithmetic; second year—the same with Book-keeping, Natural Philosophy and Chemistry. Mathematical: Arithmetic (Sanford), Algebra (Todhunter), Geometry (Chauvenet), Trigonometry, Analytical Geometry and Calculus; and this went through five years. Latin: Grammar (Bingham and Gildersleeve), Cæsar (Bingham), Prose Composition, Sallust, Ovid, Vergil, Cicero, Livy, Horace and Juvenal; and this was a five years' course. Greek: Grammar and Reader, Prose Composition (Jones), Xenophon's Anabasis and Memorabilia, Herodotus and Homer; this extended through three years. They also gave a course in French and German, each lasting two years.[2]

The school had its first destructive fire in 1882, and again in 1890. Maj. Bingham immediately after the second fire began to look for a new location. These two fires had consumed the library and apparatus; and it seemed best to move the school to some good town, where protection from fire could be had. Several places made bids for it, among which were Charlotte and Asheville. Asheville was chosen; and, as has been mentioned, it was moved there in 1891. New buildings were erected during that summer.

The city of Asheville has a world-wide reputation for

---

1. Semi-Centennial Catalogue of Davidson College, p. 17.
2. Catalogue, 1874, p. 3.

its healthfulness and its natural beauty. On one of the finest spots near by is located this school. The place is known as Bingham Heights. It is indeed a beautiful spot. The French Broad sweeps the foot of the high cliff of rocks; toward the east can be seen Black Mountain; toward the south, Blue Ridge and Pisgah; and not but a few miles away is George Vanderbilt's place, one of the greatest in the world. The buildings have the best possible ventilation and sanitary arrangements; they were made for health and utility, not for show. And too their arrangement for managing boys is excellent. They are built of brick, one story high and one room deep. Their floors are doubled, with building paper between; and beneath the whole floor is a coat of cement and slate to prevent dampness from rising. The rooms are made practically fire proof. The site is two hundred and fifty feet above the French Broad, and the drainage is perfect. The dormitories are in eight sections; and a class-room, with quarters for a teacher behind, is placed in the center of each of the sections. To move the school to a far away location and to house it in buildings so well adapted to good discipline and robust health, required much knowledge, judgment and skill. However, Maj. Bingham was fully equal to the demand; he had had a personal experience of thirty years and the traditional experience of his school for almost a hundred. To his great experience he added a careful study of the educational systems of the whole country.

The school since its removal to Asheville has extended its field of patronage, as well as made its equipment far larger and better. The number of pupils for the past six years has been about one hundred.[1] Its expenses are still higher than other schools in the State. For a school year of forty weeks three hundred dollars are

---

1. Catalogues, 1891-1897.

charged.[1] It has been a financial success to a great degree. During 1895, in spite of the hard times, more than six thousand dollars were made from the earnings above the regular expenses.[2] And its course of studies has been extended in order to meet the demands of such a location and the times and circumstances in which it exists.[3] The faculty has been doubled in the last ten years. For the school year 1897–1898 it has: Major Robert Bingham, A. M., LL. D., Superintendent; R. L. Grinnan, T. B. Lee, A. B. (University of North Carolina), S. W. McKee, A. B. (Davidson College), St. George T. Grinnan, J. S. Williams, A. B. (University of North Carolina)—Captains; M. C. Millender, M. D., Surgeon; Major Charles L. Davis (Brevet Major U. S. Army, author of "North Carolina in the Continental Lines," 1896).[4]

The charities of this institution, like most North Carolina schools, have been great. Since the beginning no worthy student has been turned away on account of the lack of means[5] In 1874, and for many years before and after this date, they made an offer of free tuition to the sons of the ministers of the gospel of any denomination; also to the orphans of ministers, candidates for the ministry and sons of deceased Masons without means.[6] This gift meant a good deal, as tuition was then one hundred and twenty-five dollars per year. Now the same offer is made, except the amount is only fifty dollars; and this reduction of fifty dollars is the same as is given in free tuition in most of the schools and colleges of the State.

The whole history of this school is interesting and

---

1. Catalogue, 1897, p. 34.
2. North Carolina Presbyterian, Dec. 24, 1896.
3. Catalogue, 1897, pp. 32–34.
4. Ibid, 1897.
5. Our Living and Our Dead, Vol. II., p. 372.
6. Catalogue, 1874, p. 3.

unique. As an instance, during the past twenty years its pupils have come from thirty-two States of the Union, and from Mexico, Brazil, Germany, Scotland, England and Siam. It has had among its numbers one who became Vice President of the United States; some of them have become Cabinet officers, Senators and members of the House of Representatives, and other prominent officials in our National Government. Its students have played a great part in this State's political, social and intellectual life. Among the eminent jurists, were Thomas Ruffin, the greatest Chief-Justice North Carolina has ever had, and Justice A. C. Avery, who retired from the Supreme Bench of this State at the close of 1896. Tod R. Caldwell, Governor of North Carolina in the troubled times of 1871-1874, Elias Carr, Governor 1892-1896, Daniel L. Russell, who is our present Governor—these and many others of great prominence are to be found among the number of pupils of this historic school.[1]

### SALEM FEMALE ACADEMY.

A brief review of the Moravian settlements in North Carolina was made in the early part of this sketch. They will be mentioned here only as far as Salem is concerned. This place was selected as the central town of all their settlements. It was chosen by Count Zinzendorf before his death; and afterwards by Frederick W. Marshall, who was then Superintendent of the whole community.[2] The hill was surveyed in 1765, and the square was laid off in 1766. The site for this central town was about eighteen miles east of the Yadkin river and between Middle Fork (Wach) and Brushy Fork (Lick).[3] The

---

1. Catalogues and points furnished by Major Robert Bingham.
2. Winkler's Winston-Salem, p. 80.
3. Reichel's History of the Moravians in North Carolina, p. 61; Martin's History, Vol. I., Appendix, pp. XLIX-LII.

square was three hundred feet long and one hundred and seventy wide. The first family house, built of logs, was completed by August, 1769. During the next year a two-story house, called the Brother's House, was erected. This was used as a church till 1771.[1] In 1772 another edifice was erected for a meeting house; and a large bell, weighing two thousand seven hundred and fifty-eight pounds, was placed in this to serve as a town clock. A two stop organ was built for the church the same year.[2] This house served them as a place of worship till 1800. In 1798 another edifice for the growing congregation was begun; and by November the 9th, 1800, it was ready for use.[3] It was a remarkable structure, and still serves them for church purposes. In this, at the same time, was built a large pipe organ with fourteen stops—for a long time the finest and largest of its kind in the whole State.[4]

The first minister of the Unitas Fratrum, for this is their real official and church name, was Rev. Paul Tiersch, who came in 1771.[5] Rev. John Daniel Kohler came from Europe to become their preacher in 1784.[6] He became Bishop in 1790; and still served the church till 1801. On June 6, 1802, Rev. C. G. Reichel, who had for some years been minister and principal of the Boys School at Nazareth, Pennsylvania, was installed as pastor of Salem.[7] During 1803, at the close of the fiftieth year of their life in North Carolina, they had a great meeting at Salem. Many representatives were there from most of the other churches of this section. At that time their members were: Salem, 290; Betha-

---

1. Reichel's History, pp. 62-63.
2. Robbins' Winston-Salem, p. 16.
3. Reichel's History, p. 105.
4. Martin's History, Vol. I., Appendix, pp. XLIX-LII.
5. Reichel's History, p. 66.
6. Ibid, p. 96.
7. Ibid, pp. 105-106.

bara, 81; Bethania, 293; Friedberg, 231; Friedland, 135; Hope, 175.[1]

This church has ever paid great attention to schools. It is stated that in 1500, forty-three years after its beginning, it had a school in each of its four hundred parishes, besides higher institutions. By 1600 their schools were the finest in Bohemia. As an illustrious example of its schools John Amos Comenius might be named.[2] As soon as a settlement was well organized, a church and a school-house were erected; they fully recognized that life amounted to little without truth and right. Salem, which signifies peace, was not slow to set on foot a movement for a school for its chilcren, especially for its girls. According to Martin, there was built on the northwest corner of the square a school-house for boys as early as 1794. To this could go the male children of the inhabitants of the town, and of those living near around. They could not enter under six years of age, nor remain longer than till the age of twelve or fourteen. In this were taught: Reading, Writing, German, English, Cyphering, History, Geography; and the rudiments of Latin, Drawing and Music were taught to some.[3]

The girls' school, which soon became known as Salem Female Academy, was opened in 1802. The regular academy building was begun October 6th, 1803. Bishop Reichel conducted the ceremony of laying the cornerstone. The whole ceremony was unique. In the northwest corner was placed a copper case in which is this, written in English and German: "In the name of God, the Father and the Son, and the Holy Ghost, in the year after the birth of our Lord and Saviour Jesus Christ one thousand, eight hundred and three, on the sixth day

---

1. Reichel's History, p. 112.
2. Manuscript (15,000 words) of Miss Adelaide L. Fries, in Salem Female Academy Library.
3. Martin's History, Vol. I., Appendix. pp. XLIX-LII.

of October, in the twenty-seventh year of the Independence of the United States of America, when Thomas Jefferson was President of them, in the fiftieth year after the settling of the first members of the Church of the United Brethren in North Carolina and in the beginning of building Bethabara, in the thirty-eighth year since the beginning of building Salem, the foundation stone of this house for a *Boarding School* of Girls was laid in a solemn manner, in the presence of the whole Congregation, with fervent Prayer to our Lord, that by the School, to be established in this House, His name may be glorified, His Kingdom of Grace be enlarged in this Country and the Salvation of souls of those, who shall be educated therein, be promoted."[1] This house was completed in 1804, and dedicated July 16th, 1805.[2] Martin's History, Vol. I., appendix, pages IXL–LII., gives a very interesting description of this building. According to him it was sixty-two feet long and forty-two deep. In the lower part were two large, and some smaller, apartments. In one of these large rooms the girls day school was kept; in the other was the dining hall for the boarding pupils. In the upper story were three large apartments, and one smaller one. In each lived from fourteen to sixteen girls under the care of two tutoresses. The small room on this story was used as a sick room. Over these rooms was a hall, sixty feet long, thirty wide and fourteen high. This was the sleeping place of the students under the care of their teachers.

The first principal of the academy was elected by the Conference of October 31st, 1802,—Rev. Samuel G. Kramsch. He was a native of Silesia and at that time English minister of the Church at Hope, North Carolina. He and his wife both had had training in boarding-

---

1. Reichel's History, pp. 116–117.
2. Ibid, pp. 119–120.

school work and management.¹ There was a girls' school in Salem a short while before the academy began. It was in the old Gemein Haus (Congregation House), which stood on the east side of the public square. The second floor of this was once a church for the congregation, but now (1800–1802) a chapel. The lower floor had three apartments. The minister occupied two of these; and the south one was used for a girls' day school.

In 1803 there were forty-two little girls in Salem, twelve of whom afterwards became teachers in the academy, one till 1856. Of the forty-two, twenty-three were pupils in the school.² Early in 1804, before the building was completed, four girls came from Hillsboro to enter as the first boarding pupils. Very soon afterwards, came two from Halifax, one from Caswell and one from Fayetteville. In 1805, two came from Camden, South Carolina, the first from that State, which, next to North Carolina, has furnished the largest number.³ The first to occupy the new building were Mr. and Mrs. Kramsch, their two daughters, twenty boarders and four teachers.⁴

Nine teachers entered into the work during 1804–1805: Miss Sophia Dorathea Reichel, daughter of the Bishop, (1804–09); Miss Maria Salome Meinung (1804–07); Miss Johanna Elizabeth Praezel (1804–08); Miss Johanna Sophia Shober (1805–06, 1807–09); Miss Johanna Elizabeth Reuz (1805–20); Miss Agnes Susanna Praezel (1805–16); Mrs. M. E. Praezel, in village girls' school, (1805–13).⁵ Of this number, Miss Praezel was the most noted. She won quite a local reputation as a fine musician. It is even said that she had learned the piano, harp and organ before she was twelve. At this

---

1. Reichel's History, p. 116.
2. Ibid, p. 118.
3. Ibid, pp. 119–121.
4. Ibid, p. 121.
5. Ibid, p. 126.

age she was made a teacher in the day school. This work was very laborious at that time, as she had to copy all the music for her pupils. She was also organist for the week-day services in the church, which were held every evening.

In 1806 the first printed circular was sent out, known as the "Terms and Conditions of the Boarding School for Female Education in Salem, N. C." The ages when girls could be admitted were eight and twelve; and at fifteen they had to leave. The expenses for the whole year amounted to about one hundred and sixty dollars, five dollars entrance money being added. The regular course of studies was: Reading, Grammar, Writing, Arithmetic, History, Geography; German and Plain Needle Work were given if desired. Music, Drawing and Ornamental Needle Work were extra.[1] Those who desired entrance had to make application. "It is desirable that such as are applied for should have had small or kine pox and measles."[2]

In those early days the home life was made as perfect as possible. The students were divided into companies of fifteen and twenty girls. Each company was in charge of two lady teachers; and these served alternate days. The teacher was always there to help and give counsel; and the principal was their pastor, father, guardian and friend. Mr. Kramsch was a botanist, and gave each girl a small garden. In this she cultivated the flowers which she collected while on her daily walks.[3]

In those early times the conveniences of traveling were very few. The horse and coach were in use in some sections; in many places, however, traveling on horseback was the common thing. It was in this way

---

1. Reichel's History. pp. 121–122.
2. Manuscript of Miss Fries.
3. Ibid.

that many girls came to Salem Female Academy. They came for hundreds of miles in company with father or older brother, and often in company with several companions. When they reached the school, the horse was sold and the saddle laid away till the girl finished her course of studies. When they once entered they remained until their education was completed; it was too much trouble to go home on vacation.[1] They did not have long summer vacations as now, but only a few days rest during the mid-summer. During these rest days the girls made themselves merry in many ways, especially by picnics and excursions into the country.

In 1806 Mr. Kramsch gave up the principalship to Rev. Abraham G. Steiner. He was a native of Bethlehem, Pennsylvania. His administration lasted about ten years, and was in every way successful. In 1807 a third room was added; and a fourth was needed soon afterwards, and was built in 1811. This same year a house was built for the principal and his family, so as to give more room for pupils. This house is still the home of the principal. The pupils came in so fast toward the latter part of his administration, that many of them could not obtain accommodations in the school building and had to lodge in private families.[2] From May, 1804, to the end of the year 1807 as many as one hundred and twenty-four girls, from North Carolina, South Carolina, Virginia, Kentucky, Tennessee and Georgia, received their education there.[3] As a rule the institution was very healthful, though at one time in 1814 there were seventy-four cases of measles.

In 1807 the first certificate of scholarship was given. Its wording is exceedingly queer: "Be it known that

---

1. Manuscript of Miss Fries.
2. Reichel's History, p. 122.
3. Manuscript of Miss Fries.

Miss ......, daughter of ...... of ...... Co., State of ......, has for sometime past resided and been a pupil in the Boarding School for Female Education in Salem, N. C., and as she is now on the point of leaving the said Institution, the Inspector and Tutoresses of the same can not withhold from her the testimony of applause due her for her general good conduct as a pupil in said Institution. She has followed her studies with all assiduity and has made good progress therein, very willingly submitted to the rules of the school, and by her good conduct and strictly moral behavior, has gained the good will and esteem of those under whom she has been placed, and the sincere regard of the whole school. Given at Salem the 29th of October, 1807, for myself, and in the name of the Tutoresses of the said Institution.

ABRAHAM STEINER, Inspector."[1]

In 1806 Mr. Steiner, on account of a failure of health, gave up the principalship to Rev. Gotthhold Benjamin Reichel; and he continued as a teacher and book-keeper. Mr. Reichel was the son of Bishop Riechel, and served the school well indeed till his death, December 20th, 1833. He was also pastor of the Salem Church from 1829 to 1833. The school increased under him, and by 1824 an addition to the building was necessary—a school-room and chapel.[2]

Some of the quaint and primitive customs during his term of office are worthy of notice. In their large common dormitory were little snow white beds. The floor was covered with white sand, swept into many different patterns. In the center stood the long table with its rows of benches. The girls were "day-keepers" by turns, two at a time, and performed all of the services for the living room, such as bringing water and carrying

---
1. Manuscript of Miss Fries.
2. Reichel's History, pp. 123-124; Manuscript of Miss Fries.

wood. Friday was a general house cleansing day. The teachers and pupils cleaned the dirty candle sticks and washed new sand for the floors. The dining hall was in the basement, and was of two rooms, one for the two youngest companies and the other for the older pupils. The girls seated themselves on benches, and the teacher sat on a stool at the head of the table. As soon as all were still, the teacher began singing the blessing, "Leave Thy Peace divine with us, we are thine." The table cloth was coarse, home-made, tow linen; the plates pewter, the knives and forks steel; and the tea or coffee was drunk from bowls without handles. On certain days this table ware had to be scrubbed with rushes. Toward the close of the principalship of Mr. Reichel, it is said that a certain lady while visiting the school was so much displeased at the table appointments, that she sent to the store and purchased China plates and cups, and cotton table clothes. Their fare was wholesome, though very plain. The boarding department was in charge of the Single Sisters until 1859; and they ran it for the support of their establishment. Nine o'clock was the hour for the pupils to be in bed; and the teachers were in by ten. Their dress was simple and made by themselves. They did not wear hats when they went to church, but caps made of white bobinet, lined with strands of floss and tied under the chin with ribbon.[1]

Upon the death of Mr. Reichel, Bishop Bechler took charge for the time. In 1834 Rev. John Christian Jacobson became principal. He was at the time of his election minister of Bethania; and he served for ten years. In 1844 he left for Nazareth, Pennsylvania, where he became principal of the Boarding School for Boys. In 1835 a new chapel was built; and by 1841 the Congregation House was given over to school pur-

---

1. Manuscript of Miss Fries.

poses alone. The school had one hundred and eighty boarding pupils in 1838; and to teach this number there were nineteen teachers, besides the principal.[1]

During the year 1840 the following circular was sent out:

"TERMS OF THE INSTITUTION FOR FEMALE EDUCATION,

| | |
|---|---:|
| Entrance | 5.00 |
| Board and Washing and Tuition, including Reading, Grammar, Writing, Arithmetic, History, Geography, the use of the Globes, Composition, Natural Philosophy, Chemistry, Botany, Latin, French, Drawing and Painting, Plain Needlework, &c per quarter | 30.00 |
| Instruction in Music per quarter | 5.00 |
| Instruction in Ornamental Needle-work per quarter | 3.00 |
| For the use of the Library per quarter | 1.00 |

Books, Stationary, Medicine and Medical attendance, and other contingent expenses, placed to account.

One hundred dollars paid in advance.

Clothes found by Parents or Guardian, or placed to account.

Bills adjusted semi-annually, and full payment to be made at the removal of a pupil. The amount of Board, Tuition, and contingent expenses may be calculated at Two Hundred Dollars, more or less for one year.

"No pupil admitted without seasonable application by letter, post-paid, mentioning name, age &c, nor unless an affirmative answer be previously given by Rev. John C. Jacobson, Principal of the Boarding School, Salem, N. C."[2]

In 1844 Rev. Charles Adolphus Bleck took charge.[3] During his administration of four years the idea of making some of the courses of studies more advanced

---

1. Reichel's History, p. 124.
2. Manuscript of Miss Fries.
3. Reichel's History, p. 124.

was incorporated. Until this time those who desired to take French had to recite to the principal at seven o'clock in the morning. When Mr. Bleck came in, a select class of eight or ten boarders and two day pupils was formed and taught by Mrs. Denke, who, as Maria Steiner, had taught in the institution from 1811 to 1828[1] and had spent two years in Europe.[2]

In 1848 Rev. Emil Adolphus de Schweinitz became the sixth principal.[3] He at once established the custom of annual examinations. These were very exciting times, and the method by which they were carried on was interesting as well as quaint. It is said that for sometime before these were to be held crowds came in coaches and on horseback; and that the whole town opened its doors to receive the visiting patrons in true hospitality. It required a week or more for the private examinations. These were conducted in the Chapel by the principal. In those times he was versed in the whole course of studies; it was not a time of specialists. It seems that the teachers taught during the year and the principal examined at the close. The last day of the examinations was always public, and was one memorable in the lives of all the students. In the Church, in which this always occurred, there were many decorations and specimens of the work done by the pupils during the past year. The first thing on the programme of that day was the roll-call, to which each pupil gave an answer by rising and making her best bow. After this came the dialogues, music and other exercises. In one or the other each girl had to take part; and often there were exercises in all of the subjects studied during the year. These public examinations during the next administration became

---

1. Reichel's History, p. 129.
2. Manuscript of Miss Fries.
3. Reichel's History, p. 124.

public entertainments, which eventually evolved into the present commencements.[1]

In 1853 Rev. Robert de Schweinitz, a brother of Emil Adolphus, took charge of the school. He held the position twelve years, and these were very important years in its history. During 1854 the first catalogue was sent out; and about the same time the old Congregation House was torn down and a new building begun. The contents of the old corner stone were placed into the new, known as the New Academy. By March 24th, 1856, the new building was ready for occupancy, and the school was moved into its larger and more handsome quarters.[2]

From the manuscript of Miss Fries, which the writer finds very interesting and accurate, and from Reichel's History of the Moravians in North Carolina, appendix, pages 192-195, the Principal's official report of the new building is given : "The dimensions of the main building are 100 feet front by 52 feet deep, with a wing at the north $70\frac{1}{2}$x$34\frac{1}{2}$ feet, and another at the south 77x44 feet. The main building, as well as the north wing, is four stories on the front, and at the rear (on account of the descent of the ground) five stories including the basement. The fronts of the house are of pressed brick, expressly manufactured for our building, and are probably some of the first of the kind made in our State."

These were very prosperous years. During the year 1856 there were three hundred and fifteen pupils, of whom two hundred and thirty were boarders. To instruct this number there were eighteen resident and eleven non-resident teachers. Up to the close of this same year, there had been in the institution three thousand four hundred and seventy students, and one hun-

---
1. Manuscript of Miss Fries.
2. Ibid; Reichel's History, p. 125.

dred and twenty-four instructors. Of this number, only two teachers and twelve pupils had died while in the school.[1] As the Civil War came on the school grew larger still; those times were the most prosperous in numbers the school ever had in its whole history. Salem Academy was regarded as a place of safety, and many pupils were sent there then on that account. The authorities of the school soon had to send out the announcement that "there was no more room; but if you will bring beds we will try to board you." These too were prosperous years in moral and intellectual growth. The school went on without a single day's interruption.[2] The din of war was near, but they went on their accustomed quiet way. That was indeed a great oasis in the desert left by devastating war around. That was a time when young hearts were bound so closely together that they have never since been disunited. Find the pupil of Salem Female Academy of those days, and you will feel that loyalty and love for institutions as you have never felt before.

Toward the close of the war Stoneman's Brigade marched upon Salem. The valuable papers were taken from the office and placed under the stone floor of the cellar of the Principal's house; and the money was hidden beneath the floor of the sitting room. When the brigade reached the town, the mayor, principal and other citizens surrendered the place and the academy, and asked for a guard to be stationed about the latter. This request for protection was granted and the school went on as if nothing had happened. The brigade was in camp south of town for about two days, but found the place so peaceful and quiet, that they soon pulled up and left. The large crowd of intelligent girls conquered

---

1. Reichel's History, p. 129.
2. Manuscript of Miss Fries.

the whole brigade, and with little trouble or inconvenience to themselves.[1] The school has been and is the greatest of all powers. It goes forth to battle quietly, but in the end conquers all things.

At the close of the war the school was full to the brim. During 1866 one hundred and fifty-two new names were added to the record-book, the greatest number of any one year. On February 21st of the same year the academy was incorporated by the legislature as a regular college. The act of incorporation is as follows: "The faculty of said School, that is to say, the President, Professors, Teachers, by and with the consent of the Trustees, shall have the power of conferring all such degrees or marks of literary distinction, or diplomas, as are usually conferred in colleges and seminaries of learning."[2] At the same time the course of studies was raised to a considerable extent. At the close of the school year 1865–1866, Mr. De Schweinitz gave up the principalship to go to Nazareth Hall, Pennsylvania.

Rev. Maximillian E. Grunert, who had been in the faculty as first professor for sometime, took charge During his superintendence the school went on prospering, till it was visited by a great scourge of small-pox. This caused great anxiety and somewhat lessened the numbers, though not a single student ever died from the disease. In 1873 he had the old building changed and improved, to very much the appearance of the new. In 1877 Rev. J. Theophilus Zorn became principal. He set on foot a school journal, known as *The Academy*, which was first issued in March, 1878, and has been published ever since. It was during this year that the first Senior Class was formed.[3]

In 1884 Rev. Edward Rondthaler became principal,

---
1. Manuscript of Miss Fries.
2. Catalogue, 1896–1897, pp. 21–26.
3. Manuscript of Miss Fries; letter from Principal J. H. Clewell.

and Rev. John H. Clewell assistant. Mr. Rondthaler was at the time pastor of the Salem congregation, and later became Bishop of the Southern Province of the Moravian Church. When he took hold the attendance was not very large, it having gradually gone down for the past several years. He brought a new life to the academy, increased its patronage, and made many advantageous improvements. As a rule the Moravian Church has been opposed to innovations; the principals have been very conservative in their methods. However, Bishop Rondthaler made many changes in the dormitories; also in the course of studies and plans of teaching.[1]

In 1885 the academy received its first endowment. The first gift was to the support of the Art Department. In consequence of the gift this department has grown to a large extent. Misses Troeger and Lewis, of New York, and Miss Siewers, have been the makers of it. The music instruction was for a long time under lady teachers, but in later years skilled men have managed it. Profs. E. W. Linebach, S. D'Anna and Fredrick Agthe, brought the work up to such a standard that in 1885 a regular course for graduation was given in this department. Profs. George Markgraff, Schmolck, Skilton and Shirley, have been its directors since that time. Another innovation of the same year was the introduction of a department of Book-keeping, Phonography and Telegraphy.[2] In 1886 the Alumnæ Association was formed. On the 10th of October, 1887, the Euterpean Society was organized, a few months later the Hesperian. In May, 1888, Dr. Rondthaler gave up the management to the present principal, Rev. John H. Clewell,[3] though he is

---

1. Manuscript of Miss Fries; points of letter from Principal Clewell.
2. Manuscript of Miss Fries; catalogues.
3. Ibid.

still superintendent of the department of languages. He is a native of Pennsylvania; graduated at the Moravian Theological Seminary at Bethlehem, and studied for some years in Europe;[1] given D. D. by the University of North Carolina in 1880.[2] He became pastor of Salem in 1877.[3] His influence as a teacher and preacher has been very marked; he is easily one of the leading characters of his church.

The present principal has made still more improvements; his administration has been wise and able. He received his education at Bethlehem, Pennsylvania, and at Union Theological Seminary, New York City.[4] Just after his coming into office, Annex Hall was erected to supply the demand for room. When this was completed a new nomenclature was adopted. The old academy now has the name of South Hall; the new academy, Main Hall, and the Bagge House, Old Annex. In September, 1889, a post-graduate course was put in; and the degree of A. B. is conferred on those who complete this course. During December, 1890, Park Hall was completed. By 1892 the literary societies had grown to such proportions that Society Hall was built for their use.[5] To a better equipment in the way of buildings have been added apparatus and a stronger teaching force. The number of students now excels the highest enrollment of the prosperous days prior to the Civil War. During the year 1896–1897 there were enrolled three hundred and twenty-four pupils. Of this number North Carolina had two hundred and fifty; and among the other seventy.four are representatives from Texas, Virginia, Georgia, South Carolina, Alabama,

---

1. Robbins' Winston-Salem, pp. 14–16.
2. General Catalogue of the University of North Carolina. p. 241.
3. Robbins' Winston-Salem, p. 16.
4. Ibid, p. 14.
5. Manuscript of Miss Fries; Catalogue 1889–1890.

New York, Tennessee, Arkansas, Florida, California, Brazil (S. A.), Mississippi, Lousiana, Kentucky, New Jersey, Pennsylvania, Massachusetts, Ohio, Iowa. Oregon, Cuba, Japan, Alaska.[1]

The course of studies is: Preparatory—History of England and the United States, Arithmetic, Algebra, Latin; Freshman—Latin Grammar, Cæsar, Arithmetic, Algebra (Wentworth, chaps. 6–12), Geometry (book I.), French History, Physical Geography, English Grammar and Composition, Natural History; Sophomore—Cicero, Sallust, Latin Composition, French or German Grammar, Arithmetic, Algebra (Wentworth, chap. 12 to end), Ancient History (Myer's), Geology, Astronomy, English; Junior—Latin Prose Composition, Vergil, French or German Grammar and Classics, Solid Geometry, Conic Sections, Algebra, Physics, Botany, Biblical Literature, Shakespeare, Mediæval and Modern History (Myer's), Rhetoric; Senior—Greek, Horace, Latin Composition, Latin authors, French or German Classics, English Literature, Trigonometry, Algebra and Geometry, Biblical Literature, Critical study of the longer English Poems, Mental and Moral Philosophy, Physiology, Chemistry, Mythology, Lectures on History and Essays.[2]

The expenses are fairly high for North Carolina schools, especially in these days. For the whole scholastic year, general tuition, room rent, lights and fuel, amount to two hundred and fifty dollars. In addition to this, Instrumental Music, Voice, Elocution, Drawing, Painting, Private French, German, Latin or Greek, Business course, are all extras; and the charge for each one of these is from twenty to fifty dollars.[3]

Thus has this old school grown and prospered till the

---
1. Catalogue, 1896-1897, p. 18.
2. Catalogue, 1896-1897.
3. Catalogue, 1896-1897, p. 36.

present day; and it will continue on and on. It has taken such deep root in the whole South, that it would require a complete reformation of society before it could be overthrown. It has become one of the historic and sacred centers of our life. It has been and is conservative, and in many ways picturesque and unique. With the beautiful campus and grounds in the rear and the lovely old Salem square on the front, it is a very attractive spot. To the outsider it has much of the air and mystery of romance, but to those within it is a place of charm as well as of work, a place where character after character has been moulded and shaped. As many as seven thousand boarding and five thousand day pupils have been instructed within its walls. Every State in the Union has been represented among its pupils, and as many as a dozen foreign countries. There have been two hundred and thirty-two teachers in the institution since its founding.[1]

The list of the distinguished alumnæ is long and famous. It would require more space than can be used here to name all of them, hence a few only will be given: Mrs. Ex-Pres. Polk (Sarah Childress), Mrs. Stonewall Jackson (Mary Morrison), Mrs. Gen. D. H. Hill (Isabella Morrison), Mrs. Martha Patterson (Martha, daughter of Pres. Johnston), Mrs. Hon. John Bell (Sallie Dickinson), Mrs. Hon. Stephen A. Douglas (Martha Martin), Mrs. Judge Van Wyck (Lydia Movenck), Mrs. R. M. Pearson (Mary McDowell), Mrs. Judge Wells of U. S. Court (Eliza Covington), Mrs. Ex-Gov. T. M. Holt (Louisa Moore), Mrs. Gen. Pender (Fannie Sheppard), Mrs. Judge Blukensderfer (Miss Kramsch), Mrs. Ex-Gov. D. L. Read (Henrietta Settle), four daughters of Postmaster-General Key.[2]

---

1. Letter from Principal Clewell.
2. Ibid.

There are but three schools of the Moravian Church in the United States besides Salem: Bethlehem, Nazareth and Lititz, Pennsylvania. However, there are quite a number in England, Germany, France and Switzerland. The academy at Salem is the property of the Moravian Church, and is governed by a Synod, which meets every three years and appoints three men to govern between the meetings. These three are the trustees of the academy. At present they are: Rt. Rev. Edward Rondthaler, D. D., president; N. S. Siewers, M. D., and Rev. James E. Hall. The school property is worth about two hundred thousand dollars. The endowment at present amounts to only about ten thousand. However, the buildings and grounds are free of rent.[1]

## THE EPISCOPAL THEOLOGICAL SCHOOL.

In 1832 Rev. L. Silliman Ives, D. D., the second Episcopal bishop of North Carolina, urged the convention to establish and equip a theological and classical school under the auspices of their church. A committee was appointed for the purpose; and they located the school near Raleigh, about one mile west of the State Capitol. They purchased one hundred and fifty-nine and one-half acres of land. To pay for this they gave their individual notes for sixteen hundred dollars. Seven thousand and five hundred dollars were borrowed from the Episcopal Fund to erect the central building. Ex-Gov. James Iredell was made chairman of the executive committee; and the whole work was pushed on with rapidity. On the 2nd of June, 1834, the school opened under very flattering circumstances. Every pupil had to be as old as fourteen, but still the institution was full the first year. During the second session

---

1. Letter from Principal Clewell.

of the first year there were one hundred and three pupils enrolled, of which eighty-three were boarders. To accommodate the rush for the next year another building of the same size as the first was ordered to be erected. The expenses for board and tuition amounted to one hundred and seventy-five dollars for the scholastic year.

The money promised on subscription came in very slowly. There were too many boys for the masters to control, and the teachers were poor in discipline. Very soon the patronage ran down, so that it was decided to close the school July, 1838. The debts by this time had amounted to about fifteen thousand dollars. The land, except twenty acres, and the furniture were sold. The trustees now proposed to leave out the classical feature and run it as an exclusively theological school. However, the Diocese did not agree to take part in this move, and the whole affair went under. It failed largely because of too great numbers during the first year and the lack of discipline and management on the part of the presiding teachers. Dr. Cogswell, Dr. Empie, Mr. De Berniere Hooper and Dr. Curtis, were its four masters.[1]

---

1. Sketches of Church History in North Carolina, pp. 297-301, by Rev. Jarvis Buxton, D. D.

## Chapter III.—Defunct Schools from 1835 to 1897.

A good many schools came into existence from 1835 to about 1870, but have long since ceased to exist. Much in the life of these is interesting. Several of them existed for about a quarter of a century and had great influence in their respective localities, and in some cases throughout much of the South. However, some of their history has been lost, and in some instances the writer has found out very little. Only those of importance will be considered here.

### CALDWELL INSTITUTE.

As early as 1833 the Presbytery of Orange appointed a committee to see after establishing a classical school in which Christian Education should be the principal aim. On this committee were several of the leading characters of the Presbytery, among whom was Rev. Joseph Caldwell, D. D., President of the University of the State. They finally decided on Greensboro as the location; and it was named Caldwell Institute after President Caldwell, who was the strongest force in the whole educational system at that time. They erected a two-story brick building on the spot just a few feet south of the present track of the Cape Fear and Yadkin Valley Railroad, through which South Elm street now runs.[1]

The school went into operation January 1st, 1836, under the guidance of Rev. Alexander Wilson, D. D. He was originally from the north of Ireland. For sometime before his coming to take charge of the school he

---

1. Messrs. R. M. Sloan and D. F. Caldwell.

had been pastor of Grassy Creek and other churches in Granville county.

Rev. Silas C. Lindsley, of New Jersey, became his assistant. He had been teaching in the Greensboro Academy five years before Caldwell Institute was begun.[1] This academy had been run in a building, used by all the denominations as a preaching place prior to 1830 and located where Ashe and Sycamore streets now corner, opposite the present residence of Mr. W. D. Trotter. According to the intention of the first committee, the principal served each pupil in the capacity of pastor. The teachers also were expected to give instruction in religious subjects. On Sunday each pupil was required to study some parts of the Bible or Evidences of Christianity, and the Westminster Catechism. Greek, Latin and Mathematics formed the basis for intellectual work.[2]

The success of the school was great even in the very beginning. By the opening of the third year another teacher was added, Rev. John A. Gretter. By the end of the sixth year one hundred students, from all parts of the State, were enrolled each year. In 1837 it received a charter from the legislature, according to which the trustees should all be of the Orange Presbytery. In 1844 Mr. Gretter resigned to become pastor of the Presbyterian Church of Greensboro, and Mr. Ralph Graves took his place. The school continued here until 1845.[3] At this time some contagious disease spread over Greensboro to a considerable extent; and at once there was a talk of moving the school to another location. The Presbytery met in Danville, Virginia, the last week of April, 1845, and decided to remove the institute at once.

---

1. Greensboro Patriot, May 24, 1845.
2. Foote's Sketches. pp. 518–519.
3. J. C. Wharton, Greensboro Patriot. December 16, 1896.

Yanceyville, Oxford and Hillsboro made bids for it. On the 11th of June it was finally decided to move it to Hillsboro.[1] After its removal, it flourished for sometime. Exactly when it closed the writer has not been able to find out. There was no school in its building at Hillsboro in 1859, when Col. Charles C. Tew established his Hillsboro Military Academy there.[2]

### GREENSBORO HIGH SCHOOL.

Immediately after the removal of Caldwell Institute the people of Greensboro took up the matter and started the High School. They used the same building. Rev. Eli W. Caruthers became the first principal. Revs. John A. Gretter and Silas C. Lindsley, and Dr. Joseph A. McLean, were his associates. The classical department was under the care of Caruthers and Lindsley; the mathematical, under Gretter and McLean; and the English was taught by all of them. The first board of trustees was composed of: William D. Paisley, John M. Morehead, John A. Gilmer, Jeduthan H. Lindsay, John M. Dick, James Sloan and Robert Gorrell.[3]

Mr. Caruthers remained principal about two years. In the *Greensboro Patriot* of December 4th, 1847, there is an advertisment of Caruthers' Classical School at Alamance, nine miles east of Greensboro. In the same paper under date of December 25th, 1847, is an advertisement of the Greensboro High School, with Rev. J. A. Gretter, principal and professor of English, and Rev. Silas C. Lindsley, professor of Latin and Greek. In this same advertisement the terms are given: tuition in the classical department fifteen dollars per session;

---

1. Foote's Sketches, p. 520.
2. Our Living and Our Dead, Vol, I., p. 498.
3. Greensboro Patriot, May 3rd, 1845.

in the English eight; board from six to eight dollars. As to how long this school continued the writer has not been able to find out with exactness. It was flourishing for somewhile, but its importance was always local. In fact, it does not deserve a place in these papers of its own force. It has been mentioned so as to give a few points on Mr. Caruthers, who was the greatest force in this part of the State for a long while and who in the line of the State's history has done comparatively a great deal. However, it has been very difficult to find out the points in his life. He deserves to be one of the best known characters in our history, but the fewest know anything of him whatever.

He was born in Rowan county, North Carolina,[1] exactly where and when the writer has never been able to find out; graduated at Princeton College with A. B. degree in 1817;[2] received the degree of A. M. between this and 1842; in 1854 given D. D. by the University of the State;[3] came to Guilford county about 1819 and became co-pastor of Buffalo and Alamance churches. Dr. David Caldwell had preached to these congregations for almost sixty years, but in 1820 he ceased to work as pastor and preacher. Mr. Caruthers at once became the full pastor of these charges; and administered to both of them until 1846. At this time Buffalo and Alamance dissolved. He remained with Alamance until July, 1861, at which time he was asked to resign. His members did not agree with his views on the Civil War. He felt that it was a vain attempt and expressed such views in private and in the pulpit. Many of his congregation were strongly in favor of it, and would not permit their noble and loyal pastor to speak opinions against it.[4]

---

1. C. H. Wiley's Alamance Church.
2. Diploma in Greensboro Female College Library.
3. General Catalogue of the University of North Carolina, p. 240.
4. Col. Joseph M. Morehead, Greensboro.

He was pastor at the same time that he was teaching at Greensboro and at Alamance. He died during November, 1865, and was buried at Alamance. During his whole life he was a strong arm of his church and a great factor in his State's culture. He and Dr. Caldwell held the pastorate of Alamance Church for ninety-three years. When his church asked him to resign, they passed unanimous resolutions in behalf of his great ability and fidelity. He never married, but chose to spend all of his time in the uplifting of his fellow-men. He was modest still progressive, liberal and diligent, his life long.[1]

He has made one of the few immortal names in the church and educational history of the State. Dr. David Caldwell can never die; neither can he who has written his life and a part of the history of his times. His first historical work was The Life of Rev. David Caldwell, D. D., published by Swaim and Sherwood, Greensboro, North Carolina, in 1842. This is a very valuable work. His second book was The Old North State in 1776—1st series, published in 1854. His third work appeared in 1856. It is known as The Old North State in 1776—2nd series. It is the best written and most accurate of all of his works.[2]

### EDGEWORTH FEMALE SEMINARY.

This institution was opened formally in 1840, though its real beginning was about thirteen years earlier. Rev. William D. Paisley moved to the little village of Greensboro in 1820. He took charge of a male academy, and later one for girls. He was the organizer of the Presbyterian Church in this town.[3] He built the house in which Mr. Robert M. Sloan, who married his third daughter, now lives. Just back of this house and be-

---

1. C. H. Wiley's Alamance Church.
2. His three books, found in some libraries.
3. J. C. Wharton, Greensboro Patriot, November 25, 1896.

## SCHOOLS OF NORTH CAROLINA. 109

tween the present residences of Mrs. Judge Dillard and George Donnell was an academy[1] for girls, as early as 1827. The first teacher in this as far as can be ascertained was Miss Judith Mendenhall. According to the 23rd of February number of the *Greensboro Patriot*, 1831, Miss Ann D. Salmon, of Fayetteville, was in charge of this female school. Then a Miss Umphries taught in the same place for a short while. Miss Mary Ann Hoye came to take charge during the year 1836. She in company with another young lady, who afterwards became Mrs. Robert G. Lindsay, came from Alexandria, Virginia. These two had charge of the female academy for about three years. Their success was so great that John M. Morehead, Governor of North Carolina 1841–1845 and one of the most noble and illustrious characters of the State, became interested in female education. Miss Hoye had made such a fine impression on his daughters while in the academy, that he at once determined to erect a fine building for the purpose of higher female education in North Carolina and the South.[2] Dr. Nereus Mendenhall, in his sketch of the New Garden Boarding School, makes the statement that Mr. Morehead built Edgeworth because his daughters, who were not Friends, could not enter this Quaker school. During 1840 he purchased a large tract of land, extending from the old homestead of the Mebanes to that which is now the property of Greensboro Female College, from West Market street on the north to his home, Blandwood, on the south. At his own expense he erected a large four-story brick building, with all the conveniences for a school. It was built upon the land now occupied by the residences of Mrs. Gov. A. M. Scales and Capt. Neil Ellington.[3]

In 1840 Miss Hoye became the principal. The school

---
1. J. C. Wharton, Greensboro Patriot, January 6, 1897.
2. Letter from Mrs. R. G. Lindsay; Messrs. R. M. Sloan and D. F. Caldwell.
3. Catalogues; Ibid.

was a great success from the very beginning. Pupils began to come from many Southern States, from Texas to West Virginia. It was the intention of Mr. Morehead to make it one of the finest female schools in the whole country; he spared neither time nor money for its success. However, it was not a money making concern to him. Among the early teachers with Miss Hoye were Misses Emily Hubbard and Eliza Rose of the literary department, Misses Nash and Kollock of Music and French, Rev. John A. Gretter of Latin, and Profs. Breitz and Brant of Music. In 1844 Miss Hoye died, and Dr. and Mrs. D. P. Weir took charge. Dr. Weir managed the business of the institution, also taught Chemistry and Natural Philosophy. They held the principalship for a short time only. Gov. Morehead secured the services of Rev. Gilbert Morgan and wife, of New York. They began their work early in 1845.[1] Mr. Morgan at once changed the course of studies, and introduced a collegiate system in the place of the academy curriculum then in operation. He seems to have understood the best methods of training and teaching, though it is said that his discipline was not correct nor well carried out. He, like those who preceded and followed him, was of the Presbyterian church. However, the school was run on a non-denominational plan.

According to an advertisement in the *Greensboro Patriot*, under the date of February 1st, 1845, their course of studies was: first department—Davie's Arithmetic, Bullion's English, Latin and Greek Grammars, Town's Spelling Book and Analysis, Webster's 8 vo. Dictionary, Woodbridge and Willard's Geography, with the use of Mitchell's Outline Maps, History of the United States, Book of Commerce, Elements of Mythology, with lec-

---

1. Mrs. R. G. Lindsay; Messrs. R. M. Sloan and D. F. Caldwell; Greensboro Patriot, February 1, 1845.

tures on Jewish Antiquities, Watt's on the Mind, with lectures on Self-Knowledge and Self-Culture, the French, Latin or Greek Language, with one ornamental branch; second department—Davie's Algebra, Legendre's Geometry, Newman's Rhetoric, Lincoln's Botany, Paley's Natural Theology, Ancient and Mediæval History, Burritt's Geography of the Heavens, and Blair's Lectures; third department—Maffett's Natural Philosophy, with experiments, Critical Study of the English Language as the Vehicle of Thought—its Etymology, Lexicography and History, Abercrombie's Chapter on Reason, with lectures as a system of Practical Logic, Smillie on Natural History, with lectures on Astronomy and Physiology, Alexander's Evidences; fourth department—Philosophy of Mind, Astronomy as a Science, Kame's Elements of Criticism, Critical Study of Milton and Shakespeare, Constitution of the United States, Principles of Interpretation, Wayland's Moral Philosophy, Guizot on Civilization, Butler's Analogy, Lectures on the Harmony of Truth, or Method and Plan of Self-Education. There was also a preparatory department, to which girls of seven and eight could go for their training necessary to enter the first collegiate class.

The first term began on the 28th day of May; and the second one, on the 13th of November. At the close of the first session the examinations took place before a committee of visitors; and the final examinations at the end of the year were public. The expenses per session of five months were: board, washing, fuel, lights and instruction in the ordinary branches $75.00; Piano $20.00; Guitar $15.00; Drawing and Painting, each $10.00; Latin, Greek and French, each $10.00; Wax-work $10.00; Shell-work $5.00; Silk and Worsted-work $5.00.[1]

---

[1]. Greensboro Patriot. February 1st, 1845. Miss Lillian Weatherly, in the College Message. May, 1897, gave these points. She obtained them from the same source as the writer.

The school was prosperous at once after Mr. Morgan took charge. By 1848 the building had more than one hundred boarders, and had to be enlarged. In addition to building more rooms for pupils they at the same time erected an Art Studio. This is now the residence of Mrs. Lucy H. Robertson. Mr. Morgan resigned during 1849-1850, and Prof. Richard Sterling, from Hampden-Sidrey College, Virginia, became principal. He was a fine teacher and won much success for the school. He served until 1862, when the doors were closed by the Civil War.[1] Soon after he took charge, the institution was at its highest point. Pupils came from all over the South. There were as many as a hundred boarders, besides the day pupils from town. There were ample scientific apparatus, a good library in the school, and a large one belonging to the principal. The course of studies was raised to a considerable extent.[2] The terms were raised in proportion. According to the catalogue of 1856-1857, board, washing, lights, fuel and tuition in English branches, amounted to one hundred dollars for five months.

In order to instruct the large crowd well, it required a good number of trained teachers. The faculty for 1856-1857 were: Richard Sterling, A. M., principal and professor of Belles-Lettres and Physical Science; Andrew J. Wood, A. B., professor of Ancient and Modern Languages; Isaac B. Lake, A. B., professor of Mathematics and Geology; Rev. J. J. Smyth, A. M., lecturer on Moral Science; Miss Sarah J. Kollock, assistant in the English Department; J. Jaques Eyers, professor of Oil Painting and Drawing; Heinrich Schneider, professor of the Piano and Harp; Miss Minna Raven, instructor in Piano and Vocal Music; Miss Bettie R. Scott, instructor in

---
[1]. Mrs. R. G. Lindsay.
[2]. Catalogue, 1856-1857.

Piano and Guitar; Miss M. Lizzie Dusenberry, instructor in Piano; Alfred M. Scales, steward; Mrs. A. M. Scales, matron.[1] A Prof. Maurice held the French department for some time. J. R. Wharton, A. B., was professor of Mathematics in 1858;[2] J. D. Campbell, A. M., was professor of Mathematics and Rhetoric in 1862.[3] Prof. Sterling, in addition to the management of the school, found time to do a good deal of writing in the way of text-books, and in publishing his own and other works. He and Prof. Campbell wrote and published Our Own Third Reader in 1863; and in 1866 The Southern Primer came from their hands. Prof. Sterling wrote and published Sterling's Southern Second Reader in 1866, and Sterling's Fourth Reader in 1865. All of these were published by Sterling, Campbell and Albright, of Greensboro.[4]

There was no school in the building from 1862 to 1868. During the war the Confederates used it for a hospital; and after the surrender it was occupied by the Federals for the same purpose. In 1868 the property was leased to Rev. J. M. M. Caldwell. Mr. Caldwell was a grandson of Dr. David Caldwell, and had had a good deal of experience with schools. He had carried on a flourishing one at Rome, Georgia, prior to the Civil War, but during this time he had moved to Statesville, North Carolina, and for a short while ran a school there. From Statesville he came to Edgeworth. In September, 1868, he opened up in this place. The faculty was composed of: Rev. J. M. M. Caldwell, principal, professor of Mental and Moral Science; Mrs. C. E. Caldwell, lady principal, English Branches; S. J. Stevens, Mathe-

---
1. Catalogue, 1856–1857. This list is given by Miss Weatherly in College Message. May, 1897. She obtained it from the catalogue in the possession of the writer.
2. J. R. Wharton, Greensboro.
3. See books published by Sterling and Campbell.
4. See their publications in Greensboro Female College Library.

matics and Ancient Languages; S. C. Caldwell, Natural Sciences; Miss Kate Pearson, English; Mrs. Kliffmuller, Art; Profs. Silge and De Smit, Music.[1] Under these faithful workers the school again became prosperous. There were about ninety boarding and seventy-five day pupils. It continued until 1871, when Mr. Caldwell's school at Rome, Georgia, again demanded his attention. He left for that place in August, 1871; and Edgeworth was never again opened. The building was then used as a residence by Mr. Julius A. Gray, a son-in-law of Gov. Morehead; and during the year 1872 it was burned.[2]

### WARRENTON FEMALE COLLEGE.

Warren county is and has always been one of the finest in the State. The section of country between the Roanoke and Tar rivers has been noted for its variety of resources, its mild climate, and especially for its hospitable and cultured people. "There were no Tories in Bute" was a saying as true as it was common; and Warren was formed from this in 1779. From this county have come many of North Carolina's greatest characters. This was the home of Hon. Nathaniel Macon, the most unique and distinguished public man in the State's whole history.[3] There was a good academy at Warrenton in the beginning of this century; and its female schools from 1841 to about 1865 were known far and wide. There were two of these, and both became equally famous. However, that which was at first called Warrenton Female Academy, and afterwards Warrenton Female College, is a few years the older.

This was founded as early as 1841, and was located on

---

1. Letter from Mr. S. C. Caldwell, Tallahasse, Florida.
2. Letter from Mr. S. C. Caldwell; Mrs. R. G. Lindsay, Messrs. R. M. Sloan, D. F. Caldwell and J. C. Wharton.
3. Wheeler's Historical Sketches, Vol. II., pp. 428-440.

the south side of the town. The trustees bought the private residence of Mr. Kemp Plummer for school purposes. To this they added the old Presbyterian Church as a chapel. Rev. N. Z. Graves, a Presbyterian preacher of Vermont, took charge as first principal. Mr. Julius Wilcox, who was Mrs. Graves' brother, was his assistant at first, and afterwards became his associate. Mrs. Sarah A. Nichols was engaged as music teacher. Messrs. Graves and Wilcox were both fine scholars and successful instructors. The institution became prosperous immediately after its opening. In 1846 Hon. Daniel Turner, who had been in the Congress of the United States for a short while, became principal of the academy; and Messrs. Graves and Wilcox built in the northern part of the town, and their school was called Warrenton Female Collegiate Institute.

Mr. Turner was a man of great ability and fine reputation. His wife was a daughter of Francis S. Key, the author of The Star Spangled Banner. Under them and their assistants the school grew very rapidly. They were made fine offers to go to California, and gave up the institution to a company of Warren's citizens in 1856. The purchasers were: William Clanton, Henry Hunter, Sr., John Buxton Williams, Nathan Milan, Jo. Seawell Jones, John E. Boyd, Horace Palmer, Sr. They at once obtained a charter and changed the name to Warrenton Female College. These men were members of the Methodist Episcopal Church South, and the school was from this on run as a Methodist institution.[1]

After the organization in 1856, Rev. Thomas S. Campbell, a member of the North Carolina Conference, became president. He had around him a large and strong faculty, among whom was Edwin E. Parham, M. A.,

---

1. Letters from Mrs. Jo. Seawell Jones, Shocco Springs, Mrs. V. L. Pendleton and Mrs. M. J. Wilcox, Warrenton, North Carolina; catalogues of both schools.

who two years afterwards became president. During
this time more than one hundred pupils were in the institution
each year; and they came from many Southern
States. There was great rivalry between this and the
sister Institute on the other side of the town. Each
watched the other, and both were strengthened by the
competition. Prof. Parham kept it up during most of
the war, but left for other fields in 1866. Dr. Turner M.
Jones removed Greensboro Female College to the buildings
during the latter part of the period from 1863 to 1873.
The institution over which he presided at Greensboro
had been burned and during the rebuilding he kept his
school at Kittrel, Louisburg and Warrenton. When Dr.
Jones came back to Greensboro in 1873, the school was
closed; and was never afterwards reopened as a college.
Mrs. Mary Williams and Miss Lucy Hawkins have been
keeping in the buildings a private school of a high grade
for some time. It had an extensive influence on the
town, the county, the State and a good deal of the South.
Its course of studies was about the same as the Institute,
Edgeworth and Greensboro Female College.[1]

### WARRENTON FEMALE COLLEGIATE INSTITUTE.

As has been stated, this school began in 1846. Messrs.
Graves and Wilcox had already made a fine reputation
in the Warrenton Female Academy; and when they
erected buildings of their own many of their former
pupils came to them. This institution continued as a
private affair. Luke Graves, M. A., came in about 1848,
and became an associate with his brother and Mr. Wilcox.
In 1853 Edwin L. Barrett took his place, and the
firm name became Graves, Wilcox and Company. In

---

1. Mrs. Jo. Seawell Jones; Mrs. V. L. Pendleton; Mrs. M. J. Wilcox. Prof. John Graham, principal of Ridgeway High School, has been very kind in giving references. Prof. E. E. Parham, Murfreesboro.

1859 Mr. Wilcox bought out Mr. Graves; and the school was run by him as principal till his death, June, 1865. From that time until 1880, when the last collegiate exercises were held, it was run by Mrs. M. J. Wilcox. It had as many as one hundred and twenty-five girls each year for a long while. Its pupils are scattered over the whole South, but most of them are to be found in North Carolina and Virginia. Its diploma graduates number one hundred and thirty-five; and the gold medal graduates eighty-two.[1]

The students were classed as first, second, junior and senior. The course of studies for diploma was: First class—Reading, Spelling, Geography, Arithmetic (Emerson's First Part), History of the United States, Natural History; Second class—Arithmetic (Davies), Geography, Penmanship, English Grammar, History of the United States, Spelling, French, Composition, Reading, Moral Lessons; Junior class—Arithmetic, Algebra (Davies), French, Latin, Greek, Rhetoric, Botany, Natural Philosophy, Composition, Chemistry, Reading; Senior class—Intellectual Philosophy (Abercrombie's), Logic, Languages, Astronomy, Elements of Criticism, Moral Philosophy, Evidences of Christianity, Geology, Anatomy and Physiology, Geometry. There was also a course for graduation with gold medals. A rather extensive course in music, drawing, painting and fancy work, was added for those who desired them.[2] The cost of board, tuition in the regular department, washing, fuel and lights, per session, amounted to about eighty-five dollars. The expense of the extras was about the same as in Edgeworth and the other female schools of that time.[3]

---

1. Mrs. M. J. Wilcox and Mrs. Jo. Seawell Jones; catalogues.
2. Catalogue, 1856-1857, pp. 12-13.
3. Ibid, p. 14.

## FLORAL COLLEGE.

This institution was chartered in 1847 and, with a short interruption during the Civil War, was in successful operation for about forty years. The location was in Robeson county, about four miles from Maxton. The main building was large and convenient. In addition to this, there were the Steward's Hall and two smaller ones on the campus. It was under the Presbyterian influence from its beginning. One of its first principals was Rev. John R. McIntosh. He was at the same time pastor of the Centre Presbyterian Church, situated in the same grove. Rev. Daniel Johnson succeeded him, and carried it on till the war broke up the school.[1] After the war it was conducted by Revs. Luther McKinnon, D. D., 1865-66, and John H. Coble, Mr. J. Luther McLean and Rev. Arch Baker. Then several different teachers ran it for a short while each, until its close about fourteen years ago. At that time the original incorporators had died and the institution had become involved in debt. Since then it has changed hands, but has never amounted to anything as an institution of learning. For a long time it had an enrollment of about one hundred students. They came from Robeson and other neighboring counties, and from several of the northern counties of South Carolina. At one time its reputation was more than local and its influence was rather strong.[2]

## CAROLINA FEMALE COLLEGE.

This school was located at Ansonville, about ten miles from Wadesboro. A joint stock company was formed in 1849, and as a result of their work a large brick building was erected, at a cost of twenty thousand dollars. This

---
1. Letter from Dr. H. G. Hill, Maxton.
2. Letter from Dr. Hill, who was kind enough to look up several points.

building contained a large chapel and twenty-four large rooms. It was ready for use by 1850. The institution received a charter during this year, and by 1851 it was opened for the reception of students. Its first president was Rev. Alexander B. Smith, of Anson county. He served but one year and a half. Then Rev. Tracy R. Walsh took charge, and held the position for ten years. The school was very successful for some time, but came very near being wrecked by the rivalry among the stockholders on political issues. It was suspended from 1862 to 1864. Rev. J. R. Griffith, of Virginia, was in charge for two years after this, and was in turn succeeded by Prof. James E. Blankinship. He held the presidency until 1868, when the institution closed as a college. During a part of these years the institution was very prosperous, having as many as two hundred students. This, like Floral, had about the same course of studies as most of the schools of its kind at the time.

About 1861 the stockholders gave the property to the South Carolina Methodist Episcopal Conference, upon the condition that the Conference would pay the ten thousand dollars' indebtedness incurred in adding rooms to the main building. However, only a very few counties in South Carolina took any interest in it, and the money was never raised. Since it closed its doors as a college, it has been run part of the time as a high school.[1]

### WESLEYAN FEMALE COLLEGE.

Murfreesboro has for almost a half century had the reputation of being a cultured town. It has had two schools in its bounds, both of which have at times had more than a local influence—the Wesleyan Female Col-

---

[1]. Prof. R. B. Clarke, the present principal of the High School; Mr. T. A. Clarke, one of the original stockholders.

lege and the Chowan Baptist Female Institute. The first of these was opened in 1853. Rev. Joseph H. Davis[1] presided over it for several years, and won some reputation for it. Revs. D. P. Wills, C. B. Riddick, J. D. Cowling, Paul Whitehead and W. G. Starr, ran it till it was burned, August 5th, 1877. It was rebuilt in 1881; and Prof. E. E. Parham, who had been at Warrenton for some time, took charge for eleven years. Rev. R. P. Troy, who had had a long experience in teaching at Pleasant Garden, Goldsboro and elsewhere, became president in 1892. It was again destroyed by fire, May 27th, 1893. It was under the Methodist Episcopal Church South, and most of its presidents belonged to the North Carolina Conference. It was very flourishing for quite awhile before its first fire. It is estimated that as many as fifteen hundred students matriculated from 1853 to 1877.[2]

### THE FAYETTEVILLE FEMALE SEMINARY.

This was built by a company of stockholders, largely of the town of Fayetteville. The corner-stone was laid June 9th, 1854. Rev. W. E. Pell, a prominent minister of the Methodist Episcopal Church South, became the first principal. Mr. W. K. Blake followed him and held the position for some time; and he was succeeded by Mr. Thomas Hooper, who carried it to its close at the breaking out of the Civil War. Since that time the building has been used for many and various purposes. Col. T. J. Drewry has his military academy in it at the present. Its patronage was never very extensive and its importance never great. It is one of the many female academies or colleges that had their beginning in the period

---

1. Deems' Annals of Southern Methodism, 1857, p. 228.
2. Letter from Mr. J. M. Wynne, Murfreesboro; Rev. R. P. Troy, Greensboro.

preceding the Civil War, and for this reason has been mentioned.[1]

22nd, 1861, when it was

This institution began in the town of Goldsboro in 1834. The Borden Hotel building was used until 1857, when a large four-story brick house was erected. The original promoters were W. K. Lane, George A. Dudley, William Carraway and Nickey Nixon; and when the new building was proposed, fifteen of Goldsboro's best citizens took stock. Rev. James H. Brent was the first president, and served until the new building was about ready for use. Then Dr. S. Morgan Closs served as president one year. Rev. S. Milton Frost was the presiding officer from 1857 to 1862. The school was then suspended until 1866, when Dr. Closs revived it and ran it for three sessions. In 1868 the charter was changed, and after that it was known as Goldsboro Female College. Prof. E. W. Adams became president when Dr. Closs left the second time, and ran it till 1871, when it was closed as a college. Rev. N. Z. Graves, who had been connected with the schools in Warrenton for several years, had a private school in the building from 1871 to July, 1874. Manuel Fetter, who had been professor of Greek in the University of North Carolina from 1838 to 1868, ran a small school in its buildings until 1879. Rev. R. P. Troy kept a classical and mathematical school till June, 1881, when the building was rented for the Graded School.[2]

### YADKIN COLLEGE.

This was a venture made by the Methodist Protestant Church, and goes back to 1859 for its beginning. This

---
1. Rev. L. L. Nash, D. D.; Prof. J. H. Myrover, Fayetteville.
2. Dr. J. F. Miller, Goldsboro; general catalogue of the University of North Carolina, p. 79; Rev. R. P. Troy; Deems' Annals of Southern Methodism, 1857, pp. 175-176.

church at the present is not very strong. It does not have a large membership, nor is it especially rich. However, it had over it for several years, seated members. It has not been able to do a great deal of work in the way of schools, especially in North Carolina. Nevertheless, many of its members have fine culture and education. It has a few good schools; Western Maryland College at Westminster, Maryland, is an instance. This, like the other churches, has felt the great need of having a school of its own; and this demand showed itself very strong during the years just before the Civil War. That was a time of many educational beginnings.

For several years prior to 1856, Revs. Alsan Gray, W. H. Wills and John F. Speight, leaders of the church, debated the question of establishing a college, in which the members could educate their sons. About this time Jamestown Female College was put in operation by some of the leading members of this church. It did not run long before it was burned down, nor was it ever rebuilt. Several plans were offered, but it was finally decided to locate a college in North Carolina. Mr. Henry Walser, who lived in the western part of Davidson county, made them the best offer. The North Carolina Conference of the Methodist Protestant Church in 1855 accepted Mr. Walser's offer, and decided to build near his home. Henry Walser, D. L. Michael, J. C. Crump and Rev. Jordan Rominger, at once began to erect a brick building, two stories high, and forty by sixty feet. Mr. Walser, however, was the liberal giver in the building enterprise. The site chosen was about eleven miles west of Lexington and three miles from Advance, the nearest depot.[1]

The school was first named Yadkin Institute. George

---

1. Rev. J. N. Garrett, Yadkin College, who has given the writer much assistance; Mr. E. E. Raper, Lexington.

W. Hege, A. B., was the first principal; and the school was opened in October, 1856. He ran it as a high school until February 22nd, 1861, when it was chartered as Yadkin College. Revs. Alsan Gray, A. W. Lineberry, David Weisner, Jordan Rominger, Thomas H. Pegram, Alexander Robbins, and Henry Walser, J. A. Davis, D. L. Michael, George W. Hege, and B. F. Smith, were made trustees. Mr. Hege was elected the first president. He served with great credit till the war broke up the school. At this time there were about eighty pupils, many of whom came from a distance. At least three-fourths of these volunteered into the Confederate service, hence the numbers were decreased so that operations were suspended.[1]

In 1867 H. T. Phillips with the assistance of F. T. Walser reorganized the institution, and ran it as a high school until 1873. His success was good. Rev. J. C. Deans went in as an associate in 1871; and the two put new force into the institution. In 1873 S. Simpson, A. B., was elected president. He was a man of untiring energies, and put in as his assistants earnest teachers. He continued with considerable success till 1884. During his administration there was an annual enrollment of about sixty students; and these came from Virginia, North Carolina and South Carolina. Many of the pupils of those times have become leaders. Hon. Z. V. Walser, the present Attorney-General of North Carolina, and E. E. Raper, are illustrations. A new building, at a cost of about seven thousand dollars, was erected by President Simpson; and many other improvements were made. He resigned and went to Western Maryland College, where he is still a professor. When he left the college closed. Rev. A. R. Morgan became principal of a high school in

---

1. Rev. J. N. Garrett and Mr. E. E. Raper.

the college building in 1887, and remained till 1889. At that time George W. Holmes, A. B., took charge; and he still runs the school.[1]

From a catalogue the following course is taken : Freshman Class, first term—Latin Grammar, Greek Grammar, Practical Arithmetic, Geography, Composition, Latin Exercises ; second term—Latin Grammar, Cæsar, Xenophon's Anabasis, Greek Grammar, Higher Arithmetic, Elementary Algebra; Sophomore Class, first term—Latin Grammar, Vergil, Ovid, Herodotus, Geometry, United States History, Natural Philosophy, University Algebra; second term—Orations of Cicero, Demosthenes de Corona, Astronomy, Trigonometry, University Algebra, German Grammar, French Grammar; Junior Class, first term—Sallust, Homer's Iliad, Chemistry, Rhetoric, German Reader, Telemaque, Analytical Geometry ; second term—Cicero de Officiis, Thucydides, Navigation and Surveying, Chemistry, French and German Extracts, Lectures on Rhetoric, General History ; Senior Class, first term—Tacitus, Geology, Metaphysics, Mathematical Astronomy, English Literature, Logic ; second term—Classical Mythology and Antiquities, Lectures on International Law, Olmstead's Mechanics, Shakespeare's Plays, Higher English.

### CHARLOTTE FEMALE INSTITUTE.

This institution was organized and opened during the fall of 1857. Rev. Robert Burwell, D. D., and his wife, who had had a select school in Hillsboro for twenty years previous, took charge. The citizens of Charlotte erected a commodious building. A good faculty was selected ; and they began work with great enthusiasm. Much success came to the school. By 1859 an addition

---

[1] Rev. J. N. Garrett and Mr. E. E. Raper.

had to be made to the building, and the teaching force was enlarged by bringing in J. B. Burwell, a son of the principal. Young Mr. Burwell graduated from Hampden-Sidney College in 1853, and since his graduation had been teaching in boys' schools in Virginia. The school was kept up by them until 1872, when they moved to Raleigh and took charge of Peace Institute. In the fall of 1871 S. J. Stevens, who had made quite a reputation in Edgeworth Seminary, was added to the faculty.[1]

When the Burwells moved to Raleigh, Rev. R. H. Chapman became principal. He carried on the school for about two and a half years, and was succeeded by Rev. Taylor Martin. In 1878 Rev W. R. Atkinson took charge. He had been for some time a teacher in Peace Institute. He kept it up for several years, and then went to Columbia, South Carolina. The institute then closed its doors. About one year ago its name was changed to Presbyterian College; and Miss Lillie Long is now building it up again.[2]

Its advertised course of studies was very much the same as in most of the schools of its kind already considered. Though most of its teachers were Presbyterians, still it was a private rather than a church school.[3]

### THOMASVILLE FEMALE COLLEGE.

This was begun February 8th, 1857, under the name of Glen Anna Female Seminary.[4] However, its real beginning goes back as far as 1849 under the title of The Sylva Grove Female Seminary. Mrs. Charles Mock ran it with success for some time. While she was at its head, it was a preparatory school to Greensboro Female Col-

---
1. Capt. J. B. Burwell, Statesville; catalogues.
2. Catalogues.
3. Ibid.
4. Catalogue, 1858.

lege.[1] After her Rev. Charles Force Deems, of the North Carolina Conference, had control of it. In his journal of 1852, under the date of September 18th, he states that he had bought the Mock place; and under the date of September 25th says that he had changed the name to Glenanna in honor of his wife. On December 24th he states that Miss Branson will open the school in January, 1853.[2] He secured a regular charter for it in 1855, and ran it for a short time thereafter.

Mr. John W. Thomas built the present building at a cost of twelve thousand dollars. He placed it upon a sure footing and secured for it a large faculty, though he did not teach himself. Miss P. L. Lathop was principal in 1858. She had as her assistants: Misses Mary E. Nelson, Sallie Winkler, M. C. Shelly, C. Cunningham and Jennie Thomas.[3] There were as many as one hundred and fifty pupils at the breaking out of the Civil War. Through the great energy and correct judgment of Mr. Thomas it was kept up through those stormy times. In 1867 its name was changed to Thomasville Female College. It ran on with considerable success until 1873, when it was closed for some time in consequence of the death of Mr. Thomas.[4]

In 1874 the property was purchased by Prof. H. W. Reinhart. He ran it for ten years as sole proprietor, and with a large amount of success. In 1884 Rev. J. N. Stallings bought a half interest and became co-principal.[5] The institution continued here until March, 1889, when the whole plant, faculty and students, were tranferred to High Point.[6] For some time before this the school had been going down, and Mr. Stallings was made offers

---
1. Greensboro Patriot, June 30, 1849.
2. Charles Force Deems, by his Sons, pp. 118-115.
3. Catalogue, 1858.
4. Ibid, 1878-1879.
5. Ibid, 1883-1884.
6. Catalogue of High Point Female College, 1891-1892.

to move it to High Point. On the 11th day of March, 1889, the High Point Female College received a charter; and on the 15th of the same month the school was transferred to its new quarters. It was kept up here for about four years only and then closed its doors. It had served for a long while, and its service was fairly good. As many as a dozen teachers were connected with it during half of its existence. Its course of studies was equally as high as in any female school of those times. It was a private institution from its beginning, and its principals were of different churches.

### JUDSON COLLEGE.

This institution deserves mentioning more for the great attempt that was made rather than for what it accomplished. As early as 1858 the Baptist west of the Blue Ridge began to work up a college for girls. The Salem Association, which met at Old Salem Church, August 6th, 1858, considered the matter, and pledged about nine hundred dollars for the building. A little later that year the Western Convention adopted the college and appointed trustees. The name of Hendersonville Female College was agreed on. At the next convention it was reported that the building had been let to the contractor at a cost of $11,089. However, it was a long time before this building was ready for occupancy. In October, 1882, it was completed; and it had cost about $15,000. During this long period of building the name was changed three or four times. It was at one time known as the Western North Carolina Female College, and at another Judson Female College, and finally Judson College.[1]

Rev. J. B. Boone, with four or five teachers, ran the

---

1. Catalogue, 1890-1891; The North Carolina Journal of Education, December, 1891, pp. 67-69.

institution from its beginning to June, 1889. They won some success, though the patronage was local in most cases. Dr. R. H. Lewis, A. M., was elected president in June, 1889, and managed it for three years. He had been teaching for about thirty years. He had taught in Cumberland, Warren, Granville, Lenoir and Henderson counties; also in Oxford Female Seminary, Kinston College and the University Normal School. He had been teaching in Kinston since 1877; and he still runs a select school there. When he undertook the principalship of Judson, he surrounded himself with five good teachers and began the work with much promise. They offered a rather high course of studies, and granted A. B. and A. M. degrees; and these were open to both sexes. The enrollment during the second year of his administration was about one hundred and twenty. These came from Buncombe, Edgecombe, Haywood, Henderson, Jackson, Madison, Mecklenburg, Mitchell, Polk, Swain, and Yancey counties. The debt incurred on the building had never been paid, and the whole plant was sold under mortgage in 1892; and since then it has been used as a private school and for hotel purposes.[1]

### HORNER AND GRAVES.

This, like Bingham, was one of the very best equipped boy's schools of its time. It was first opened at Oxford in 1851 by James H. Horner, A. M., LL. D.[2] Mr. Horner was a pupil of the Bingham School and graduated at the University of North Carolina with A. B. degree in 1844.[3] He was the sole principal until 1870, when R. H. Graves, Sr., A. M., came in with him. Mr. Graves had grad-

---

1. Catalogue, 1890-1891; The North Carolina Journal of Education, p. 67; letter from Dr. Lewis, Kinston.
2. Catalogue of Horner's School, 1897-1898.
3. General Catalogue of University of North Carolina, p. 149.

uated at the University with A. B. in 1836; was a tutor of mathematics in the same 1837-1843; and for some time after this was a teacher in the same department in Caldwell Institute, of Hillsboro.[1] The school under the name of Horner and Graves remained in Oxford until 1874. In January of this year they moved to Hillsboro. Col. Charles C. Tew had founded the Hillsboro Military Academy in 1859, and carried it on with fair success until the Civil War was in full blaze. In consequence of his death at Sharpsburg and the decline of the military spirit at the close of the war, the school was never reopened as a military institution. Mrs. Tew died in 1870, and in 1872 Mr. Paul C. Cameron, of Hillsboro, bought the property. The location was excellent and the building well suited for a boy's school. He made offers to Horner and Graves, whose success at Oxford had been much more than local. They accepted his offers and transferred their training school to Hillsboro.[2] However, they did not continue together there but two years, when Mr. Horner went back to his old place. Mr. Graves carried on the school for about two years after the separation.[3]

This school, though of but short life, had a strong influence in training boys for college. The course of studies was high, and the manner of discipline rigid. The faculty was strong: J. H. Horner, A. M.; R. H. Graves, A. M.; Hugh Morson, Jr.; R. H. Graves, Jr., B. Sc., C. and M. E.; Maj. D. H. Hamilton; A. W. Venable, Jr. Mr. Morson has been in the Raleigh Male Academy for a long time; Mr. Graves afterwards became the famous mathematical professor in the University of North Carolina.[4]

---

1. General Catalogue of University of North Carolina, p. 134.
2. Our Living and Our Dead, Vol. I., pp. 498-500.
3. Letter from Profs. J. C. and J. M. Horner.
4. Catalogue, 1874-1875; General Catalogue of the University, p. 134.

## WILSON COLLEGIATE INSTITUTE.

Rev. Charles Force Deems, D. D., who was president of Greensboro Female College from 1850 to 1854[1] and was connected with several more North Carolina schools at different times, was the first principal. Immediately after the session of the North Carolina Conference in 1858, the citizens of Wilson made an appeal to Dr. Deems to establish a school for boys and girls at that place. They erected buildings at a cost of about ten thousand dollars and supplied them with seven thousand dollars' worth of furniture. They gave Dr. Deems two-thirds of all this property, and proposed to pay his expenses on a trip to Europe.[2] The school was dedicated January 13th, 1859, under the name of St. Austin's Institute; and the first session began on the 17th of the same month. By the close of this session eighty-two girls and ninety-three boys had enrolled. Miss Mary Wade Speed was principal of the girl's seminary; and Capt. James D. Radcliff had control of the boys. Courses in English, Mathematical and Classical branches were offered. Dr. Deems remained at its head for four years.[3]

Then D. S. Richardson, A. M., had charge for a short while, until the school was suspended by the war. The buildings were used for a hospital by the Confederate army. After the war Mr. Richardson came back and ran it for about four years. He was followed by E. M. Nadal. In 1871 Warren and William Woodard bought the property; and Sylvester Hassell, A. M., became principal in January, 1872. He was at its head until

---

1. Catalogue of Greensboro Female College, 1894–1895, p. 4; Charles Force Deems, by his Sons, p. 108.
2. Charles Force Deems, by his Sons, pp. 151–153; letter from Rev. Sylvester Hassell, Williamston.
3. Charles Force Deems, by his Sons, pp. 155–156.

1886. Then Silas E. Warren purchased the property, and was its principal until his death, 1894.[1]

Mr. Hassell was a man of fine native ability and culture. His school was a high grade academy at first, but was afterwards changed into a college, under the name of Wilson College. His pupils came from many of the counties of the northeastern part of the State. He gave them a fine and extensive training in most of the branches then taught in the smaller colleges. The institution by the name of Wilson College was the result of the union of the Institute and the Female Seminary. The Seminary had for some time been run by John De Berniere Hooper, A. B., A. M., assisted at one time by Rev. William Hooper, D. D. Mr. John DeB. Hooper ranks among the finest teachers the State has produced. He had a service in this line for forty-one years; was professor of Latin and French 1838–1848, and of Greek and French 1875–1885, in the University of North Carolina; was twenty-one years in private school work.[2]

The faculty in 1875 was: Sylvester Hassell, A. M., president, Physics, Ethics; J. B. Brewer, A. M., Mathematics, Chemistry; J. H. Foy, Ancient and Modern Languages; D. G. Gillespie, Book-keeping, Banking; E. M. Nadal, Mathematics; Miss Mollie A. Southall, Music; Mrs. J. B. Brewer, instructor in Music; Miss Bettie A. Chandler and Mrs. S. N. Biggs, English branches; Miss Bertha Tripp, Drawing, Painting.[3]

---

1. Letter from Rev. Sylvester Hassell; Mr. T. J. Hadley, Wilson.
2. Dr. Dred Peacock; General Catalogue of the University of North Carolina, pp. 53, 79 and 149.
3. Catalogue of Wilson College, 1875–1876.

## Chapter IV.—Schools of the Present.

In this, as in the last chapter, only the schools of more than local importance will be considered. There have been many worthy high grade schools that the writer can not speak of in this short sketch. Besides the numerous academies that can not be mentioned, there are many church or private institutions making battle against the powers of darkness still in the Old North State. Among these are representatives of each church—Baptist, Presbyterian, Quaker, Methodist, Episcopal, German Reformed, Lutheran, Christian, Catholic. In each the school can not be considered correctly without taking note of the church; nor would the church amount to very much without the school's influence. They have both grown side by side, and into and out of each other. These will be treated in the order of the time of their opening.

### WAKE FOREST COLLEGE.

This is distinctly a Baptist school. It stands at the head of all the other institutions of this denomination, and is the equal of any of the church institutions of the State. Its history has been inseperably connected with the growth and development of the Baptist church. In order to present the real conditions and circumstances under which the school was born and has grown, a very brief summary of the early history of this church will be given.

As early as 1695 there were some of this faith to be found among the colonists of North Carolina.[1] Some

---

1. History of Grassy Creek Baptist Church, p. 17.

came for adventure, and others for religious liberty. The first church was organized by Paul Palmer in 1727; and this was on the Pasquotank river, now known as Shiloh Church.[1] This at once became very active. Its members soon organized many churches in Gates, Chowan, Perquimans, Pasquotank, Camden and Currituck counties. In 1729 the second church was gathered together at Mcherrin, near Murfreesboro.[2] In 1758 the Sandy Creek Association was formed in Randolph county with nine churches. This is the oldest association in the State and the fourth in age in the United States.[3] In 1765 the Kehukee Association was formed in Halifax county[4] with eight churches. Four years later the Grassy Creek Association was organized in Granville county. This county was then, and has been since, full of Baptists. Until 1770 the Sandy Creek Association included South and North Carolina and Virginia, but at the Convention of October (14th) of the same year a division was made; and the churches of this State continued under the Sandy Creek Association.[5]

Their growth was rapid until the battle of Alamance, not far from Sandy Creek Church. After this the strong measures of Gov. Tryon drove about fifteen hundred families from this section; and the church was at a stand still for some time. During the Revolution many of the leaders of this church took a very active part. In the very first of this century a great revival swept over the State, and many additions were made to all of the churches of this denomination. About this time a movement was begun to unite all of the churches of this State into one organization for the purpose of education

---

1. History of Grassy Creek Baptist Church, p. 17; Rev. J. D. Hufham, D. D., Biblical Recorder, December 8, 1897.
2. Dr. Hufham, Biblical Recorder.
3. History of Sandy Creek Baptist Association, p. 62.
4. Ibid. p. 42; History of Kehukee Baptist Association, pp. 27-31.
5. History of Grassy Creek Baptist Church, pp. 72-74.

and missions; and this was accomplished about twenty-seven years later, when the Baptist State Convention and Board of Missions were organized at Greenville in 1830.[1]

It was during the latter part of this attempt to unite on missionary and educational work that there came about the schism. Until 1825 all the Baptists had believed in missions and Sunday schools as far as these ideas were then known, but from this until 1830 there gradually grew an opposition party. This opposition named itself Primitive Baptists, though in reality it is the younger, and the progressive side assumed the name of Missionary Baptists.[2] The opposition has always been opposed to culture and progressive industry, hence is very weak. It has had no schools, and its influence has amounted to very little. On the other hand the real Baptists have taken unto themselves the light and power of the school-room. They have grown in numbers and strength until they are to-day about the strongest religious power in North Carolina; and this State, with three hundred thousand of this faith, is the greatest Baptist Commonwealth in the Union.[3]

During the struggle for State organization for educational purposes a number of strong and heroic preachers took part: Samuel Wait, John Armstrong, Thomas Meredith, J. Culpepper, W. R. Hinton, A. J. Battle, N. Richardson, James McDaniel, T. D. Armstrong, John Purefoy, Eli Phillips, W. H. Merrit, P. W. Dowd, J. Lowell, William Burch, William Dowd, J. Goodman, Joel Gulledge, W. P. Biddle, James Dennis, Eli Carrol, Thomas Crocker, John Monroe, John Kerr, William Warrell, W. H. Jordan, Q. H. Trotman, G. W. Hufham, George Fennel, William Hooper, G. W. Thompson, D.

---

1. Dr. Hufham, Biblical Recorder, December 8, 1897.
2. History of Grassy Creek Baptist Church, p. 93.
3. J. W. Baily, Editor Biblical Recorder, Address at Wilmington, May 8, 1897.

S. Williams, A. J. Spivey, Josiah Crudup.[1] They did well their parts, and Wake Forest College owes its founding to them. Through the efforts of different ones of this number the Chowan, Neuse and Raleigh Missionary Societies and the North Carolina Benevolent Society were organized previous to 1830. During March (26–29) of the same year these united to form the State Convention.[2]

This Convention held its first meeting at Cross-Roads Church, Wake county, in 1831. There were fifty-one delegates present, from about twenty counties.[3] It was reported that $819.90 had been collected during the year for education and missions. Revs. Samuel Wait, Thomas Meredith, William Hooper and John Armstrong were the leaders of this Convention; and they were deeply imbued with the educational spirit. The following resolution was passed: "Resolved, that the Convention accept the offer of Elder John Armstrong to educate young men of the ministry, and that the Board of the Convention be authorized to send such young men as they approve to him (he having been a teacher since his coming to North Carolina) or to some school, and to defray their expenses as far as the funds of the Convention will admit."[4]

At the Convention of 1832 a proposition was made to establish a school of their own on the manual labor plan. Dr. Calvin Jones had a fine farm in Wake county of six hundred and fifteen acres, valued at $2,500. He was a liberal man as well as a believer in education, and offered to give $500 on his farm, provided the church would raise the other $2,000. J. G. Hall, W. R. Hinton,

---

[1]. J. S. Purefoy, Wake Forest Student, Vol. VI., p. 181.
[2]. Ibid, p. 182.
[3]. Ibid, p. 182.
[4]. Memoir of Rev. John L. Pritchard, pp. 19–23; J. S. Purefoy, Wake Forest Student, Vol. VI., p. 182.

John Purefoy, A. S. Wynne and S. J. Jeffreys were appointed a committee to obtain the required money with which to purchase the farm.[1] At the Convention of the next year, which met at Dockery's meeting-house in Richmond county, Stephen A. Graham, Joseph B. Outlaw, Alfred Dockery, David Thompson and Samuel S. Biddle were made a committee to secure a charter for Wake Forest Manual Labor Institute,[2] to be located on Dr. Jones' farm, sixteen miles from Raleigh.

The charter for Wake Forest Institute was secured with a good deal of difficulty. The legislature of 1833–1834 had a large number of members opposed to the Baptist doctrine and church. For a while it seemed that the charter would not be granted. However, after much discussion it passed the lower house. When it was brought to a vote in the senate there was a tie, but the speaker, Hon. William D. Moseley, an alumnus of the University of North Carolina, cast his vote in favor of the institution. Though a charter was granted, it was a meager affair. The trustees were not allowed to hold more than fifty thousand dollars of real and personal estate; and this was subject to taxation. Too, the charter was only of twenty years' duration.[3]

Rev. Samuel Wait, D. D., was the real founder and first president of the institution. According to the statement made in the general catalogue, he was elected in 1832. Dr. Smith, on page 102 of his History of Education in North Carolina, says that the election took place May 10, 1833. The school was not opened till February, 1834.[4] Dr. Wait was born in Washington county, New York, December 19th, 1789. He graduated

---

[1]. J. S. Purefoy, Wake Forest Student, Vol. VI., p. 183.
[2]. Ibid, Vol. VI., p. 183; Vol. XV., p. 201.
[3]. Catalogue of Wake Forest College, 1889–1890, copy of the Charter; J. S. Purefoy, Wake Forest Student, Vol. VI., p. 184.
[4]. General Catalogue of Wake Forest College, p. 3; Memoir of Rev. John L. Pritchard, p. 23; J. S. Purefoy, Wake Forest Student, Vol. VI., p. 184.

at the Columbian College, Washington, D. C. It is said that he was a tutor for some time in the same institution, and that he came South to obtain money for the college. The Newbern church called him as their pastor in 1827.[1] He was very active in the cause of general culture and education in his adopted State. He had much to in organizing the State Convention and the Board of Missions. In connection with Rev. Thomas Meredith he labored for the church newspaper, *The Baptist Interpreter*, which was first published at Edenton in 1833; this was transferred to Newbern the next year and had its name changed to *Biblical Recorder*; and from there it came to Raleigh in 1838, where it has since remained.[2]

His services to the infant school, of which he was the head for about eleven years, were arduous and distinguished. He had begun with $169 and twenty-five boys. When he gave up the presidency, he had erected a large brick building at a cost of $15,000, increased the patronage many fold and changed the little institute into a college. After his resignation, he was president of the Oxford Female Seminary from 1851 to 1857; and served the churches in Caswell county as pastor till his death, July 28th, 1867.[3] He was president of the board of trustees of Wake Forest from 1845 to 1866.[4]

Along with Dr. Wait in the early struggle was Rev. John Armstrong. He became financial agent at the same time that Dr. Wait assumed the principalship; and was the teacher of Ancient Languages from 1835 to November, 1837.[5] A new building was needed at once, and subscriptions for the same were begun in February,

---

1. Smiths' History of Education in North Carolina, p. 102.
2. Dr. Hufham, Biblical Recorder, December 8, 1897.
3. J. B. Brewer, Wake Forest Student, Vol. XV., pp. 201–211; J. S. Purefoy, Wake Forest Student, Vol. VI., p. 182; Smiths' History of Education, p. 102.
4. General Catalogue, p. 9.
5. Ibid, p. 18.

1835. C. W. Skinner and D. S. Williams gave $500 each; and Mr. Armstrong obtained about $17,000 in subscriptions. The trustees gave out the contract for a building at a cost of $15,000. Before the building was completed great financial depression spread over the country. By November, 1836, they were in debt $2,010.55. In 1838 Dr. Wait took the field as agent, while Rev. J. B. White became president *pro tem*. On January 2nd, 1841, they secured $10,000 as a loan from the literary fund of the State. This put them in better circumstances, though the debt on the old building was not entirely paid until 1849. Rev. J. S. Purefoy was the great force in this financial crisis.[1]

The manual labor idea was a failure, and was abandoned in 1838. The labor of the student was worth but three cents an hour and amounted to very little. The idea was better than the remuneration to the student. The first circular of expenses was: board $5 per month; tuition in Latin and Greek $2; English branches $1.50; washing 75 cents—total for ten months $92.50.[2] By an act of the legislature the charter was amended and the name changed to Wake Forest College, December 28th, 1838. This amendment gave them far greater privileges. The time was extended fifty years and the trustees could hold $250,000 free from taxes. When the college came into existence, the courses and terms were raised.[3] According to their circulars of 1839 the expenses per year were: tuition $45; room rent $2; bed and bedding $4; wood $2; servants' hire $2; deposit for repairs $2. Board and washing could be had for $8 per month.[4]

Dr. Wait resigned November 26th, 1844; and Rev.

---

1. General Catalogue, p. 4; J. B. Brewer, Wake Forest Student, Vol. XV., pp. 201-210.
2. J. S. Purefoy, Wake Forest Student, Vol. VI., pp. 184-185.
3. Catalogue, 1889-1890, copy of Amendment.
4. Given also by Smith, History of Education, p. 105.

William Hooper, D. D., LL. D., was elected his successor October 17th, 1845. He assumed control at the beginning of the next year.[1] He was a conspicuous character in the teaching profession, having served with great ability for sixty-six years; was a grandson of William Hooper, the signer of the Declaration of Independence;[2] born near Wilmington, North Carolina, 1782; took from the University of North Carolina A. B. in 1809, A. M. in 1812 and D. D. in 1857; was professor of Ancient Languages in the same 1817-22 and 1828-37, of Rhetoric and Logic 1825-28; was a professor in the South Carolina College for a time before becoming president of Wake Forest.[3] Dr. Hooper held the presidency but two years. However, he did much in this short time. He gave assistance in rescuing the institution from the great debt that had been incurred, though it was about one year after his resignation that this was paid in full. His work in the Convention for the organization, as a trustee and as a president, was alike distinguished.

Rev. John B. White, D. D., was elected the third president in 1849, and held the position until June, 1852, when Prof. W. H. Owen was president *pro tem* for two years.[4] It was during the first year of Dr. White's administration that the indebtedness was paid and a small endowment fund begun.[5]

Washington Manly Wingate, D. D., became president in June, 1854, and was the head and guide until his death, February 27th, 1879.[6] He was the greatest presiding officer this institution has ever had. He brought it from a small college with little equipment and practically no endowment to the front rank of Southern colleges.

---
1. General Catalogue of Wake Forest College, pp. 8 and 18.
2. General Catalogue of the University of North Carolina, p. 53.
3. Ibid, pp. 79-80 and 149.
4. General Catalogue, pp. 3-4.
5. J. B. Brewer, Wake Forest Student, Vol. XV., pp. 201-210.
6. General Catalogue, pp. 4 and 18.

His life for a quarter of a century was the life and light of the institution. He was born in Darlington, South Carolina, March 22nd, 1828; graduated with A. B. from Wake Forest in 1849; studied theology at Furman University, South Carolina, for two years; from 1852 to 1854 agent for his *alma mater*.[1]

When he took hold, the institution needed a strong mind to guide it and an energetic one to extend its sphere. From 1854 to 1861 it rose rapidly and firmly. When the devastation of war had swept the fruits from our soil, it required even greater force to bring back resources and life. Duties were suspended in May, 1862, and it was not reopened until 1866. At the State Convention of 1856, which met at Raleigh, $25,000 were pledged for the endowment fund. Dr. Wingate had increased this amount to $46,000 by 1861. When the war closed the whole fund was worth only $11,700. However, new and greater efforts were made on this line, and from 1866 to 1883 about $40,000 more were secured.[2] He not only worked to equip the college with apparatus and strong teachers, but toiled to make true men out of his students. He labored, as few others have, for a deep and general culture. Through his college duties he still kept up the ministry, being at different times pastor of the churches in Oxford, Franklinton, Selma and elsewhere. He was a power in conventions, assemblies and in all kinds of educational or religious work.[3]

Rev. J. D. Hufham, D. D., who is now the greatest North Carolina Baptist, says of him: "We have lost the greatest man we had among us. For twenty-five years he was the central figure, the greatest power of North Carolina Baptists. He had a vigorous, comprehensive and subtle intellect. In law, or statesmanship,

---

1. Manuscript on Wingate; General Catalogue, p. 24.
2. General Catalogue, p. 4.
3. Manuscript on Wingate.

or any of the professions which require the knowledge and management of men, he would have risen to eminence. He was a great moral philosopher, a great preacher, the best I have ever heard, and a wise and successful pastor. He ruled the boys through their respect for him and their faith in him. He was a brave man, a true man; still he was as tender and gentle as a woman."[1]

In 1879 Rev. Thomas Henderson Pritchard, D. D., became president. He held the position until June, 1882.[2] He had had such a useful career and was so well and favorably known, that he perhaps of all was the very man to advertise the college to the whole church. He was born in Charlotte, North Carolina, February 8th, 1832; graduated with A. B. from Wake Forest in 1854; ordained minister in 1855; three years preacher and teacher in Hertford; two years a student under Dr. John A. Broadus in Charlottesville, Virginia; pastor of Franklin-Square, Baltimore, for three years; pastor of First Baptist Church of Raleigh for about thirteen years; twenty-three years a trustee of his *alma mater*; for some time associate editor of the *Biblical Recorder*; after resigning the presidency of Wake Forest, pastor at Louisville, Kentucky, Wilmington and Charlotte, North Carolina; died in Charlotte, May 23rd, 1896.[3]

Rev. W. B. Royall, D. D., professor of Greek, was chairman of the faculty from June, 1882, to November, 1884, when Rev. Charles Elisha Taylor, D. D., assumed the presidency. He was born in Richmond, Virginia, October 28th, 1842; entered Richmond College at fifteen and would have graduated in 1862 but for the war; joined the army April 17th, 1861; at the University of Virginia 1865–70, where he graduated; traveled for some

---
1. Manuscript on Wingate.
2. General Catalogue, pp. 4 and 18.
3. Wake Forest Student, Vol. XV., pp. 521–534.

time in Europe;[1] was assistant professor of Latin and German 1870-71, and professor of Latin and German from 1871 to 1884, in Wake Forest;[2] in 1889 the University of North Carolina gave him Litt. D.[3] He still guides the institution, and with great ability and success.

On December 31st, 1883, the endowment fund reached $100,000. During this year Mr. J. A. Bostwick, of New York, gave his first gift—$10,000. Two years afterwards he gave the Bostwick Loan Fund, to aid indigent young men; and in 1886 he added $50,000 to the endowment. During July, 1890, the same liberal giver offered to add one-half to whatever amount, up to $50,000, might be raised by March 1st, 1891. Then began one of the greatest canvasses ever made in this State. Hundreds of poor men, women and children gave their mite; and by the stated time $26,000 had been secured. By this about $40,000 were added, and the fund amounted to $194,000.[4] At the present time (1897) this fund exceeds $200,000.[5] In addition to a large increase of funds, there have been erected three more commodious buildings. The Heck-Williams Building was erected in 1878 by Col. J. M. Heck and Mr. John G. Williams, of Raleigh. The Wingate Memorial Building was erected in 1880 by the friends of the institution. The Lea Laboratory, for the most part built through the generosity of Mr. Sidney S. Lea, of Caswell county, was completed in 1888.[6]

The faculty has been: Samuel Wait, Philos., Lit., 1834-45; Thomas Meredith, Math., Nat. Philos., 1834-37; John Armstrong, Anc. Langs., 1835-37; Charles R. Merriam, tutor of Husbandry, 1834; Graves (1835) and Wilcox (1836), tutors; John B. White, Math., Nat.

---

1. Dr. Hufham, Biblical Recorder, December 8, 1897; letter from President Taylor.
2. General Catalogue, p. 20.
3. General Catalogue of the University of North Carolina, p. 242.
4. General Catalogue, pp. 4-5.
5. Catalogue, 1896-1897.
6. General Catalogue, pp. 5-6.

SCHOOLS OF NORTH CAROLINA. 143

Philos., 1837–49; D. F. Richardson, Anc. Langs., 1837–39; Stephen Moore, Adjunct of Langs., 1838–39; George W. Thompson, tutor, 1838; D. F. Richardson, Hebrew, Rhet., 1839–43; Stephen Moore, Greek, Lat., 1839–43; E. W. West, tutor, 1841–42; William Hays Owen, Anc. Langs., 1843–58; William Tell Brooks, tutor, 1843–46; William Hooper, Philos., Lit., 1845–49; Samuel S. Satchwell, tutor, 1846–47; W. T. Brooks, Asst. Anc. Langs., 1846–58; Archibald McDowell, tutor, 1847; John B. White, Philos., Lit., 1849; William T. Walters, tutor, 1849–52; Willie Person Mangum, Jr., tutor, 1849–50; Benjamin Wesley Justice, tutor, 1850–52; John Mitchell, tutor, 1852; W. T. Walters, Math., 1852–68; James Henry Foote, tutor, 1853; Thomas H. Pritchard, tutor, 1853; W. M. Wingate, Philos., Rhet., 1854–79; William Cummings, Chem., Min., Geol., 1854; William Gaston Simmons, Chem., Nat. Hist., 1855–88; Benson Field Cole, tutor, 1856; Robert H. Marsh, tutor Anc. Langs., 1856; Samuel P. Smith, tutor, 1859; J. H. Foote, Anc. Langs., 1859–66; William Royall, Lang., 1859–70; William Baily Royall, tutor, 1866–68; Luther Rice Mills, Adjunct Math., 1867–71; W. B. Royall, Asst. Langs., 1868–71; John C. Scarborough, tutor, 1869–71; Charles Meredith Seawell, tutor, 1870; Charles Elisha Taylor, Asst. Lat., German, 1870–71; L. R. Mills, Math., 1871– ; W. B. Royall, Greek, French, 1871– ; C. E. Taylor, Lat., German, 1871–84; L. W. Bagley, tutor, 1877; W. L. Poteat, tutor, 1878–80; Neill Dockery Johnson, tutor, 1878; T. H. Pritchard, Philos., Lit., 1879–82; Charles Wesley Scarborough, tutor, 1879–82; William Royall, Modern Lang., 1880; W. L. Poteat, Asst. Nat. Hist., 1880–83; Charles Henry Martin, tutor, 1882; Eli E. Hilliard, tutor, 1882–83; Exum Green Beckwith, tutor, 1883; William Furney Marshall, tutor, 1883; W. L. Poteat, Nat. Hist., 1883–88; C.

E. Taylor, Philos., Hist., 1884–; Edwin McNeill Poteat, Asst. Lat., 1885; James Reynolds Duggan, Chem., 1886–88; George W. Manly, Lat., 1886–90; Walter H. Michael, Asst. Lat., Math., 1886–88; Charles E. Reese, Chem., 1888; W. H. Michael, App. Math., Phys., 1888–90; E. G. Beckwith, Asst. Math., 1888; John Bethune Carlyle, Asst. Lat., 1888–91; Aaron E. Purinton, Chem., 1888–89; Benjamin Franklin Sledd, Mod. Lang., 1888–94; Charles Edward Brewer, Chem., 1886–; Thomas Stafford Sprinkle, Phys. Cult., 1889–91; George Washington Greene, Lat., 1890–91; John F. Lanneau, Phys., App. Math., 1890–; J. B. Carlyle, Lat., 1891–; Jas. Constantine Maske, Asst. Langs., 1891–94; Enoch Walter Sikes, Phys. Cult., 1891–94;[1] William J. Ferrell, Asst. Math., 1892–; Needham Y. Gulley, Law, 1893–95, Law and Polit. Sci., 1895–; Hendren Gorrell, Mod. Lang., 1894–; Robert W. Haywood, Asst. Greek, Lat., 1894–96; Walters Durham, Phys. Cult., 1894–95; George W. Paschal, Asst. Greek, Lat., 1896–; Willis R. Cullom, Bible, 1896–.[2]

The present faculty, consisting of twelve professors, two assistant professors and three tutors, is very strong. With the exception of the University, there is not a more able or consecrated set of intellectual workers in the State. There are among them students and graduates of the University of Virginia, Leipsic (Germany), Johns Hopkins, Washington and Lee, and Chicago University.[3] At the last State Convention, held in Oxford, E. W. Sikes, M. A., Ph. D. (Johns Hopkins University), was elected to the Chair of History. Before this, History had been under the charge of the president or a professor of some other department. From this new department very much may be expected. The Baptists have already done

---
1. General Catalogue, pp. 18–20.
2. Catalogues, 1893–1896.
3. News and Observer, Raleigh, August 18, 1897.

a great deal for their history. Rev. J. D. Hufham, D. D., is now doing some fine work; and Dr. Sikes will no doubt give a greater impetus to the historical spirit, which is just now beginning to move, correct and enlighten our State. The publications of the faculty have not been very many, though there is at present quite a tendency toward authorship. Drs. Hooper, Wingate, Walters and Brooks published some pamphlets, mainly of sermons. Dr. William Royall published a book on Latin Syntax, also one on Ethics. During the summer of 1896 Dr. Gorrell and Prof. Sledd brought out a new edition of The Princess of Cleves. Prof. Sledd published a book of poems, From Cliff and Scaur, in December, 1897. President Taylor has written a Life of Matthew Tyson Yates, which is to be published during the year 1898.[1]

The course of studies is fairly high for Southern institutions. For entrance into college classes two years in Latin, one in Greek, a fair knowledge of English, Arithmetic, Algebra to equations of the second degree, Elementary Botany, Physiology, Physical Geography and Zoology, are required. The following collegiate schools are given: Latin Language and Literature, three years and seminary work; Greek Language and Literature, three years and seminary; English Language and Literature—Rhetoric, History of Literature, Old and Middle English, History of Language; Modern Languages—French and German Languages and Literature, two years and advanced work in each; Pure Mathematics—Algebra, Geometry, Trigonometry, Analytical Geometry, Differential and Integral Calculus; Physics, Applied Mathematics, Astronomy; Chemistry—General, Inorganic, Organic, Applied Chemistry, Mineralogy; Biology—General Biology, Botany, Zoology, Human Physiology, Geology;

---
1. Letter from President Taylor.

Moral Philosophy—Psychology, Ethics, Logic, Christian Evidences, History of Philosophy; History and Political Science—History, Political Economy, Constitutional Government; Law—Common, Statute, International, Constitutional; Bible, two years. B. A., M. A. and B. L. degrees are conferred.[1]

The two literary societies, Euzelian and Philomathesian, were founded in 1837 and have grown with the institution. Their influence has been deeply felt in all forms of the college life. In 1890 the Scientific Society was organized, and in 1895 the Historical Society. These have already shown their usefulness in promulgating a scientific and historical spirit, that some day will bless the State.[2] Along with the institution and the different societies has grown the library, until it now has 11,500 volumes.[3] One of the institution's most effective agencies for intellectual, literary and college life, has been the *Student*. This began its career in January, 1882, and has now grown to be among the leading school papers.[4]

Upon the whole Wake Forest College has had a very honorable record. Since its founding about four thousand different students have been within its walls. Almost five hundred of these have become ministers of the gospel; and many others have won eminence in law, politics, medicine, merchandising, manufacturing and teaching. Each year adds to its strength in facilities and patronage. During 1892–1893 the enrollment was 191. Since that it has gradually increased to 197, 221, 260 and to 263 for the year 1896–1897.[5] The present

---
1. Catalogue, 1896–1897, pp. 20–46.
2. Ibid, pp. 53–55.
3. Letter from President Taylor.
4. Catalogue, 1896–1897, p. 56.
5. General Catalogue; Catalogues since 1892.

policy is vigorous and aggressive. This institution, with its church, has made a very active fight against State aid to higher education. That it has aided its welfare thereby cannot be proven; the future only can tell.

### DAVIDSON COLLEGE.

The Presbyterian settlements in North Carolina have already been spoken of somewhat at length; so also have their early schools. It has been shown that they were a strong element in the political, religious and educational life of this State during the latter part of the eighteenth century. While other churches, especially the Baptist and Methodist, have grown rapidly during the nineteenth century, the Presbyterian has gone side by side of these. It still has great influence and power and now, as a century ago, firmly believes in its institutions of learning. The strongest of these for more than fifty years has been Davidson College. It has been to them what Wake Forest has been to the Baptists—a source of life as well as of light.

This institution was located in the northern part of Mecklenburg county, midway between Charlotte and Statesville, twenty-two miles from each,[1] in the year 1837. Not far from this had been the classical schools: Crowfield, Sugar Creek, Queens' Museum, Zion-Parnassus, Providence, Rocky River, Poplar Tent, Centre, Bethany and others. The idea of having a Presbyterian college in this community was in vogue as early as 1820. It was at a convention held in Lincolnton in September of this year that the first steps were taken. In this gathering were many from a large area of both the Carolinas. They resolved to establish a school by the name of Western College, and appointed a board of trustees.

---

1. Catalogue, 1896–1897, p. 42.

They felt the great need of having a high grade institution in their own midst; the University was rather far away for those times of few conveniences for traveling. A charter was granted, and the board of trustees made attempts to secure money with which to erect a building. Success did not come to them, why the writer does not know. They gave up the whole affair in 1824.[1]

The idea among many Presbyterians was not by any means dead; it was taking a new hold. At the Presbytery of Concord, which met at Prospect Church in Rowan county during March, 1835, Rev. Robert Hall Morrison is said to have introduced the following resolution: "Resolved, That this Presbytery, deeply impressed with the importance of securing the means of education to young men, within our bounds, of hopeful piety and talents, preparatory to the gospel ministry, undertake (in humble reliance upon the blessing of God) the establishment of a *Manual Labor School;* and that a committee be appointed to report at the next meeting of the Presbytery the best measures for its accomplishment and the most favorable places for its location."[2] Revs. Robert H. Morrison, John Robinson, Stephen Frontis and Samuel Williamson, with Robert Burton, William Lee Davidson, John Phifer and Joseph Young, were made the committee.[3]

During August of the same year it was reported that a farm of four hundred and ninety-six acres had been contracted for. This belonged to William Lee Davidson; and they were to pay him $1,521 by the first of the next year. Mr. Morrison had by this time obtained in subscriptions $18,000, and Rev. P. J. Sparrow $12,392, making in all more than thirty thousand dollars. These

---

1. Semi-Centenary Addresses, pp. 30-31.
2. Minutes of Concord Presbytery, Vol. III., p. 107, copied edition, given in Semi-Centenary Addresses, pp. 33-34.
3. Semi-Centenary Addresses, p. 8.

reports were made on the 25th of August, 1836; and on the next day it was decided to name the school Davidson College, after Gen. William Davidson, who fell like a hero fighting for liberty at Cowan's Ford.[1] An invitation was at once sent to the Bethel Presbytery, of South Carolina, to join in this new enterprise. The invitation was accepted October 10th, 1835. Soon after this the Morganton Presbytery, which included the territory west of the Catawba river, also came in.[2] They selected a site two miles from Old Centre Meeting-house and one and a half from the Iredell line. On this they began to erect the buildings in the summer of 1836.[3] The Stewards' Hall, the President's House, a home for the teacher of languages, now known as "Tammany," and four blocks of brick dormitories, were completed within a short while.[4]

On March 1st, 1837, the college opened. Rev. Robert Hall Morrison, D. D., pastor of Sugar Creek, president and professor of Mental and Moral Philosophy; Rev. Patrick Jones Sparrow, D. D., of Salisbury, professor of Ancient Languages; Mortimer D. Johnston, A. M., tutor of Mathematics—these were the faculty for the first year.[5] Dr. Morrison was the strongest personality in the educational movement of that time, and was elected the first president of the infant college. He was chosen by the three Presbyteries of Concord, Bethel and Morganton. He was born in Cabarrus county, North Carolina, September 8th, 1798; graduated with A. B. from the University of the State in 1818; ordained minister April 21st, 1821; served the churches at Providence, Fayetteville

---

1. Semi-Centenary Addresses. p. 34; Foote's Sketches, p. 521; Davidson Monthly, Vol. VII., p. 195.
2. Semi-Centenary Addresses, p. 35; Davidson Monthly, Vol. VII., p. 195.
3. Ibid, p. 35
4. Ibid. p. 37.
5. Semi-Centenary Addresses. p. 38; Foote's Sketches, p. 321; Davidson Monthly, Vol. VII., p. 196.

and Sugar Creek; received D. D. from the University of North Carolina 1838, and A. M. from the College of New Jersey; after resigning the presidency of Davidson was pastor of Unity and Macpelah churches; died May 13th, 1889.[1]

Dr. Morrison resigned early in 1840. He had worked for the institution with such enthusiasm and force that his health became very poor, hence his resignation. During his short term of office much was done—the school had been organized and started on its way. During the first session there were about sixty students; and there were not good accommodations for more than forty-eight. More rooms were soon added, and by the end of his administration there were about one hundred pupils each year. The manual labor idea, from which they at first expected many good results, soon proved a failure, and was abandoned in 1841. There was no graduating class until 1840. However, there were public examinations and orations at the close of each spring term. The first attempt to secure a chemical apparatus and a library was made during the second year, but with little success.[2]

A charter was granted and ratified December 28th, 1838. However, there was a good deal of difficulty in securing this, as a large number of the legislature at that time opposed the idea of giving a grant to an institution under the church. By this charter the trustees were to be chosen by the Presbyteries of Concord, Bethel and Morganton, and any other Presbyteries of the State that might afterwards wish to join these in the educational enterprise. The original trustees were: John Robinson, Ephraim Davidson, Thomas L. Cowan, Robert H. Burton, Robert H. Morrison, John Williamson, Joseph

---

1. Semi-Centenary Addresses, pp. 88–39; Semi-Centennial Catalogue, p. 13; General Catalogue of the University of North Carolina, p. 132.
2. Semi-Centenary Addresses, pp. 91–107.

W. Ross, William L. Davidson, Charles W. Harris, Walter S. Pharr, Cyrus L. Hunter, John D. Graham, Robert Potts, James M. H. Adams, David A. Caldwell, William B. Wood, Moses W. Alexander, D. C. Mebane, James W. Osborne, Henry N. Pharr, John M. Wilson, P. J. Sparrow, James G. Torrence, John L. Daniel, Pierpont E. Bishop, George W. Dunlap and John Springs.[1] By article first of the constitution, none were eligible to a trusteeship but "members in full communion of the Presbyterian Church."[2]

When it came to the qualifications of teachers, the constitution was still more rigid. According to the third section of the second article, they were compelled to take the following vows: "I do sincerely believe the Scriptures of the Old and New Testaments to be the word of God, the only infallible rule of faith and practice. I do sincerely adopt the Confession of Faith of the Presbyterian Church in the United States of America, as faithfully exhibiting the doctrines taught in the Holy Scriptures. . . . . . . . .
I do solemnly engage not to teach anything that is opposed to any doctrine contained in the Confession of Faith, nor to oppose any of the fundamental principles of the Presbyterian Church Government, while I continue a teacher or professor of this Institution."[3]

The text-books used during Dr. Morrison's administration were: Day's Algebra, Olmstead's Natural Philosophy and Astronomy, Turner's Chemistry, Gibson's Surveying, Hedge's Logic, Locke on the Human Understanding, Blair's Rhetoric, Paley's Evidences of Christianity, Adam's Latin Grammar, Cæsar's Commentaries, Sallust, Vergil, Cicero, Horace, Livy, Valphy's Greek Grammar, Greek Testament, Graeca Minora and Ma-

---
1. Semi-Centenary Addresses. pp. 48–49; Semi-Centennial Catalogue, pp. 2–3.
2. Foote's Sketches, p. 522.
3. Ibid. p. 522.

jora.¹ And in connection with this course of studies Rev. Patrick Jones Sparrow deserves more than a mere mention. He it was who did a great part of the teaching during the first three years. He was born in Lincoln county, North Carolina, in 1802; served his church in many ways before becoming professor of languages in Davidson; president of Hampden-Sidney College, Virginia, for some time after 1842; died in Alabama, November 10th, 1867.²

Rev. Samuel Williamson, A. M., D. D., became president in July, 1841. He gave the longest service of any presiding officer—thirteen years; and his administration was distinguished, especially so when the difficulties under which he labored are considered. The manual labor idea had failed and the institution was in poor financial circumstances; and it was by his great energy and tact that it was kept alive. During a great part of his presidency, he was pastor of the College Church, attended to his official duties and at the same time taught Rhetoric, Logic, Natural Philosophy, Mineralology, Geology, Chemistry, Evidences of Christianity, Moral Philosophy, Metaphysics, Political Economy and International Law. At no time during his administration did the income support more than two regular professors, and that too in a meager way. Many plans were attempted to secure more money, among which was the sale of twenty-year scholarships. About four hundred of these were to be sold to raise $40,000, with which to endow two professorships. This plan, while it brought in some money at the time, was ruinous in the end. They proposed to sell tuition twenty years in advance at five dollars per year. The Civil War destroyed its proceeds, while the scholarships remained good.³

---

1. Semi-Centenary Addresses, p. 98.
2. Ibid, pp. 39-40; Semi Centennial Catalogue, p. 14.
3. Ibid, pp. 50-52, 109-119; Davidson Monthly, Vol. VII., p. 196.

Dr. Williamson was born in York county, South Carolina, June 12th, 1795; graduated at South Carolina College in 1818; pastor of Providence Church from 1822 to 1840, when he became professor of Mathematics in Davidson; given D. D. by Washington College in 1847; pastor of Hopewell and Steel Creek 1855-1857; preacher in Arkansas 1857-1882, where he died March 12th, 1882.[1] His influence upon the inner life of his students was great; he made a deep impression upon them, one that remained a life-time. There were one hundred and seventy-three A. B. graduates under him. Many of these became distinguished in after life. Among this number were W. P. Bynum, a member of the Supreme Court of North Carolina, and J. M. Baker, a judge of his adopted State, Florida, and a member of the Confederate States Senate.[2]

Just as Dr. Williamson was giving up the presidency a great gift came to the institution. By the will of Maxwell Chambers, dated November, 1854, a legacy of one-fourth of a million dollars was left to the college. However, as their original charter did not allow the trustees to hold but two hundred thousand dollars, about $45,000 of this went back to his next kin, Hon. David F. Caldwell. The legislature at once gave the trustees the power to hold a half a million, but this action was too late to save all of the legacy. Mr. Chambers deserves a high place in the history of this institution. It was by means of his gift that the college was placed in good financial circumstances, a chapel and dormitories erected, and laboratories and library equipped. He had been very successful in business in Charleston, South Carolina, and in Salisbury of this State. He was a great giver to

---
1. Semi-Centenary Addresses, pp. 50-52, 109-119; Davidson Monthly, Vol. VII., p. 196; Semi-Centennial Catalogue, p. 14.
2. Semi-Centenary Addresses, p. 115.

the needy of his fellow-men, and in many ways assisted in the betterment of his country.[1]

On January 24th, 1855, Rev. Drury Lacy, D. D., was elected the third president. He began his duties in July, 1855, and served till July, 1860. He was born in Prince Edward county, Virginia, August 5th, 1802;[2] graduated at Hampden-Sidney College in 1822, and at the Union Theological Seminary in 1832; pastor of the Presbyterian Church in Newbern and Raleigh from 1833 to his election as president of Davidson; teacher in Raleigh 1865–1880; given A. M. in 1839 and D. D. in 1852, by the University of North Carolina; died in Jonesboro, North Carolina, August 1st, 1884.[3] He was a man of fine scholarship and great earnestness, but soon found the rigid and tiring work of administering the affairs of the college burdensome. Two hundred and seventy-one pupils were enrolled and fifty-five graduated during his term of office. He was professor of Metaphysics as well as president; and managed the affairs of erecting the chapel building.[4]

Associated with him were Rev. E. F. Rockwell, D. D., Gen. D. H. Hill, Col. J. A. Leland, C. D. Fishburne, and W. C. Kerr. With these teachers began that period of rigid drilling, that has since been characteristic of the institution. Rockwell in Latin, Fishburne in Greek, Hill and Leland in Mathematics and Science, worked the boys so hard that there came about an unpleasant disturbance in 1854–1855, in consequence of which some of the students left. These were men who became eminent in different lines; and while they taught in Davidson they accepted no standard but that of true and high scholarship.[5]

---

1. Semi-Centenary Addresses, pp. 53–54; Davidson Monthly, Vol. VII., p. 196.
2. Ibid, p. 55; Davidson Monthly, Vol. VII., p. 197.
3. Ibid, p. 56; Semi-Centennial Catalogue, p. 16; General Catalogue of University of North Carolina, p. 239.
4. Semi-Centenary Addresses, pp. 127 and 129.
5. Ibid, pp. 122 and 124.

Gen. Hill, though by far better known as a soldier, still had a very honorable and extensive career as a school-man. He was born in York county, South Carolina, July 21st, 1821; graduated at West Point 1842; professor of Mathematics in Washington College, Virginia, 1847–1853; superintendent of the North Carolina Military Academy, Charlotte, 1859–1860; became Lieutenant General of the Confederate States Army July 10th, 1863; editor of the Land We Love 1866–1869; author of Elements of Algebra; president of the University of Arkansas 1877–1884, and of Middle Georgia Military and Agricultural College 1885–1889; died at Charlotte, North Carolina, 1889.[1] Prof. Kerr also deserves more than a mention. He was born in Guilford county, North Carolina, in 1827; took from the University of the State A. B. 1850, A. M. 1852 and Ph. D. 1879; student at Harvard 1853–1855; computer in the office of the Nautical Almanac 1852–1857; geologist of North Carolina 1864–1882; author of many valuable reports and works on the Geology of this State; died in 1885.[2]

In 1860 Rev. John Lycan Kirkpatrick, D. D., became president. He came at a time when high hopes were in the college atmosphere. The new building had been completed at a cost of from $85,000 to $90,000. There was a great attempt to secure the best possible teachers; and the salaries were raised from twelve to fifteen hundred dollars. It seemed that a new and far greater era awaited the institution. But when the Civil War came on everything was brought to a standstill, though duties were not entirely suspended until a short while before the surrender. There were from four to six teachers and several young boys in the college halls most of the time during those gloomy years. However, only two classes

---

1. Semi-Centennial Catalogue, p. 15; Lieut.-General Hill, by Judge A. C. Avery.
2. General Catalogue of the University of North Carolina. pp. 159 and 241; Semi-Centennial Catalogue, p. 16.

graduated. These were in 1861 and 1864, and they were small. The course of studies was very irregular and in many cases very low. The institution for the time being became a high school, with doors open to the youth of the South wandering from place to place. Dr. Kirkpatrick was a great preacher and power, and had his circumstances been at all favorable would have accomplished much. He had done his best, but the institution seemed almost ruined; and he resigned in 1866 to accept a chair in Washington College, afterwards called Washington and Lee University.[1] He was born in Mecklenburg county, North Carolina, January 13th, 1813; graduated at Hampden-Sidney College 1832; licensed to preach in 1837, and was pastor at Lynchburg, Virginia, Gainsville, Alabama, and Charleston, South Carolina; professor of Moral Philosophy and Belles-Lettres in Washington College 1866–1885, the year of his death.[2]

When the war closed the funds of the college were almost gone, and still the scholarships sold in 1851 were to be paid in free tuition. It seemed to the trustees necessary to repudiate these scholarships or to reduce the faculty to three members. They chose the former and made strenuous efforts to bring back life to the almost lifeless institution. In 1866 Rev. George Wilson McPhail, D. D., LL. D., was elected president. They gave him six strong teachers; and he was the professor of Mental and Moral Philosophy. They all began work with zeal, and the results were far better than any one had ever expected. There were not more than twenty pupils during the first year of his administration, but as prosperity began to return the numbers increased rapidly, until in 1870 there was an enrollment of one hundred and twenty-five.[3]

---

1. Semi-Centenary Addresses, pp. 56–57, 131–139.
2. Ibid. p. 57; Semi-Centennial Catalogue, p. 17.
3. Semi-Centenary Addresses, pp. 58–59, 141–146.

Dr. McPhail was of delicate constitution, and the burdens of bringing back life and patronage to the college proved too much for him. His death occurred while he was in the office, in the midst of the Commencement of 1871, June 28th. He was a great man and his influence upon his students remained through life. During his short term of five years much was done to build up and strengthen every phase of the college. In this time sixty young men graduated, one in 1867 and three in 1868. He was born in Norfolk, Virginia, December 26th, 1818; graduated at Yale 1835; pastor in Virginia and Pennsylvania 1842-1861; president of LaFayette College, Pennsylvania, 1860-1862; principal of the Female Seminary in Norfolk 1860-1867.[1]

Upon the death of Dr. McPhail, John Rennie Blake, A. M., professor of Physics since 1861, was made chairman of the faculty. His term of office continued until 1877. These six years were among the most prosperous the institution ever had. It was a time of many needed changes and universal good will. His administration compares very favorably with that of any of the presidents. He and his co-laborers, for the members of the faculty were each alike responsible for a part of the administration, increased tuition fees, introduced entrance examinations in order to raise the standard of scholarship, extended the management of the college to the Presbyteries of Georgia, Florida and South Carolina, put a financial agent into the field, and raised the curriculum to a great extent. During these six years one hundred and three students graduated, and two hundred and five matriculated.[2]

Prof. Blake, in addition to his regular department and the chairmanship, was clerk of the faculty, librarian,

---

1. Semi-Centenary Addresses, p. 59; Semi-Centennial Catalogue, p. 18.
2. Ibid. pp. 60-61, 147-154; Davidson Monthly, Vol. VII., p. 197.

treasurer of several funds and of the college; and received no extra pay for all these extra duties. He held his professorship until 1885, a period of a quarter of a century. This was the longest term in the whole history of the college to that time; and since there has been but one of the same duration—that of William Joseph Martin, A. M., LL. D., who was professor of Chemistry from 1869–1896. He was born in Greenwood, South Carolina, 1825; graduated at the University of Georgia 1846; teacher in South Carolina 1846–1853, and in the Presbyterian Female College of Greensboro, Georgia, 1853–1856; student in Harvard 1856–1857; professor in La Grange Synodical College, Tennessee, 1857–1861; professor of Physics, Chemistry and Geology in Davidson College 1861–1869, Natural Philosophy and Astronomy 1869–1885. After his resignation in 1885, he retired to private life in Greenwood, South Carolina.[1]

In 1877 Rev. Andrew Doz Hepburn, A. M., D. D., LL. D., was elected the seventh president; and he kept the office until June, 1885. He was very successful in stirring up new ambitions and hopes in his students and as a president did much, though he was not in accord with the trustees toward the latter part of his administration. One hundred and twelve students graduated under him, and three hundred and eighteen matriculated. He resigned in 1884 in consideration of the difference of opinion between himself and the trustees. He went back to Miami University, Ohio, of which institution he afterwards became president.[2] He was born in Williamsport, Pennsylvania, November 14th, 1830; graduated at the University of Virginia 1852; professor of Logic and Rhetoric in the University of North Carolina 1860–1867; professor in Miami University till 1873;

---

1. Semi-Centennial Catalogue, p. 18; Davidson Monthly, Vol. XII., p. 245.
2. Semi-Centenary Addresses, pp. 61–63, 156–165; Davidson Monthly, Vol VII., p. 197.

professor of Latin and French in Davidson College 1874–1875, and while president had the department of Metaphysics and English Literature; given LL. D. by the University of North Carolina in 1881.[1]

On August 4th, 1885, Rev. Luther McKinnon, D. D., was elected president. He was born in Richmond county, North Carolina, October 31st, 1840; graduated at Davidson 1861 and at Columbia Theological Seminary 1864; principal of Floral College 1865–1866; pastor at Goldsboro 1866–1871, at Concord 1871–1883, and at Columbia, South Carolina, 1883–1885. In consequence of ill health he retired from the presidency in 1888, and now lives at Clinton, North Carolina.[2] The number of students was only ninety-eight the year before he took hold, but during his first term there were one hundred and fifteen. Though he had had no experience in school work, still his influence in his church was so strong that patronage began to increase rapidly and new forces began to look to the college.[3]

Upon the resignation of Dr. McKinnon, Rev. John Bunyan Shearer, M. A., D. D., LL. D., assumed the presidency, and he still holds the position. He was born in Appomattox county, Virginia, 1832; graduated at Hampden-Sidney College 1851, at the University of Virginia 1854, and Union Theological Seminary 1858; pastor in Chapel Hill 1858–1862 and in Virginia 1862–1870; president of Stewart (now South Western Presbyterian University), Tennessee, 1870–1879, professor in same 1879–1888; D. D. from Hampden-Sidney College and LL. D. from South Western Presbyterian University.[4]

His administration has shown steady progress from

---

1. Semi-Centenary Addresses, p. 62; Semi-Centennial Catalogue, p. 19; General Catalogue of the University of North Carolina, pp. 80 and 241
2. Semi-Centenary Addresses, pp. 63–64; Semi-Centennial Catalogue, p. 21; letter from Dr. McKinnon.
3. Semi-Centenary Addresses, p. 64.
4. Semi-Centennial Catalogue, pp. 21–22.

the beginning. When he assumed control there were enrolled about one hundred boys, but for the past few years there have been upon average one hundred and sixty-five.[1] The endowment fund left by the war amounted to about $70,000; and a good deal of this was unproductive. By 1892 this had been increased to $110,000, and this whole amount was well invested. The above amount, with twelve thousand dollars worth of land in Minnesota, is their present fund.[2] There are now on the campus, in addition to the main building, the Y. M. C. A. Hall, Gymnasium, Old Chapel, two Society Halls, Oak Row, Elm Row and Tammany. The library has 11,000 volumes; the three laboratories of Chemistry, Mineralology and Physics, are well supplied with apparatus. The two literary societies have been strong factors in the literary and social growth of the student life. *The Davidson Monthly*, which with the beginning of the school year 1897-98, changed its name to *The Davidson College Magazine*, is now in its fourteenth volume; and it has contributed no little to the welfare of the institution.[3]

The regular professors from the beginning have been: Robert Hall Morrison, A. M., D. D., Sci., Math., 1836-40; Patrick Jones Sparrow, D. D., Langs., 1837-40; Samuel Williamson, A. M., D. D., Math., 1840-41, Chem., Mental and Moral Philos., Rhet., 1841-50, Mental and Moral Philos., Rhet., 1850-54; Samuel Blain Owen Wilson, A. M., Langs., 1841-53; Mortimer Davidson Johnston, A. M., Math., Nat. Philos., 1841-53; Elijah Frink Rockwell, A. M., D. D., Chem., Nat. Philos., 1850-52, Chem., Geol., 1852-54, Lat., Mod. Hist., 1854-68; James Ruet Gilland, A. M., Langs. 1852-54; Daniel Harvey Hill,

---

1. Catalogues, 1888-1897.
2. Catalogue, 1896-1897; Davidson Monthly. Vol. VII., p. 197.
3. Catalogue, 1896-1897; Davidson Monthly, Vols. I.-XIII. and Davidson College Magazine, Vol. I.

Math., Nat. Philos., 1853–54, Math., Civil Engineering, 1854–58; Clement Daniel Fishburne, A. M., Greek, Anc. Hist., 1855–60; Drury Lacy, A. M., D. D., Moral Philos., Sacred Lit., Evidences of Christ., 1855–61; John Adams Leland, A. M., Ph. D., Nat. Philos., Astr., 1854–60; Washington Caruthers Kerr, A. M., Ph. D., Chem., Mineralology, Geol., 1855–65; Alexander McIver, A. M., Math., 1859–69; Victor Clay Barringer, A. M., Belles-Lettres, 1860–65; John Lycan Kirkpatrick, D. D., Mental and Moral Philos., Evidences of Christ., 1860–66; William Bingham Lynch, A. M., Greek, Anc. Hist., 1860–64; John Rennie Blake, A. M., Phys., Chem., Geol., 1861–69, Nat. Philos., Astr., 1869–85; George Wilson McPhail, D. D., LL. D., Mental and Moral Philos., 1866–71; John Monroe Anderson, A. M., Eng., Logic, Evidences of Christ., 1866–73, Eng., Polit. Philos., 1873–74; Wilson Gaines Richardson, M. A., Ph. D., Langs., 1866–74; Charles Phillips, D. D., LL. D., Math., Astr., 1868–69, Math., Engineering, 1869–75; William Joseph Martin, Chem., Geol., Nat. Hist., 1869–87, Chem., 1887–96; James Fair Latimer, A. M., Ph. D., LL. D., Metaphysics, 1872–73, Psychol., Logic, Ethics, 1873–75, Greek, German, 1875–83; Andrew Doz Hepburn, A. M., D. D., LL. D., Lat., French, 1874–75, Mental Philos., Eng. Lit., 1875–85; William Mynn Thornton, A. B., Greek, German, 1874–75; John Russell Sampson, A. M., Lat., French, 1875–83; William Waller Carson, C. E., M. E., 1877–83; William Daniel Vinson, M. A., Math., 1883–97; William James Bingham, M. A., Lat., French, 1883–87; Luther McKinnon, D. D., Ethics, Bible, 1885–88; William Samuel Graves, M. A., B. L., Greek, German, 1885–87, Lat., French, 1887–93; William Spencer Currell, M. A., Ph. D., Eng., Psychol., Pol. Econ., 1886–94; Henry Louis Smith, A. M., Ph. D., Nat. Philos., 1887– ; John Bunyan Shearer,

M. A., D. D., LL. D., Bible, Moral Philos., 1888– ; Caleb Richmond Harding, A. M., Ph. D., Greek, German, 1888– ; W. R. Gray, Ph. D., Latin, French, 1893– ; Thomas P. Harrison, Ph. D., Eng., 1895– ; William J. Martin, Jr., M. D., Ph. D., Adjunct Nat. Sci., 1895–96, Chem., 1896– ; J. L. Douglas, Math., upon death of Dr. Vinson, August 20th, 1897.[1]

The acting professors have been : William Nathaniel Dickey, Nat. Philos., Astr., 1860–61 ; Stephen Frontis, French, 1860–61 ; Robert Lewis Harrison, M. A., Greek, German, 1875–76 ; William Scott Fleming, A. M., Greek, German, 1883–85 ; William Nelson Mebane, A. B., Greek, German, 1884–85 ; Chalmers Colin Norwood, A. M., Nat. Philos., Astr., 1885–87 ; Gonzales Lodge, Ph. D., Greek, German, 1886–88. Paul Patterson Winn, A. M., Langs., 1871–74, and Samuel Barnett, A. M., 1874–77, have been adjunct professors. The following have been tutors : M. D. Johnston, A. M., Math., 1837–41 ; T. M. Kirkpatrick, A. M., 1841–49, and P. P. Winn, A. M., 1869–71, Langs ; C. Mc. Hepburn, A. B., 1880–81, J. P. Paisley, A. B., 1881–84, S. R. McKee, 1887–88, R. R. Stevenson, 1888–89, T. E. Winecoff, 1889–90, Banks Withers, 1890–91, W. L. Lingle, 1890–93, Math. J. B. Wharey, A. B., 1893–95, and F. F. Rowe, A. B., 1896–97, have been instructors.[2]

Among the list given above are many of great ability and influence. They graduated from many of the leading institutions in America, and some studied in Europe. Their devotion has been as great as their ability. They have labored heroically for the cause of christian education, and there are many evidences of the splendid results from such labors. President Shearer was the first to make the fight against State aid to higher institutions

---

1. Semi-Centennial Catalogue, pp. 13–22 ; Catalogues, 1888–1897 ; Memorial Number Davidson College Magazine, October, 1897.
2. Semi-Centennial Catalogue, pp. 22–24 ; Catalogues, 1888–1897.

of learning in North Carolina. He, however, has now almost abandoned the attempt. During the first fifty years, one thousand eight hundred and sixty pupils matriculated in the institution; and a great part of these received their only education there. Of the whole number of matriculates during those years one hundred and ninety-three entered the ministry.[1] All over this State and the whole Southland can be found pupils of these teachers; and wherever they have gone they have become good and intelligent citizens. There are not many authors among this large faculty; the majority of them were too busy in making men to make books. As far as the writer can ascertain the list is as follows: Gen. D. H. Hill, Elements of Algebra, Sermon on the Mount, Crucifixion of Christ; W. C. Kerr, a great number of reports on the Geology of North Carolina; W. G. Richardson, Latin Pronunciation in American Colleges; A. D. Hepburn, Rhetoric; J. B. Shearer, Bible Course Syllabus.[2]

There are and have been for sometime three courses leading to degrees—A. B., B. S., and A. M. The first two require four years, and the A. M. can be taken in one year after having completed either of the others. For entrance one must stand on Arithmetic, Algebra to equations of the second degree; Gildersleeve's Latin Primer, Reader and Grammar, Exercise Book, Cæsar, Cicero's Orations Against Catiline; Goodwin's Greek Grammar and Reader (comprising the first two books of the Anabasis), White's Beginners' Greek Book; English Grammar.[3]

The course of studies for A. B. is: Freshman Class: Latin—Select Orations of Cicero, Livy, Gildersleeve's Exercise Book, Composition; Greek—Xenophon's Hel-

---
1. Semi-Centenary Addresses, p. 65.
2. Semi-Centennial Catalogue, pp. 15–22.
3. Catalogue, 1896–1897.

lenica (Blake), Lysias, Goodwin's Greek Grammar (revised edition), Winchell's Greek Syntax, Goodell's Greek in English; Mathematics—Bowser's College Algebra, Olney's University Algebra, Phillips & Fisher's Geometry; Physics—Gage's Elements of Physics; English—Genung's Outlines of Rhetoric, Strang's Exercises in English, Composition, English Classics; Biblical Instruction—A Reference Bible, Bible Course Syllabus (Shearer), a Bible Dictionary, Coleman's Historical Text-Book and Atlas of Biblical Geography. Sophomore Class: Latin—Cicero pro Milone, Horace (Chase and Stuart), Private Reading, Gildersleeve's Grammar, Composition; Greek—Herodotus, Homer (Seymour's School Iliad), Goodwin's Grammar, Seemann's Mythology, Pennell's Ancient Greece, Composition; Mathematics—Phillips & Fisher's Geometry, finished, Jones' Drill Book in Trigonometry, Algebra, finished; Chemistry—Remsen's Briefer Course, Lectures; English—Genung's Practical Rhetoric, and Rhetorical Analysis, Poetics, Selections from English and American Authors, American Literature, Compositions twice a month; Biblical Instruction—same books as in the Freshman Class, and Prideaux's Connection of Sacred and Profane History (Harper). Junior Class (studies elective, five to be chosen): Latin—Plautus' Menaechmi, and Pseudolus, Tacitus' Annals, Private Reading, Gildersleeve's Grammar, Allen's History of Rome, Latin Composition; Greek—Demosthenes, Euripides, Greek Literature (Jebb), Greek Poets in English Verse, Goodwin's Grammar, Composition, Lectures; Mathematics—Hardy's Analytic Geometry, Venable's Notes on Solid Geometry, Hardy's Calculus; Physics—Cumming's Electricity Treated Experimentally, Houston and Kennelly's Alternating Currents, Lectures; Chemistry—Remsen's Laboratory Manual, Venable's Qualitative Analysis (second edition), Lectures; English—Old English Language and Literature, Middle English Language and Literature, Lectures, Essays; History—Green's Short History of the English People, Myer's Mediæval and Modern History, Topical Investigation; Political Economy—Perry, Jevons, Taussig, Wells; French—Whitney's French Grammar, Erckmann-Chatrian's Waterloo Petite Histoire du Peuple Francais (Lacombe), Private Reading; German—Joynes-Meissner's Grammar, Grimm, Anderson, Hauff, and other prose writers; Biblical Instruction—Bible, Syllabus, Bible Dictionary, Coleman, Robinson's English Harmony, Lectures, Evidences. Senior Class (studies elective, five to be chosen): Latin—Juvenal (Hardy), Phormio and Andria of Terence, Pliny's Letters, Private Reading, History of Roman Literature (Cruttwell); Greek—Thucydides, Sophocles, Æschylus, Aristophanes, Lectures, Comparative Grammar, Gayley's Mythology; Mathematics—Byerly's Differential Calculus, Byerly's Integral Calculus, Lectures; Applied Mathematics—Church's Descriptive Geometry, Davies' Surveying, Henck's Field Book for Engineers; Astronomy and Meteorology—Young's Astronomy, Waldo's Elementary Meteorology, Lectures; Mineralogy and Geology—Foye's Handbook of Mineralogy, Le Conte's Elements of Geology, Lectures; Chemistry—Thorpe's Quantitative Chemical Analysis, Remsen's Organic Chemistry; Logic (first term)—Davis' Elements of Logic (Deductive and Inductive); Constitutional History (second term)—Wilson's State, Myer's General History; English—English Literature, Poetics, Shakspere, Milton, Browning, Tennyson, Lectures, Essays; Mental and Moral Philosophy—Elements of Psychology, (Davis), Haven's History of Philosophy, Lectures; French—Whitney's French Grammar, Selections from Erckmann-Chatrian, Corneille, Racine, Moliere, and

Victor Hugo, Private Reading, Composition; German— Joynes-Meissner's Grammar, Hosmer's German Literature, Composition, Lessing, Goethe, Schiller; Bookkeeping and Commercial Law (to be taken as an extra or eclectic study)—Text-books reserved.[1]

### THE TERMS OF EXPENSES ARE:

| | | | | |
|---|---|---|---|---|
| Tuition—first Term, | $25 00 | second Term | $35 00 | $60 00 |
| Room rent, " | 10 00 | " | 15 00 | 25 00 |
| Incidentals, " | 6 00 | " | 9 00 | 15 00 |
| Medical fee, " | 1 00 | " | 2 00 | 3 00 |
| Deposit for damages to buildings, etc., | | | | 2 00 |
| Day board, in families, per month, | | | from 9 00 to | 10 00 |
| Day board, in club, per month, | | | from 6 00 to | 8 00 |
| Wood, per cord, | | | from 1 25 to | 1 50 |
| Lights, about, | | | | 2 00 |
| Washing, per month, | | | from 1 00 to | 1 25 |

[2]

### GUILFORD COLLEGE.

For the present purposes enough has been said about the Quaker settlements in North Carolina. Their attitude on the educational question demands further consideration. George Fox, their founder, was a strong advocate of its advantages and necessity. But, owing to the peculiar circumstances of their settlement in this State, their real educational condition was not known until 1830; and it was then very poor.[3] At a Yearly Meeting of this year committees were appointed to find out and report the real condition. To a Meeting of 1832 was made the following report: "There is not a school in the limits of the Yearly Meeting that is under the care of a committee, either of a Monthly or Preparative Meeting. The teachers of Friends' children are mostly not members of our Society, and all the schools are in a

---
1. Catalogue, 1896-1897, pp. 24-26.
2. Ibid, 1896-1897, p. 55.
3. Dr. Nereus Mendenhall, Guilford Collegian, November, 1889, pp. 63-64.

mixed state." This report moved the Meeting to appoint a committee to get up and send out an address on education. Dougan Clark, Jeremiah Hubbard, Nathan Mendenhall, Joshua Stanley and David White, constituted the committee. They sent out an address, a part of which was: "We believe that the Christian and literary education of our children consistent with the simplicity of our profession is a subject of very deep interest, if not of paramount importance in supporting the various testimonies that we profess to bear to the world, and even to the very existence and continuance of the Society."[1]

At the same Meeting they began to raise money, and secured $370.55 in subscriptions. Forty-five members were appointed a committee to buy a farm, locate the school and draw up plans for the building and management. Plans were laid before the Yearly Meeting of 1832 and adopted, and about $1,200 were pledged for carrying them out. The school was located and a charter secured from the legislature in 1833. The charter was obtained through the efforts of Mr. George C. Mendenhall, the most prominent Quaker in politics of that time. There was then great opposition to the Friends, because of their decided views on anti-slavery questions. Had a charter for a Quaker school been asked for, it would have been refused. The committee appointed for this purpose copied a charter from that of a school at Clemmonsville and left blank the name. This was passed, and afterwards New Garden Boarding School was inserted in the blank space.[2]

The site chosen was about six miles northwest of Greensboro and on land just obtained by purchase and given by Mr. Elihu Coffin. By 1834 the Friends in

---
1. Dr. Mendenhall, Guilford Collegian, November, 1889, pp. 63-64; President L. L. Hobbs, The Earlhamite, January, 1888, p. 74.

2 Dr. Mendenhall, Guilford Collegian, November, 1889, pp. 64-65; President Hobbs, The Earlhamite, January, 1888, p. 74; Catalogue, 1888-1889, p. 9.

England had given as much as two thousand dollars. In 1837 Mr. Joseph J. Gurney gave $488.88. Two years later Mr. George Howland, of the New England Yearly Meeting, made a gift of $1,000, and later an equal amount. Mr. Roland Greene, of Rhode Island, and the Meetings of New York, Philadelphia and Baltimore, were very liberal in giving to this work. Nathan Hunt and Jeremiah Hubbard were perhaps the most active and influential of the Friends of this State in behalf of the proposed institution. From these gifts and the credit of the North Carolina Yearly Meeting for five thousand dollars buildings were erected. The main building was 126x40 feet; and it was completed for the opening, August 1st, 1837.[1]

There were twenty-five boys, and the same number of girls, enrolled the first day. Mr. Dougan Clark and his wife were the first superintendents. They were both influential members of the Society and served the school with great credit until December 2nd, 1842. Then came: Joshua and Abigail Stanley, 1842–47; Thomas T. Hunt and wife, 1847–49; Nereus Mendenhall, David Marshall, Aaron Stalker, 1849–59; Jonathan E. Cox, 1859–64; John Carter, 1864–68; school rented to Jonathan E. Cox, 1868–71, and leased to Mr. Cox and Ezra M. Meader, 1871–72; George N. Hartley, 1872–78; Jeremiah S. Cox and wife, 1878–80; Jesse M. Bundy and wife, 1880–87. At this time the office of superintendent was abolished.[2]

The school at once began to make itself felt. The following is a circular from the trustees made in 1848: "We think it must be apparent to all that the school has

---

1. Dr. Mendenhall, Guilford Collegian, November, 1889, pp. 65–66; President Hobbs, The Earlhamite, January, 1888, p. 75; Catalogues, 1888–1897; Week's Southern Quakers and Slavery, p. 301.

2. Dr. Mendenhall, Guilford Collegian, December, 1889, pp. 103–106; President Hobbs, The Earlhamite, January, 1888, pp. 76–77; Week's Southern Quakers and Slavery, p. 301.

been of great benefit to our youth,—nay, to society at large. It has furnished, not only to our body, but to the country, many well qualified teachers; and thus, through them, directly exerted an influence for good which will continue to spread, and which will no doubt be felt by future generations." From the beginning instruction was given in English Grammar, Spelling, Reading, Scriptures, Latin, Greek, French, Logic, Arithmetic, Algebra, Geometry, Mensuration, Natural Philosophy, and Physiology. At first no one except the children of Quakers could become pupils, but this narrow idea was soon abandoned.[1] During 1850 there were ninety-four students, forty of whom were not Friends.[2]

Some of the quaint customs of those early days are very interesting. The girls were kept away from the presence of the boys except on rather rare occasions. There was a uniform simplicity of dress; and the Quaker bonnet and coat were rigidly adhered to. "Roaching" the hair and wearing whiskers were forbidden. During the summer-time recitations were heard before breakfast.[3] These rules speak for themselves: "In school you are to refrain from laughing, talking, whispering, or making a noise with your feet; learning your lessons in silence; and when repeating them to your masters or mistresses you are to speak audibly, deliberately, and distinctly. In the evening after supper you are again to collect yourselves together, and after the calling of your names, retire to your bed chambers and undress in as much stillness as possible, folding up your clothes neatly and putting them in their proper places."[4]

From 1850 to 1856 the school was very prosperous as to numbers, but as to finances a failure. There were 128

---
1. President Hobbs, The Earlhamite, January, 1888, p. 86; Dr. Mendenhall, Guilford Collegian, February, 1890, pp. 161-162.
2. Week's Southern Quakers and Slavery, p. 301.
3. Dr. Mendenhall, Guilford Collegian, February, 1890, p. 161.
4. President Hobbs, The Earlhamite, January, 1888, p. 76.

students in 1853, 143 in 1854, and 179 in 1855. From 1856 the numbers declined, in consequence of sickness and the panic which spread over the country in 1857.[1] During this year it was found out that the institution was badly in debt, owing to a bad system of keeping accounts and collecting. By 1858 the indebtedness amounted to $4,173 above all the assets; and later it was as large as $27,245.52, with only about $20,000 worth of land, buildings and furniture. In 1860 a committee was appointed by the Yearly Meeting to consult with the trustees as to paying off the debt by selling the whole plant and its appurtenances. The advertisement of the sale was made, but before the transaction took place it was decided to refer the whole matter again to the Yearly Meeting. By the Yearly Meeting of 1861 the financial obligations were assumed, and $3,000 were subscribed. Soon after this about $15,000 were raised by the other Meetings, especially the Indiana and Baltimore; and by 1865 it was reported that the whole debt had been liquidated.[2]

In 1861 Jonathan E. Cox rented the school; and he ran it as a private enterprise during the whole of the Civil War. When peace came in 1865 the Friends again desired to control it as their own institution. This was the beginning of a new and greater era. Through all of its past difficulties the school had wielded a great influence—it was the greatest institution in Southern Quakerism. Each year from this on hopes looked brighter. The Quakers were making a steady growth in North Carolina, though in a very quiet way.[3] In 1881 Francis Thompson King and Dr. J. C. Thomas, of Baltimore, gave $22,000. A part of this was used in repair-

---

1. Week's Southern Quakers and Slavery, p. 301.
2. Ibid, p. 302; Dr. Mendenhall, Guilford Collegian, December, 1889, pp. 104-105, January, 1890, pp. 126-127.
3. Week's Southern Quakers and Slavery, pp. 302, 317.

ing and enlarging the old building, and in making King Hall out of the church, given to the school by the Yearly Meeting in 1882. In 1885 King Hall was burned, but the institution stopped only a day; and during the summer of the next year it was rebuilt. In the fall after the fire Archdale Hall was erected as a boys' dormitory.[1] The school was now almost ready to change its name and to enlarge its sphere of work; and this was done in 1888 when it was rechartered as Guilford College.[2]

During the first fifty years of the school's life there were at the same time a superintendent and a principal. The former was the treasurer, and the latter at the head of the school-room work. The principals have been: Jonathan L. Slocum, 1837-38; John L. Clark and James Chase, 1838-39; Nereus Mendenhall, 1839-42; Alfred H. Lindley, 1842-44; Jonathan W. Albertson, 1844-46; Nereus Mendenhall, 1846-47; William Nicholson, one term of 1847; Samuel D. Coffin, 1847-49; Nereus Mendenhall, 1849-52; Dougan Clark, 1852-56; John R. Hubbard, 1856-60; Nereus Mendenhall, 1860-66; A. Marshall Elliot, one term of 1866-67; Samuel C. Collins, 1867-70; Pendleton R. King, one term of 1870-71; George N. Hartley, 1871-78; L. L. Hobbs, 1878-84; Joseph Moore, 1884-88.[3] Among these were many of fine ability and deep consecration, but Dr. Nereus Mendenhall ranks as the most distinguished and unique. He was born August 14th, 1819; took his literary degree at Haverford College and M. D. at the Jefferson College of Medicine, both in Pennsylvania; principal of the New Garden Boarding School four different times; a civil engineer in the survey of the Western North Carolina Railroad; teacher in the Penn Charter School of Philadel-

---

1. Dr. Mendenhall, Guilford Collegian, January, 1890, pp. 128-129; Catalogue, 1888-1889, pp. 12, 14.
2. Catalogues, 1888-1897.
3. President Hobbs, The Earlhamite, January, 1888, p. 77.

phia; a leader in the religious and educational movements of his church; one of the greatest teachers of the State; died October 29th, 1893.[1]

With the opening of the school year 1888–1889 began a greater life. In the place of a high school course and faculty were instituted a college curriculum and teaching force. Prof. Lewis Lyndon Hobbs, who had been connected with the Boarding School since 1876, became the first president; and he still serves with much success. He was born at New Garden, now Guilford College, North Carolina, in 1849; entered Haverford College in 1872, where he received A. B. and A. M.; professor of Greek and Mathematics in New Garden Boarding School, 1876–78; principal of the same, 1878–84, and professor of Greek and Latin, 1884–88.[2]

During his administration many improvements in the way of buildings and equipment have been made. A large Y. M. C. A. Hall was erected in 1891–1892; and the Duke Science Hall is now (February, 1898,) ready for use. The endowment fund amounts to fifty thousand dollars. The course of studies is almost as high as that of any of the leading colleges in the State. The graduates enter the Senior Class at the University of North Carolina without examinations. The faculty from the beginning of the college has been composed of from seven to twelve members; and all of these have had fine training for their special work. The library has grown with the other features until it now has four thousand volumes; and the cabinet of Natural History is among the very finest in the State. Two degrees, A. B. and B. S., are given. The college course embraces four years; and a two years preparatory department is annexed. By the endowment fund and the rigid economy of the

---

[1]. Mrs. Mary Mendenhall Hobbs, Guilford Collegian, November, 1893, pp. 57–63, and December, 1893, pp. 98–105; Week's Southern Quakers and Slavery, p. 131.

[2]. Guilford Collegian, Vol. VIII., May, 1895, p. 217; Letter from President Hobbs.

administration the expenses are kept down to a low point. For a year of thirty-eight weeks only $171.00 for the college course and $157.00 for the preparatory are charged. The institution is co-educational still, as it has been through its whole history. The numbers for the past nine years have ranged from about 140 to 209, and these have been somewhat equally divided among the sexes. The Quakers have always advocated that in most respects woman is equal intellectually to man; and New Garden Boarding School and Guilford College have shown to the people of North Carolina that there is much of truth in such views.[1]

The faculty for 1896–1897 was: Lewis Lyndon Hobbs, A. B., A. M., Haverford College, president, Latin, Mental and Moral Philosophy; Mary E. Mendenhall, B. S., Guilford College, English Literature, Rhetoric; J. Franklin Davis, A. B., A. M., Haverford College, Greek, German; George W. White, A. B., Haverford College, treasurer, Mathematics; A. W. Blair, A. M., Haverford College, Natural Science, History; Louisa Osborne, A. B., Earlham College, governess, assistant in Latin; Lydia N. Blair, A. B., Earlham College, English, principal of preparatory department; Lillian J. Hill, Drawing, Painting; Myra Alderman Albright, Music; Samuel H. Hodgin, A. B., Guilford College, assistant in preparatory department; Laura D. Worth, B. S., Guilford College, graduate of Boston School of Gymnastics, Physical Training. Some of these have been connected with the college since its beginning. Among the other teachers who have been in the faculty at different times are: John W. Woody, A. B., A. M., LL. B., History, Political Science, 1888–94; Elwood C. Perisho, B. S., Mathematics, 1888–93; Gertrude W. Mendenhall, B. S., Natural Science, 1888–91; Mary M. Petty, B. S., Latin,

---

1. Letter from President Hobbs; Catalogues, 1888-1897.

History, 1890–93; Walter W. Haviland, A. B., Mathematics, 1892–96.[1] There have been but two authors among the faculty. In 1891 Prof. Woody published Elements of Pedagogy;[2] and Prof. Davis has written a translation of an Anglo-Saxon Grammar.

Thus has this quiet still interesting old school grown from year to year; and it increases in strength and utility as the days go by. As the Quaker Society has been a unique and beneficial element, so has this institution been an educational power in this State. Many of its pupils have become leaders in the various fields of life; Dr. Braxton Craven is an illustrious example. There are a good many proofs that its fine influence has been appreciated. Among these is the gift of B. N. and J. B. Duke. These generous men in the fall of 1897 gave ten thousand dollars, with which to erect the Science Hall.[3] With this additional equipment the college starts out on a more hopeful era.

### TRINITY COLLEGE.

A brief sketch of the eighteenth century Methodism in North Carolina has already been given. A few points in reference to its growth and development during the past ninety-seven years will here be considered. In 1800 six thousand, three hundred and sixty-three whites, and two thousand, one hundred and nine negroes, were reported from this State.[4] Twenty-eight years after this the Virginia Conference, of which North Carolina was a part, had thirty-five thousand, two hundred and ninety-five members.[5] In 1838, the year after the formation of the North Carolina Conference, there were reported from

---

1. Catalogues, 1888–1897.
2. Prof. Woody's book in Greensboro Female College Library.
3. Guilford Collegian, April, 1897, pp. 208–241.
4. Minutes of the General Conferences, Vol. I., p. 92.
5. Ibid, Vol. I., p. 558.

## SCHOOLS OF NORTH CAROLINA. 175

this Conference nineteen thousand, two hundred and eight members;[1] and at the same time the northeastern part of the State belonged to the Virginia Conference; the southwestern, to the South Carolina Conference; the western, to the Holston Conference. Since that time Methodism has had a rapid growth. The North Carolina Conference, which embraces the eastern half of the State, now has a membership of sixty-five thousand, five hundred and fifty-four;[2] and the Western North Carolina Conference has sixty-eight thousand, seven hundred and sixteen.[3]

In 1838 there were no institutions of learning to aid the church. Now there are within both conferences Trinity College, Greensboro Female College, Weaverville College, Davenport College, Littleton Female College, and Louisburg Female College; and the high schools of Trinity, Burlington and Jonesboro.[4] Several of these schools do not belong to the church; they are only under its protection. Each conference annually assesses its membership five thousand dollars for educational purposes.[5] Trinity College alone receives funds from both conferences. The whole of the five thousand assessed by the North Carolina Conference is for Trinity College. In the Western Conference this amount is distributed as follows: Trinity College, $2,900; Weaverville College, $1,500; Trinity High School, $300; General Board of Education, $300.[6] Since 1856 Trinity College has played a great part in the growth of the Methodist Church; it has been to this denomination what Wake Forest and Davidson have been to the Baptists and Presbyterians. Too, it has taken a high place in our social, educational and political life.

---

1. Minutes of the General Conferences, Vol. II., p. 525.
2. Minutes of the North Carolina Conference, 1897, p. 22.
3. Minutes of the Western North Carolina Conference, 1897, p. 22.
4. Ibid, pp. 34-35; Minutes of the North Carolina Conference, 1897, p. 45-46.
5. Ibid, p. 23; Ibid, p. 45.
6. Ibid, p. 34.

It had its beginning in 1838, though under the name of Union Institute. It was first established, and remained until 1892, in the northwest corner of Randolph county, about five miles to the south of High Point. Many prominent families lived in this section—the Grays, Harpers, Leaches, Hogans, Browns, Johnsons, Mendenhalls, Englishes, Tomlinsons and others.[1] On the north were Quakers; and on the south, Methodists. From the union of these came the name of the institute. The first school out of which Trinity grew was begun by Rev. Brandtly York, D. D., in 1838. He at first taught a common school at Brown School-house, an old dilapidated log structure, about 16x20 feet. This was located almost a mile southwest of the present site. In the summer of 1838 his patrons built a new log house, 24x36 feet, a few yards northeast of the place where the college building was afterwards erected. When his school of about fifty pupils, girls and boys, moved into the new quarters, about August 12th, the name of Union Institute was adopted.[2]

The school at once became prosperous, and in a short while there was need of more room. By 1840 another building was ready for use. It was a framed house, 30x65 feet, and divided into two rooms. Soon after the erection of this structure there came about a disposition on the part of the Methodist children to make fun of the Quaker "thee" and "thou," in consequence of which the most of the Friends withdrew their girls and boys. This brought about a great decrease in the patronage. Dr. York's health had been poor for some time. The decrease of prosperity and his poor health caused him to resign in 1842. The school had made a beginning and,

---

1. Dr. Craven, Centennial of Methodism in North Carolina. p. 179.
2. Hon. W. M. Robbins on Trinity College—Its Antecedents—Early Days—Founders, clipping in Trinity College Historical Museum, from Raleigh Christian Advocate, published soon after his death; Rev. B. A. York, Raleigh Christian Advocate, August 30, 1898.

though Dr. York retired at this early period, it had been a decided success.¹ Rev. Baxton Craven, who had been an assistant for a short while, became principal immediately upon Dr. York's resignation; and he it was who brought about those great changes and guided the destiny of the institution for forty years.² Dr. York was a pioneer in education. He was born in Randolph county, North Carolina, January 3rd, 1805, died October 7th, 1891; educated himself in English Grammar, Rhetoric, Logic, Moral and Mental Philosophy, Latin, Greek and Mathematics; ordained minister of the Methodist Church in 1837; principal of Clemmonsville High School, Davidson county, 1842–46; Olin, 1851–56; York Institute, Alexander county, 1856 till the war broke it up; Ruffin Badger Institute, Chatham county, 1869–73; professor of Logic and Rhetoric in Rutherford College, 1873; New Salem and Randleman High School, 1881–85; traveler and lecturer in North and South Carolina, Virginia and Arkansas; teacher for about seventy years and preacher for sixty; instructed fifteen thousand pupils, preached five thousand sermons and delivered three thousand lectures; blind for about forty years.³

The first year that Mr. Craven taught he was guaranteed two hundred dollars, and as much more as he could make from the school. He did not have a regular assistant for some time; some of the best pupils in the higher classes often aided him in the lower class work. During the period 1843–1850 from twenty-eight to one hundred and eighty-four students matriculated annually, the

---

1. Hon. W. M. Robbins on Trinity College—Its Antecedents—Early Days—Founders, clipping in Trinity College Historical Museum, from Raleigh Christian Advocate, published soon after his death; Rev. B. A. York, Raleigh Christian Advocate, August 30, 1893; Centennial of Methodism in North Carolina, p. 180; Dowd's Life of Braxton Craven, p. 41.
2. Dowd's Life of Braxton Craven, p. 113.
3. Rev. B. A. York, Raleigh Christian Advocate, August 23 and 30, 1893; Autobiography of Dr. York in manuscript; Rev. M. H. Hoyle, The Western North Carolina Methodist, January 9, 1892.

general average being about one hundred. The income of this period was from $300 to $1,800 a year; and at the same time about $224 were given annually to indigent students. The standing of the academy was high, and its pupils came from many sections of the Carolinas and Virginia. Mr. Craven was but twenty years of age when he assumed the principalship; and as he grew in mental strength, his school became larger and more effective. In January, 1851, it was rechartered under the name of Normal College and begun its second era. During the first twelve years of its existence it had grown from a little common school to a first class academy. At the beginning of this new era, it had a small library and two literary societies—Columbian (1846) and Hesperian (1850).[1]

In 1845 the following subjects were in the course: English Grammar, Composition, Elocution, Rhetoric, Logic, Mental and Moral Philosophy, Arithmetic, Algebra, Geometry, Surveying, Mensuration, Analytical Geometry, Natural Philosophy, Astronomy, Latin and Greek Grammar, Latin and Greek Authors, Botany, Chemistry, Geology, Geography, and Anatomy. The terms of those days were very low: tuition per session $5; board and washing per month $4.50; a few other small items of expense.[2] All of the above subjects were taught by Mr. Craven; and he was at the same time doing advanced work as a student in Greek, Latin, Hebrew, History, Political Economy, and several other branches.[3] In 1850 he went to Randolph-Macon College and stood examinations on the whole course of studies

---

[1]. Dr. Craven, Centennial of Methodism in North Carolina, pp. 180-181; Dowd's Life of Braxton Craven, pp. 42, 48, 52, 53; Hon. W. M. Robbins.
[2]. Greensboro Patriot, February 28th, 1845.
[3]. Dowd's Life of Braxton Craven, p. 55.

of that institution, and obtained the A. B. degree; A. M. from the University of North Carolina in 1851; D. D. from Andrew College, Tennessee, and LL. D. from the University of Missouri; born August 26th, 1822, and died November 7th, 1882.[1]

At the North Carolina Conference of 1851 the first connection between the church and school was made, though this was not at all close. The school ran its own affairs and supported itself, while the Conference endorsed it and appointed a visiting committee for the same. The normal feature was a failure in the end. During its continuance (until 1859) many students took this course only and went out known as graduates of the college, though in reality they had had but a short common and high school training. However, this plan brought temporary assistance in the way of a loan from the literary fund of the State. In 1853 the charter to Normal College was amended, and the institution was given power to confer degrees and to perform all other acts usually granted to such schools. Section 9 of this amended charter is: "Be it further enacted, that the President and Directors of the Literary Fund are hereby directed to loan to the Trustees of Trinity College the sum of Ten Thousand Dollars out of any money not otherwise appropriated, at six per cent. interest, to be paid semi-annually, upon said Trustees giving bond and good security for the same." For some time it seemed that the proper security could not be obtained. Hon. John A. Gilmer, of Greensboro, then a trustee, came to the rescue of President Craven, and the money was secured. By means of this fund the first brick building, now known as the old part, was erected.[2]

---

1. Dowd's Life of Braxton Craven, pp. 55, 56, 125; North Carolina Sermons, Vol. II., p. 12; General Catalogue of the University of North Carolina, p. 289.
2. Dr. Craven, Centennial of Methodism, pp. 181-183; Dowd's Life of Braxton Craven, pp. 56-57; Catalogue, 1896-1897, copy of amended charter.

From this on the institution prospered more and more each year. The first graduating class was in 1853, and was composed of D. C. and L. Johnson.[1] The faculty consisted of from four to six members.[2] The average matriculation from 1853 to 1857 was one hundred and eighty-seven; and the annual income was about $5,000, with $450 given to poor students. In 1858 the trustees gave over the property, worth about $30,000, to the North Carolina Conference. By the legislature of the next year the college was entirely vested in the Conference and its name was changed to Trinity. With this transfer of property and change of name the normal feature came to an end, and the Governor of the State was no longer *ex officio* president of the trustees.[3]

The institution had become denominational, but for a long time after this the church gave no financial assistance. Dr. Craven gave his school to the Conference and his great life to the Methodists of North Carolina, but they have been very slow to return value for value. The truth is, that the Methodist Church of this State has never stood square by its institutions of learning. It has stood still and allowed its greatest character to kill himself; and several times its noblest institution has almost fallen from the lack of appreciation and loyalty. Dr. Craven might easily have made himself rich from Trinity College as a private school. His soul was too large for such selfishness; he gave forty of his best years, his money and all of that rare and rich personality, the superior of which this State has never produced. He is one of the few immortal names in our whole educational history.

From 1859 to 1862 the college was at its highest point

---

1. Catalogue, 1896–1897, p. 109.
2. Catalogues, 1854–1859.
3. Dr. Craven, Centennial of Methodism in North Carolina, p. 184; Dowd, pp. 62–63.

of prosperity. The matriculations each of these years averaged two hundred and four. The income amounted to $7,500, besides the losses and gifts to poor boys. Everything seemed favorable for an endowment fund and a far greater life to the institution. The committee, appointed by the Conference in 1858 to secure funds with which to erect another building, had obtained in subscriptions $15,000. They were about ready to build another brick structure of the same size as the first, but the war came on and put a stop to improvement and almost to life itself.[1] The faculty of 1860-1861 was: B. Craven, D. D., president, Metaphysics, Rhetoric, Logic; Lemuel Johnson, A. M., Mathematics; W. T. Gannaway, A. M., Latin, Greek; I. L. Wright, A. M., Natural Science, Modern History; O. W. Carr, A. B., tutor of Greek and English Literature; L. W. Andrews, A. B., tutor of Mathematics.[2] These were doing fine work, and Trinity College was taking a high rank among Southern schools. Four years were required for graduation after entering the freshman class; and to enter this one had to stand on Arithmetic, English Grammar, Latin Grammar and Reader, Cæsar, Ovid, Vergil's Bucolics and six books of the Aeneid, Greek Grammar and Reader (or Graeca Minora), St. John's Gospel in the Greek Testament, Ancient and Modern Geography, Algebra to equations of the second degree.[3]

In 1863, Dr. Craven resigned the presidency and was pastor of Edenton Street Church in Raleigh for two years. Prof. Gannaway was president *pro tem* during this time. The college exercises were kept up, though with but few students, until April, 1865, when Gen. Hardee's troops encamped near by.[4] With the excep-

---

[1]. Dr. Craven, Centennial of Methodism in North Carolina. p. 185; Dowd, p. 63; Raleigh Christian Advocate, Feb. 22nd, 1882, reprint from Trinity College Herald.
[2]. Catalogue, 1860-1861.
[3]. Ibid.
[4]. Dr. Craven, Centennial of Methodism in North Carolina. p. 186.

tion of Dr. Craven, the faculty was not diminished through those gloomy years. There was but one graduate in 1864—E. H. Tapscott, and none in 1865.[1] During this period about twenty young ladies matriculated; and this was a pleasant and profitable innovation. Those were indeed trying days; they tested the college in a severe way.[2] In this connection the long and faithful services of Prof. Gannaway deserve consideration. When he retired from the faculty in June, 1892, he had been with the institution for thirty-five years, the longest period of service, with the exception of that of Dr. Craven, in its whole history. He was born in Wythe county, Virginia, June 10th, 1825; entered Emory and Henry College in 1840 and graduated in 1845; took A. M. from his *Alma Mater* in 1852; principal of Floyd Institute, Virginia, 1845–1854; principal of Masonic Institute at Germanton, North Carolina, 1854–1857; in Trinity College, Greek and Philosophy 1857–58, Greek and Latin 1858–63, Greek, Latin and French 1863–66, Greek and Latin 1866–70, Latin and History 1870–83, Latin, History and French 1883–86, Latin 1886–92.[3] He still lives at Trinity, North Carolina; and is the same gentleman and scholar that he has ever been.

During the fall of 1865 Dr. Craven was again elected president. The school reopened in January, 1866. The numbers at first were small, but the prospects brightened each year. The college was now in good financial circumstances, the debt to the literary board having been paid by Dr. Craven individually. The patronage increased rapidly, until there were matriculated over two hundred boys in 1870. During the period 1866–1876 there was an annual average of one hundred and fifty-

---

1. Catalogue, 1896–1897, p. 111; Prof. Gannaway, Trinity Archive, May, 1893, pp. 324–330.
2. Prof. Gannaway, Trinity Archive, May, 1893, pp. 324–330.
3. Prof. Gannaway, Autobiography, Trinity Archive, April, 1893, pp. 277–280.

six; and the income was about $6,000 a year.[1] In 1871 there was a great demand for more room, and $10,000 were asked from the Conference of this year. The church agreed to raise the amount, and upon the promise Dr. Craven began to erect the Chapel. It was ready for use by June, 1875. When completed it had cost $14,000. The amounts collected from the ten thousand dollar subscriptions were less than $3,000; and in 1877 the debt on the building was $9,725. This was a great burden upon the president to the hour of his death.[2]

Dr. Craven, in his address to the Conference of 1876 at Raleigh, made the following statement: "From the first, a period of thirty-four years, the statistics are as follows: losses, six thousand and sixty dollars; gratuitous tuition, eleven thousand three hundred dollars; deaths at college, thirteen; expulsions, twenty-five; conversions, eleven hundred and fifty-seven. The whole number of graduates is one hundred and ninety-eight; of these seventy-eight have received A. M.; thirty-four are lawyers; physicians, thirteen; preachers, twenty-eight; teachers and professors in colleges, twenty-five. . . . . . Fifteen of the graduates are members of the North Carolina Conference, and thirty-six, being one-fifth of the whole Conference, were educated in whole or in part at Trinity."[3] To these remarkable statements may be added that the institution was then worth as much as $40,000, of which amount $30,000 had been made from the receipts of tuition.[4]

For several years before Dr. Craven's death the patronage was becoming small. In 1878–79 there were matriculated 114; in 1879–80, 101; in 1880–81, 117, and dur-

---

1. Dr. Craven, Centennial of Methodism in North Carolina, p. 186; Dowd, pp. 66–67.
2. Dowd's Life of Braxton Craven, pp. 68–69.
3. ' Dr. Craven, Centennial of Methodism in North Carolina, pp. 186–187.
4. Ibid, p. 188.

ing 1882–83, the year after his death, 100.[1] It seemed that he had lost his hold on the church to a great extent. He had stood and fought like a hero for almost forty years, but now he saw his own dear institution on the decline. The heavy debt incurred in erecting the chapel bore heavily upon his shoulders; and too, many of the strongest members of his church were fighting instead of assisting him. He had either made a serious mistake, or his fellow-churchmen were very jealous of his noble work and influence. It has been said that he was by far too ambitious for a bishopric, and consequently made enemies out of many of his once strongest friends. There is much of truth in this accusation. But if it were entirely true, it would be no excuse for such cold-blooded action on the part of his fellow-churchmen. He had done them a service, the like of which this country has rarely seen; and still they opposed him on every side.

Upon the death of Dr. Craven, November 7th, 1882, Prof. W. H. Pegram was elected chairman of the faculty; and he held this position during the year 1882–1883. In this connection Prof. Pegram's long and loyal services to the institution deserve mentioning. He graduated at Trinity College in 1873; tutor in Natural Sciences 1873–75; professor in the department of Natural Sciences from 1875 to the present.[2] At the commencement of 1883 Rev. Marquis Lafayette Wood, D. D., was elected president, but he held this position only a little more than one year. He was born in Randolph county, North Carolina, October 23rd, 1829; graduated at Normal College in 1855; joined the North Carolina Conference the same year; missionary to China 1860–1866; given D. D. by Rutherford College and the University of North Carolina in 1884; died November 25th,

---

1. Catalogues, 1878–1883.
2. Catalogues, 1873–1897; Trinity Archive, October, 1894, p. 39; Manuscript of Prof. J. F. Heitman.

1893.[1] When he began his administration, the college was in a bad condition in many ways. There was no money, and general demoralization prevailed. The first year under him opened with about sixty boys, and there were eighty at the beginning of his second year. He was not by any means able to pay his faculty in full. The Conference had promised the institution $2,500 for 1883-1884, but only about $800 of this were collected. He had been in pastoral duties so long that the rigid work of attending to the affairs of a college, especially when it was in such a deplorable condition as Trinity then was, was not attractive to him; and he resigned at the Conference of 1884.[2]

The financial condition of the ten years from 1875 to 1885 is shown by the following figures:

|  | Annual Salary of each professor. | Actually Paid. | Annual Deficit. |
|---|---|---|---|
| 1875-76 | $1,000 | $550.47 | $449.53 |
| 1876-77 | 1,000 | 525.15 | 474.85 |
| 1877-78 | 1,000 | 415.99 | 584.01 |
| 1878-79 | 1,000 | 394.61 | 605.39 |
| 1879-80 | 1,000 | 398.54 | 601.46 |
| 1880-81 | 1,000 | 304.15 | 695.85 |
| 1881-82 | 1,000 | 231.83 | 778.17 |
| 1882-83 | 1,000 | 572.30 | 427.70 |
| 1883-84 | 1,000 | 500.00 | 500.00 |
| 1884, fall term, ½ year | 500 | 350.00 | 150.00 |

[3]

President Crowell, in speaking of the above figures, says: "In these nine and a half years each professor, salaried at $1,000, left in the college $5,366.96; four professors have virtually given to Trinity College in this time the total amount of $21,067.84, or an annual gift from each professor of $554.41. The faculty has given more to Trinity in these nine and a half years than the Conference probably ever has. In short, it is plain that a small faculty has been for several years really main-

---
1. Journal of the North Carolina Conference, 1893, pp. 43-46; General Catalogue of the University of North Carolina, p. 242.
2. Prof. Heitman's Manuscript.
3. President Crowell's Report to the North Carolina Conference of 1888, pp. 28-29.

taining a college belonging to a Conference of 82,000 people. This college could never have been carried on had these men left upon finding out that their salaries were not to be paid. They remained for their loyalty to the church-college; they sacrificed their independence; involved themselves frequently because of the uncertainty of income. They gave, and gave, and gave more than all others put together. Their debts were not paid by the lapse of a year, yet the Conference never expects to pay this enormous arrearage in salaries. Certainly no other institution of the church which every member, lay and clerical, vows to support has met with such experiences as her highest educational institution—Trinity College."[1]

At the Conference of 1884 the college was given up to a committee, composed of J. W. Alspaugh, J. S. Carr and J. A. Gray. These generous men offered to pay into the institution $2,500 a year for two years, on the condition that the Conference would raise the same amount. The proposition was accepted and the committee took charge at once. Dr. Wood retired as president at the close of the fall term of 1884. Rev. John Franklin Heitman was elected chairman of the faculty, and he acted in this capacity until June, 1887. He was born in Davidson county, North Carolina, April 17th, 1840; student in Trinity College 1861–62; in the army 1862–65; graduated from Trinity College in 1868; principal of the Kernersville High School 1868–69; became a member of the North Carolina Conference in 1869; professor of Greek and German, German and Metaphysics, Greek and Metaphysics, Metaphysics and Theology in Trinity College 1883–91; headmaster of Trinity High School 1891–95.[2]

---

1. President Crowell's Report to the North Carolina Conference of 1888, pp. 28–29.
2. Prof. Heitman, Autobiography, The Carolina Wesleyan, January 1st, 1892.

His chairmanship brought about good though quiet results. At the beginning the faculty was increased by A. W. Long, A. B., and H. H. Williams, A. M. Mr. Long was the first regular professor of English the college ever had; until that time the work in English had been distributed among the professors of other departments. During the two years which the committee had charge and managed affairs through Prof. Heitman $1,000 were spent in repairs and the faculty were paid in full; and this had been done but few times, if ever, in the history of the institution. The $2,500 promised from the Conference was by no means collected in full either year, still the committee stood by their promise and gave to the college $5,000. By their timely and generous assistance they saved its life. When they gave it back to the Conference of 1886, it was in a far better shape than when they assumed its control.[1] They had shown to the church that with a little money Trinity College could live and prosper, though its great founder was dead. Prof. Heitman, by his rigid economy and close attention to business, had performed a great service. He took hold at a time when the old college had almost fallen and enemies were fighting on every side; and through it all he stood firm and discharged his duty. At the Conference of 1886, Rev. S. B. Jones, D. D., of South Carolina, was elected president. He, however, did not accept; and the management again fell upon Prof. Heitman. In June, 1887, Rev. J. F. Crowell, A. B., was inaugurated as president and the new regime began.[2]

Prof. Crowell was but twenty-eight years of age when he assumed control of the college, still was full of energy

---

[1]. Manuscript of Prof. Heitman; Journals of the North Carolina Conference, 1884–1886.

[2]. Catalogue, 1887–1888; Manuscript of Prof. Heitman; The Carolina Wesleyan, January 1st, 1892.

and of these methods of school work. He was a native of Pennsylvania; a regular A. B. graduate of Yale University, and two years a post-graduate in the same.[1] He entered into the work with an enthusiasm that overcame all obstacles. The institution was still in poor financial circumstances. There was at the time of his election practically no endowment fund, the gift of $3,000 made by Dr. Siddell in 1883 having been used for other than endowment purposes; and the Conference collection for the year 1887 was only $2,241.26.[2] At the special meeting of the trustees, April 5th, 1887, at which Prof. Crowell was elected president, Mr. J. S. Carr gave $10,000 for this fund. During the next year this amount was increased to $25,000 more. The Centenary Church of Winston became responsible for the president's salary, $1,800 per year for the first three years of his administration; and the Winston Chair of Political and Social Science was designated from this gift. In 1889 Mrs. W. H. Avera gave property worth about $2,500 to establish a department of Biblical Literature in honor of her husband.[3]

The requirements for entrance examinations were raised to a considerable extent, and these examinations were exacted of every matriculate. The whole course of studies began an expansion. A larger and far more enthusiastic faculty constituted the teaching force. In 1891–1892 there were in active service eleven full professors (including the president) and five instructors. This was by far the largest and strongest faculty the college had ever had; and it has never been so large since. During the first two years of President Crowell's term of office almost a revolution had been brought about: a new life had been infused into the old institu-

---
1. The North Carolina Teacher, October, 1887.
2. Journal of the North Carolina Conference, 1887, p. 53.
3. Letter from Dr. Crowell, Northampton, Massachusetts; Catalogues, 1887–1890.

tion and its surroundings; the curriculum had been modernized and deepened; standards of scholarship changed and raised; patronage increased and many new friends made. It now seemed best to move the college to some live town for purposes of mutual benefits. Raleigh offered $35,000 in cash and a site. At the Conference of 1889, at Greensboro, a resolution to accept the offer of Raleigh was made; and after a great discussion, in which Dr. Crowell (Litt. D. from the University of North Carolina, June, 1889,) was the controlling force, the resolution passed by a vote of 143 yeas and 41 nays. A committee, consisting of Walter Clark, J. F. Crowell and J. W. Mauney, was appointed by this Conference to secure legislation in reference to moving the institution.[1]

Soon after this action Mr. Washington Duke proposed to Rev. E. A. Yates, D. D., then pastor of Trinity Church, Durham, North Carolina, that in case Raleigh failed to make good her promises he would give $35,000 for a building and $50,000 on the endowment, if Trinity College would move to Durham. When the citizens of Raleigh heard of Mr. Duke's proposition, they decided to release the college authorities from their contract. Then Mr. J. S. Carr, the great philanthropist of many noble causes, offered to give a tract of sixty-two and one-half acres of land, valued at $25,000. Other citizens of Durham subscribed several thousand dollars. These offers were accepted, and the college was located about one mile west of the thriving little city of Durham. In this connection Rev. R. F. Bumpass, the pastor of Main Street Church, Durham, should be mentioned as having had a good deal of influence upon Mr. Duke in his great gift.[2]

Then began the building. By the fall of 1892 every-

---

[1]. Journal of the North Carolina Conference, 1889, pp. 25-27; Letter from Dr. Crowell; Catalogue, 1889-1890.
[2]. Letter from Dr. Crowell; Catalogues, 1889-1897.

thing was ready for occupancy and the institution was transferred. This would have taken place one year earlier, had it not been for the crush of the great tower in the main building. The plant when completed was among the very finest in the whole country: the Main Building erected at a cost of about $85,000; the College Inn, containing seventy-five dormitories, chapel, dining hall and parlors, $34,000; the Technological Building, $8,000; five residences for the faculty; water-works and electric lights in all of the buildings; and the Main Building and College Inn heated by hot air. The buildings had cost about $150,000, the most of which had been given by Mr. Washington Duke. This building enterprise was the greatest mistake that Dr. Crowell and the building committee ever made. Seventy-five thousand dollars would have erected all the buildings the institution needed, or will ever need. Had economy been shown here, there would now be about $75,000 more in the endowment fund. Great empty buildings, with little equipment in the way of apparatus, libraries and teachers, do not by any means make a true college. This mistake was recognized after it was too late to correct it. It brought on for the most part the great trouble that came to the institution during 1892–1893.[1]

When the college was transferred to Durham, the preparatory department remained at the old place under the guidance of Prof. Heitman. The first year at the new place opened up fairly well as to the patronage, but troubles came thick and fast. The faculty was cut down to twelve members, one of whom was Judge A. C. Avery, who had a law class only twice a week. During the fall term the salaries were paid only in part, a very small part at that. At a special meeting of the trustees about the middle of the fall term President Crowell and the

---

1. Letter from President Crowell; Catalogues, 1891-1897.

members of the faculty were called in and questioned as to the causes of the general demoralization and complaint. For some time the relation between the president and the faculty had been very strained, and in some ways unpleasant. At this special meeting resolutions were passed in reference to the relations of the officials of the institution; and H. J. Bass, V. Ballard, W. H. Branson and E. J. Parrish were appointed a finance committee. This committee relieved the president of all financial duties.[1]

This financial arrangement turned out well, and the salaries were paid during the spring term of 1893. The most of the money came from Mr. B. N. Duke and brothers. It was at this emergency that Mr. Duke offered sixty $50 scholarships. These gave tuition to sixty worthy boys and at the same time paid into the college $3,000 a year.[2] Still the real troubles had only been settled in part; the faculty and president were still in bad faith with each other. Something was wrong somewhere. When the trustees had their meeting during the latter part of the spring term of this year, they found affairs in a bad condition. They then began to open their eyes; before this most of them had looked at college affairs from a distance. It had come to the point that the president or the faculty must resign. The president of the trustees asked Dr. Crowell to hand in his resignation. He, however, was given the opportunity of defending himself before them. At the close of his defense, they voted to give him another year as an experiment. When this news was made known, J. M. Bandy, F. E. Welch, S. B. Weeks, R. L. Flowers, C. L. Raper and D. A. Houston, handed in their resignations; and a short while before this J. M. Steadman and J. L.

---

1. Letter from Dr. Crowell; Catalogue, 1892-1893; Resolutions of the Trustees, fall of 1892; the writer was a member of the faculty during this stormy year.
2. Catalogue, 1892-1893.

Armstrong had done the same thing. Of this number all retired in June of that year except R. L. Flowers, who remained professor of Mathematics.[1]

This was really the greatest crisis the institution ever had: the place was new and in some parts unfinished; general demoralization prevailed among some of the students; the new plant required $10,000 a year for heat and light; the faculty were not paid, and in many cases their condition was ignored or unappreciated; Mr. Washington Duke had stopped giving; and for some time it seemed that the end had come. Who was to blame? This is exceedingly difficult to answer in full. Some have said that President Crowell was the sole cause; others have said that the faculty in having their irregular meetings and in rebelling somewhat against the higher authorities were the cause. The truth is that neither the president, faculty nor trustees were alone to blame; all three together had made the mistakes that brought on the crisis. The president had driven his faculty from him by his insincerity, by his attempt to absorb all the power into his own hands and by not paying any attention to the experience and requests of his colleagues. The faculty were perhaps too ready to find fault and to talk the failings of the college to the student body and to the world. The trustees are to be blamed for allowing such enormous extravagance in building and in not keeping themselves acquainted with their institution's affairs and real condition.

The writer should hear make an explanation. He was in this whole scene, and remembers well those stormy faculty meetings and thrilling events of the year 1892–1893. Personally he was on good terms with President Crowell, but he could not help recognizing a good many

---

[1] Catalogue, 1893–1894; Letters from those who resigned; the writer as an eye witness.

of his failings. At the same time he was in friendly relations with all the members of the faculty, and still he saw that they went to extremes. He did not meet in those irregular meetings on the part of some of the faculty, nor did he ever talk about the administration to the students or the public. He could not agree with the administration as he felt that a teacher should and sent in his resignation. Though he was in the midst of the fight and still has the faculty and President Crowell as his personal friends, he dares to make a free and frank statement and to treat the whole matter in a perfectly fair way.

Dr. Crowell remained president during the year 1893–1894, but at the meeting of the trustees, May 1st, 1894, he sent in his resignation. The trustees, however, re-elected him with a unanimous vote, but he saw fit to decline this and retired July 1st, 1894.[1] He had given the college the seven best years of his life. Though it had had many trials during the latter part of his administration, still he had done a greal deal for the institution. He had found it a small college and had placed it among the first institutions of the land. He had given to the student body a zeal for true scholarship and intellectual attainments. He had given it a fine faculty of specialists; also had taken out of his own pocket as much as $14,000,[2] though a poor man. His services have not as yet received their due consideration and appreciation, but as the years go by he becomes a greater president and man. He made mistakes, many of which were due to the fact that he did not know the North Carolina people; on the other hand he performed a great work. In the days to come he will be recognized as one

---

1. His two letters to Col. J. W. Alspaugh, published in The News and Observer, May, 1894.
2. Letter from Dr. Crowell; Catalogue, 1887–1894; Books of the building committee and treasurer.

of Trinity's greatest and most consecrated leaders. The church and trustees owe him a debt that they have made few efforts to pay. They have, however, recognized him as one of their benefactors by naming the Technological Building, erected by him at a cost of $8,000, the Crowell Science Building.[1]

During the summer of 1894 Rev. John Carlisle Kilgo, A. M., of Wofford College, South Carolina, was elected president. He took hold at the beginning of the fall term of that year; and still guides the institution. He was born at Laurens, South Carolina, July 22nd, 1860; student in Wofford College 1880-1881, from which he was forced to leave on account of poor eyes; taught 1882; licensed to preach May 27th, 1882, and became a member of the South Carolina Conference in December of the same year; pastor of the Bennettsville circuit, Timmonsville, Rock Hill, Little Rock—all in South Carolina 1882-1888; financial agent of Wofford College 1888-1890; professor of Political Economy and Metaphysics in Wofford College 1890-1894; A. M. from Wofford 1892; D.D. from Wofford and Randolph-Macon 1895.[2] He entered into the work with great enthusiasm and hopes, and has done much to place the college on a better footing. He is easily the greatest preacher of the Methodist Church in the State, and by his great sermons and addresses has made a lasting reputation. He has increased the endowment by $100,000; the productive fund is now $125,000 and the property is worth $200,000.[3] He has made his student body characteristic and loyal. His fight against State aid to higher education has been intense and able, though it seems that he has accomplished very little thereby. The institution is now coeducational.

---

1. Letter from Dr. Crowell; Catalogue, 1896-1897.
2. Trinity Archive, October, 1894, pp. 2-3; Catalogues, 1895-1897.
3. Letter from President Kilgo; Journal of the North Carolina Conference, 1897.

This plan was inaugurated by Dr. Crowell; and it has now by the gift of $100,000, given by Mr. Washington Duke, December 10th, 1896, become an established feature. This gift was made on the condition that women be admitted on equal terms with men.[1]

The donations to the institution during the last ten years have been large for Southern schools. The college has had enough given to it in this time to be in the best financial condition of any school in the country. However, it is still in rather poor circumstances. The following have been the main gifts: J. S. Carr, $10,000 endowment and land worth at least $25,000; J. F. Crowell, $14,000; Dr. J. A. Cunninggim, George Watts, J. A. and J. M. Odell, each $1,000; W. R. Odell, $500; Washington Duke, $275,000; B. N. Duke, brothers and Mrs. R. E. Lyon, $7,500 a year for three years; B. N. Duke $2,550 on Dr. Crowell's salary, salary of private secretary for some time, deficits on current expenses, often amounting to $7,000, for the past three years. There have been a great many more generous donors. The library, which has about 10,000 volumes, has received a large number of small gifts; so has the historical museum.[2]

As far as the writer can find out the faculty of the college has been as follows: Rev. Braxton Craven, A. M., D. D., 1851–82; Rev. A. S. Andrews, D. D., 1851–54; Hon. W. M. Robbins, A. M., 1851–54; L. Johnson, A. M., tutor, 1853–55, 1855–84; I. L. Wright, A. M., 1855–65; W. T. Gannaway, A. M., 1857–92; O. W. Carr, A. M., tutor, 1855–63, 1866–78; Rev. J. H. Robbins, A. M., tutor, 1855–59; Rev. J. H. Speed, A. B., 1856–57; R. H. Skeen, A. M., 1858–60; L. W. Andrews, A. M., tutor, 1860–63; J. W. Young, 1864–65; Rev. Peter Doub, D. D.,

---

1. Mr. Duke's letter, The News and Observer, December 11, 1896.
2. Letter from President Kilgo; Mr. Duke's books; Letter from Dr. Crowell; Catalogues, 1857–1897.

1866-70; W. C. Doub, A. M., 1866-73; Rev. J. H. Tucker, A. M., 1871-72; Rev. W. H. Pegram, A. M., tutor, 1873-75, 1875-; C. P. Frazier, A. B., asst. professor, 1878-79; J. D. Hodges, A. M., 1879-82; Rev. J. M. Ashby, A. M., 1882-83; Rev. J. F. Heitman, A. M., 1883-91; Rev. M. L. Wood, D. D., 1883-84; J. A. Elliot, A. B., tutor, 1884-85; N. C. English, A. M., 1885-92; J. M. Bandy, A. M., 1885-93; H. H. Williams, A. M., 1885-86; A. W. Long, A. B., 1885-87; Dred Peacock, tutor, 1886-87; G. N. Raper, tutor, 1886-88; J. L. Armstrong, A. M., 1887-93; J. H. Hathcock, tutor, 1887-88; William Price, A. B., 1888-89; F. E. Welch, A. B., 1889-93; Rev. L. W. Crawford, A. M., 1890-93; J. S. Bassett, Ph. D., instructor, 1890-91, 1894-; J. M. Steadman, B. S., 1891-93; H. A. Aikins, Ph. D., 1891-92; S. B. Weeks, Ph. D., 1891-93; B. C. Hinde, A. B., 1891-94; W. I. Cranford, Ph. D., tutor, 1890-91, instructor, 1891-92, 1893-; W. T. McDowell, A. B., tutor, 1891-92; B. B. Nicholson, Ph. B., tutor, 1891-92, 1893-94; R. L. Flowers, instructor, 1891-93, 1893-; Hon. A. C. Avery, LL. D., 1892-93; C. L. Raper, A. B., instructor, 1892-93; D. A. Houston, A. B., instructor, 1892-93; J. L. Weber, A. B., 1893-94; E. T. Bynum, A. B., instructor, 1893-94; A. H. Merritt, A. B., 1893-; Rev. Olin Boggess, A. B., B. D., 1893-95; Jerome Dowd, 1893-; Edwin Mims, M. A., 1894-; Rev. J. C. Kilgo, A. M., D. D., 1894-; M. H. Arnold, A. M., 1894-95; M. H. Lockwood, E. E., 1894-97; F. S. Aldridge, tutor, 1895-96; W. H. Adams, tutor, 1895-97; W. P. Few, Ph. D., 1896-; J. I. Hamaker, Ph. D., 1897-; P. V. Anderson, C. C. Weaver, Z. F. Curtis, and S. L. Dent, tutors, 1896-97.[1]

The faculty at present, as it has been for some time, is able and conservative. There are among its members

---

1. Catalogues, 1851-1897; W. H. Pegram, Trinity Archive, October, 1894; News and Observer, August 26, 1897.

Ph. D. graduates of Johns Hopkins, Yale, Harvard and Cornell, and students of the U. S. Naval Academy and German Universities.[1] The publications of the faculty do not number many volumes, but are equal to those of any North Carolina institution. They are as follows: Common School Grammar by Brandtly York in 1854, which with his High School Grammar has gone through four editions;[2] Dr. Craven's Revisal of Bullion's English Grammar, 1863; L. Johnson, Common School Arithmetic, 1864; Analytical Arithmetic by J. M. Bandy, 1890; English Grammar by J. L. Armstrong, 1891; several historical works by S. B. Weeks and J. S. Bassett; Jerome Dowd, Sketches of Prominent Living North Carolinians, 1888, Life of Braxton Craven, 1896.[3] The students have had four publications: *The College Herald*, 1881–82; *Trinity Magazine*, 1883; *Trinity Archive*, now in its 12th volume; *Historical Publication*, 1897.[4]

The course of studies is as high as that of Davidson, given in another part of these sketches. Since the college moved to Durham there has been no regular preparatory department. However, there have been several classes of sub-freshman work. At the last sessions of the North Carolina and Western North Carolina Conferences it was decided to introduce a preparatory department, beginning with the fall of 1898. For the past three years none but A. B. and A. M. degrees have been given. Dr. Crowell had brought in B. S. and Ph. B.; also had organized a Law department under Judge A. C. Avery, a department of Theology under Rev. L. W. Crawford upon the completion of which B. D. was given, a department of Civil Engineering with C. E. degree under Prof. J. M. Bandy. All three of these depart-

---
1. The News and Observer, August 26, 1897.
2. Rev. B. A. York.
3. Works in the writer's library; also in Greensboro Female College Library.
4. Ibid.

ments had an existence of but little more than two years. The plan of President Kilgo has been to limit the field and intensify the work. The terms are very low in consideration of the advantages; $50 only are charged for tuition per year.[1]

Thus has Trinity College grown, labored and suffered. It has had a very interesting history, though it has not been written; and this sketch is by far too brief. The internal history of the old college, like that of every school, can not be written in words, but only in the lives and hearts of those who have been connected therewith. Trinity College has shown itself in many an emergency. It has now a brighter field. The present arrangement of having two full professors in the department of English will produce results as yet not hoped for. The historical work begun by Dr. Weeks and now kept up under Dr. Bassett has been able; and really this institution is among the pioneers in such work. The Historical Society organized in 1892 still becomes deeper and stronger; and its collection, known as the historical museum, is becoming large and valuable.[2]

## ST. MARY'S SCHOOL.

This has been one of the famous private schools for girls of the State. While the principals have been members of the Episcopal Church, still the church had nothing to do with the school until 1895. At that time it was made a Diocesan institution.[3] The property was purchased by the Diocese of North Carolina in May, 1897, at a cost of $50,000; and Bishop J. B. Cheshire has taken the field to secure $100,000 for an endowment fund.[4] It has had a long and interesting existence, and

---
1. Catalogues, 1887–1897.
2. Catalogues, 1891–1897.
3. Letter from Principal Bennett Smedes.
4. The News and Observer, May 15, 1897.

## SCHOOLS OF NORTH CAROLINA. 199

its history deserves to be written in detail. However, these sketches have already become too extensive, and the remaining part will have to be given in somewhat condensed form.

The school was opened in 1842 by Rev. Aldert Smedes, D. D., and since then it has never closed its doors. Its location is about one mile from the State Capitol. With an oak grove of twenty acres and six quaint buildings, it is a very attractive spot. This has been made sacred by the great ability and consecration of its founder. He was its guide and almost its very life for thirty-six years. He was great and conspicuous in his church, but greater still in his school work. He has made St. Mary's a household word in as many as five thousand homes all over the South; during the first fifty years, 1842–1892, there were enrolled forty-seven hundred and fifty different pupils. His charities were far greater than most people can or will give. He had an income apart from his school, hence did not make this a mere money making concern. His chief aim was to train lady-like, refined and Christian women.[1] He was born in New York City, April, 20th, 1810; educated at Columbia College, Transylvania University, Kentucky, and the General Theological Seminary of his church in New York; assistant rector of Christ Church, New York City, and rector of St. George's Church, Schenectady, New York; D. D. from the University of North Carolina in 1854;[2] died at Raleigh, April 25th, 1877.[3]

At his death his son Rev. Bennett Smedes, A. M., took charge, and he has run it to the present.[4] His father had set a high example and standard to follow, still the

---

1. Dr. K. P. Battle's Centennial Address on Raleigh, 1892, p. 70; Dr. Battle, North Carolina University Magazine, November, 1893; Bishop Cheshire, Semi-Centennial Address at St. Mary's, 1892; Our Living and Our Dead, Vol. III., p. 115.
2. General Catalogue of the University of North Carolina, p. 240.
3. Dr. Battle, North Carolina University Magazine, November, 1893.
4. The News and Observer, May 15, 1897; Letter from Principal Smedes.

son has in no way fallen short. During 1896–1897 there were enrolled one hundred and fifty-five pupils, and the faculty consisted of fifteen members. Among the strongest teachers under Dr. Aldert Smedes were: Misses E. A. Evertson and O'Connor; Mesdames Clement and Gonye; and Mrs. Iredell. There have been equally as strong ones under the administration of Mr. Bennett Smedes. Among these may be mentioned as leaders: Mrs. Kate de R. Meares; Misses M. E. J. Czarmouska and E. D. Battle. The library of the school contains twenty-five hundred volumes; and the principal's of the same size is open to the pupils. There has been but one author among the teachers—Mrs. Annie C. Ketchum, Lotus Flowers and a text book on Botany. *The Muse* is the name of the students' publication. The course of studies is not much different from that of Salem Female Academy already considered. The terms have recently been reduced. For tuition in English Branches, Latin, Class Singing and Elocution, washing, use of the library, Music from an assistant, $240 are charged.[1]

### ASHEVILLE FEMALE COLLEGE.

This school goes back to 1842 for its beginning.[2] Its early history has not been ascertained. However, the writer has made every effort to do so, but has met with no success and little appreciation. It was the property of the Holston Conference of the Methodist Episcopal Church, South, until 1866, when it passed over to a joint stock company, composed for the most part of Asheville citizens. Drs. Erasmus Rawley and Cummins were among the presidents before the Civil War. When it became the property of the stock company Dr. James S. Kennedy was elected president; and he held this posi-

---
1. Catalogue, 1896–1897; Letter from Principal Smedes.
2. Catalogue, 1897–1898; Letter from Prof. B. E. Atkins, Gastonia.

tion for about ten years. Then Rev. J. R. Long served as presiding officer for two years. From 1878 to 1879 the institution was suspended.[1]

In September of 1879 Rev. James Atkins, A. M., D. D., assumed control, and was at its head for ten years. Rev. S. N. Barker, of Texas, was president 1889–1890; and B. E. Atkins, A. M., 1890–1893.[2] In the fall of 1893 Dr. James Atkins, who had been president of Emory and Henry College, Virginia, for four years, came back. He again had control until the summer of 1896, when he was elected Sunday School Editor of the Methodist Episcopal Church, South. During the year 1896–1897 it was kept up by Mrs. James Atkins. Last summer the property was sold to Archibald A. Jones, A. M. In 1887 the present building was erected by Dr. James Atkins at a cost of $30,000. During the eighteen years with which he was connected with it, as president of the faculty or of the trustees, it had an annual enrollment of about one hundred and fifty; and the pupils came from almost every State in the South and from Massachusetts, Ohio, Illinois and Nebraska.[3] The course of studies was equally as high as that of any of the female schools in the State; and the faculty was composed of about twelve members. Board, furnished rooms, fuel, lights, and tuition in the literary branches, cost $225 per year of thirty-eight weeks; Music, Art, Elocution, Book-keeping, French, German, were extras and cost from $10 to $35 each.[4]

Mr. Jones, who was president of Central Female College, Lexington, Missouri, 1889–1897, has enlarged the faculty, extended the curriculum and increased the expenses to a considerable extent. The faculty for 1897–

---

1. Letter from Prof. B. E. Atkins.
2. Ibid.
3. Ibid; Catalogues, 1890–1898.
4. Catalogues, 1890–1896.

1898 is composed of fourteen members. The courses advertised in English, Latin, Greek, French, German, Mathematics, Physics, Chemistry, Geology, Philosophy, and History, are as extensive as those given by any of the higher institutions for men in the State. There is a preparatory department of considerable scope. It is very probable that this will have about all of the pupils, and that the high courses given in the catalogue are only ideal standards. Board, lights, heat, tuition in regular courses, for scholastic year amount to $325; and Music, Art and Elocution are extras and cost from $15 to $45.[1]

### GREENSBORO FEMALE COLLEGE.

This institution ranks among the very first in age and influence. Its history has been varied and interesting. It was born and reared as a child of the Methodist Church; and, though at one time it was almost forsaken by the church, it still loves and supports its dear old mother. Its charter was ratified December 28th, 1838; and this was the second regularly chartered female college south of the Potomac.[2] The Wesleyan Female College of Macon, Georgia, which claims the record of being the first regularly chartered college for women in the world, had its charter confirmed by the legislature of that State December 23rd, 1836.[3] There are several female schools, like Salem Female Academy, older than either of these institutions, but they were not recognized by law as colleges at such an early date.

By 1830 the Methodists of Greensboro were strong enough to build a church. A short while after the church was erected, a little school was begun for the children of the members. Miss Phoebe Judson was in

---

1. Catalogue and circular announcements for 1897-1898.
2. Dr. T. M. Jones, Centennial of Methodism in North Carolina, p. 163.
3. C. E. Jones' Education in Georgia, p. 91.

charge of this for some time.[1] This school was the beginning of the movement to establish Greensboro Female College. In 1837 the trustees of the school sent a petition to the Virginia Conference, which met at Petersburg, Virginia, January 31st. It was at this time and place that the North Carolina Conference was given a separate existence; and the petition from the trustees of the school in Greensboro set forth the necessity of having a female institution of high rank under this new Conference. Revs. Moses Brock, Peter Doub and Samuel S. Bryant were appointed a committee to consider this petition. They, after careful deliberation, introduced to the Conference resolutions, which were adopted and are as follows:

"*Resolved*, 1. That the Conference will co-operate with the trustees of Greensboro Female School, provided that one-half the number of the board of trustees shall at all times be members of the North Carolina Conference.

"*Resolved*, 2. That the board thus constituted shall petition the Legislature of North Carolina for a proper charter for a seminary of learning, to be called the Greensboro Female College.

"*Resolved*, 3. That the Conference appoint Moses Brock, Hezekiah G. Leigh, William Compton, Peter Doub, John Hank, James Reid, Bennett T. Blake, William E. Pell and Samuel S. Bryant, trustees, to carry into effect the object contemplated by the previous resolutions.

"*Resolved*, 4. That the Bishop be requested to appoint an agent for the purpose of raising funds for this object.
                              MOSES BROCK, Chairman."[2]

Rev. Samuel S. Bryant was appointed financial agent. Revs. Moses Brock, Ira T. Wyche and James Reid followed him in the same position. During the latter part of 1837 two hundred and ten acres of land, on the western

---
1. Miss Ruth York, College Message, November, 1897.
2. Dr. Jones, Centennial of Methodism in North Carolina, pp. 160-161.

side of Greensboro, were purchased at a cost of $3,350. Forty acres were laid off for college purposes, and the remaining part was sold in town lots for about as much as the original tract had cost. The money for the building came in very slowly; those were times of great business and financial depression. The trustees, however, went on with the work, and borrowed money on their individual notes. In September, 1843, the corner stone was laid and by the summer of 1845 the building was completed. It was built of brick, three stories high, and contained thirty-six rooms. From first to last it had cost as much as $20,000, a large part of which was still unpaid. Some time later the debt incurred in the building was consolidated by a loan of $7,000 from the literary fund of the State. Rev. Peter Doub, D. D., was perhaps the most active and influential of all those who took part in this educational enterprise. During those early days Mrs. Susan Mendenhall, of Guilford county, made a gift of $4,000, one of the largest individual donations ever made to the institution.[1]

On February 1st, 1846, the first faculty was elected, and Rev. Soloman Lea, A. M., became president. He was born at Leasburg, Caswell county, North Carolina, November 21st, 1807; graduated with A. B. from the University of North Carolina in 1833; A. M. from the same in 1838; tutor in Randolph-Macon College 1835-37; president of Farmville (Virginia) Female Seminary 1841-43; principal of Somerville Female Institute, Leasburg, 1847-92; died April 30th, 1897.[2] The first work of the college began April 15th, 1846. The faculty was

---

[1] Dr. Jones, Centennial of Methodism in North Carolina, pp. 161-162; C. C. Weaver, Trinity Archive, November, 1896; Catalogues, 1892-1898, historical sketches.
[2] General Catalogue of the University of North Carolina, p. 161; Rev. R. H. Broom, North Carolina Christian Advocate, June 2, 1897; Dr. Jones, Centennial of Methodism in North Carolina, p. 162; Letters from Rev. Soloman Lea to President F. L. Reid, March 25, April 21, 1893, Greensboro Female College Library; Miss Wilhelmina Lea, Trinity Archive, February, 1898.

composed of five members. The course of studies was very much the same as in Edgeworth Female Seminary at that time. The expenses were as follows: board and tuition in the preparatory department, five months, $62-$65; board, washing, fuel, lights, tuition in college course, with Music, French, Drawing, Painting and Needle-work, five months, not more than $100.[1]

The first term was of but three months duration, and there were enrolled sixty pupils. During the fall term of the first year there were one hundred, sixty of whom were boarders. The income from the students for the first term was not sufficient to pay the salaries in full, but during the second after the salaries were paid there was a surplus. The salary of the president was $1,000; matron, Mrs. S. Blake, $1,000; Rev. Bennett T. Blake, professor, $500; Mrs. Sophia Lea, Music, $500; Miss Phoebe Judson $300. Mr. Lea did his best to make the college a success; and he succeeded well, though several occurrences of an unpleasant nature took place. There was a great deal of discord in the faculty. Mr. Blake, who was a prominent member of the Conference, was professor of Mental and Moral Science, chaplain, secretary of the trustees and treasurer of the college; and he wanted to have a very large part of the management in his own hands. He, Mrs. Blake and another member of the faculty, whom Mr. Lea calls the "Northern mischief maker," stirred up discord unless they were allowed absolute authority. Mr. Lea soon found out that he could not run the college with such discordant elements in its faculty, and resigned in December, 1847.[2]

Upon the resignation of Mr. Lea, Rev. Albert Micajah Shipp was elected to the presidency. He took hold in

---

1. Catalogue, 1846; Greensboro Patriot, February 7, 1846.
2. Journal of Greensboro Female College, 1846-1885, p. 40; Greensboro Patriot, December 11, 1847; Manuscript of Mr. Lea in Greensboro Female College Library, written to President Reid in 1893.

January, 1848, and resigned June, 1850. During his term of two and one half years the institution prospered even beyond the highest expectations. Twenty-six young women graduated under him, and the finances were put in a somewhat better shape.[1] Though he was not connected with it long enough to be considered one of its great presidents, still he was one of the greatest characters ever within its walls. He was born in Stokes county, North Carolina; graduated with A. B. degree from the University of North Carolina in 1840, A. M. in 1845; D. D. from Randolph-Macon College 1859; LL. D. from the University of North Carolina 1883; pastor at Charleston, Columbia, Sumter and Cheraw, South Carolina, and Fayetteville, North Carolina; professor of Mathematics and French in Greensboro Female College at the same time he was president; professor of History in the University of North Carolina, 1849–1859, and of French 1850–1853; president of Wofford College, South Carolina, 1859–1875; professor of Exegetical Theology in Vanderbilt University 1876–1886, of which he was dean of the theological department and vice chancellor for three years; wrote History of Methodism in South Carolina 1884; died at Cheraw, South Carolina, July 27, 1887.[2]

In June, 1850, Rev. Charles Force Deems was elected the third president. He was so well and favorably known that it seemed that a new era had begun when he assumed the management. He was born in Baltimore, Maryland, December 4th, 1820; student at Dickinson College, Pennsylvania, 1834–1839, where he graduated; preacher in New York City 1839–40; agent of the American Bible Society in North Carolina 1840–1842; adjunct professor of Logic and Rhetoric in the University of

---

1. Journal of Greensboro Female College, 1846–1885, p. 40; Greensboro Patriot, December 11, 1847; Manuscript of Mr. Lea in Greensboro Female College Library, written to President Reid in 1893; Dr. Jones, Centennial of Methodism in North Carolina, p. 164; Catalogues, 1892–1898.
2. General Catalogue of the University of North Carolina, pp. 80, 207, 241; Letter from Miss Susie V. Shipp, Cheraw, South Carolina.

North Carolina 1842-1848; professor of Natural Science in Randolph-Macon College 1848-1849; D. D. from Randolph-Macon 1853; founder of the female schools in Thomasville and Wilson; founder and pastor of the Church of the Strangers in New York City 1870-1893; LL. D. from the University of North Carolina 1877; founder and editor of the American Institute of Christian Philosophy 1881-1893; editor of five different papers; author of as many as twenty volumes; died in New York City, November 18th, 1893.[1]

He brought new life and methods, and the school became very prosperous. During the first scholastic year under him one hundred and thirty-seven pupils matriculated; and this was the enrollment for the next year. The rooms were all filled, and many more pupils would have entered had the accommodations been sufficient. President Deems asked the trustees for more room. They were already burdened with the debt of the first building and were unwilling to increase this. It was in this emergency that President Deems in 1852 made the $20,000 proposition. It was as follows: that the North Carolina Conference collect and pay over $20,000 to the trustees; that the trustees give board and tuition to the daughters of all the ministers of the Conference at that time, and afterwards to ten annually during the life of the institution. This at the time seemed a splendid proposition, though in the end it was not successful. The offer was accepted on the part of the Conference, and many of the preachers went to work to raise the money. Revs. William Closs, D. D., and William Barringer secured a large part of it.[2] It was not until the

---

1. Charles Force Deems, (autobiographical and biographical), by his Sons, pp. 17, 61-65, 80, 94, 95, 98, 108-121, 191-222, 222-236, 274, 308-323, 348; General Catalogue of the University of North Carolina, pp. 80, 240; Dr. F. L. Reid, the Alumni Quarterly of the University of North Carolina, January, 1895.
2. Dr. F. L. Reid, the Alumni Quarterly of the University of North Carolina, January, 1895; Dr. Jones, Centennial of Methodism in North Carolina, pp. 164-165; Catalogues, 1851-1853; Journal of Greensboro Female College, 1846-1895, pp. 656-684.

fall of 1856 that any benefits came to the ministers, and the full amount was not paid to the trustees until May, 1860.[1]

Before anything was done in the way of enlarging the building Dr. Deems retired, December, 1854. Though he was the presiding officer for only four and a half years, still he had increased the faculty, appliances and patronage; and he made a reputation for the college in the way of scholarship.[2] In this connection it is well to bring to light a few points of the internal workings of the president and trustees. From the beginning there had been somewhat of a disposition on the part of the latter to assume too much of the management of college affairs in their own hands. The trustees elected the president and expected him to run the institution so as to make fine profits for them, but they gave him little choice in selecting teachers and in paying them what their services were worth. A minority of the trustees had enough influence on the majority to thwart all plans for improvement and scholarship. While the income for 1852–1853 was $7,330, the salaries were only $4,710, giving a profit of $2,620.[3] In spite of such fine profits, the executive committee of the trustees cut down the salaries of three members of the faculty. Mr. Lea and Dr. Shipp had resigned largely on account of such mismanagement on the part of the trustees. Dr. Deems endured it for some time, but on May 18th, 1853, he sent in his resignation. The writer has a copy of this before him and bears witness that the whole is very interesting reading. It is scathing, still pleasant and true. It shows the deep grasp that Dr. Deems had of the true educational problems. His first resignation was not ac-

---
[1]. Day Book of Greensboro Female College, 1855–1863; Dr. Jones, Centennial of Methodism in North Carolina, p. 167.
[2]. Dr. Jones, Centennial of Methodism in North Carolina, p. 165; Catalogues, 1851–1853; Charles Force Deems, by his Sons, pp. 108–117.
[3]. Journal of Greensboro Female College, 1846–1885, p. 676.

cepted, and he remained as president until December, 1854.[1]

At this time Rev. Turner Myrick Jones, who had been professor of Mathematics and Ancient Languages for one year, became president; and he remained at its head until his death, June 30th, 1890. He was born in Franklin county, North Carolina, June 4th, 1819; graduated at Randolph-Macon College with A. B. and A. M.; D. D. from Trinity College 1870; private teacher in Warren county 1844-1846; principal of Ridgeway Male Academy 1846-1847; principal of Midway Academy, Franklin county, 1847-1850; principal of Louisburg Male Academy 1850-1853, when he came to Greensboro Female College.[2] He was one of the most noble and cultured teachers this State has produced. As a teacher and guide of young women he has no superior, and with the exception of Dr. Smedes no equal.

When he took hold the institution was not by any means in a solid condition. The financial report of 1855 shows that $10,000 were still unpaid on the first building; and this was to be raised from tuition. The patronage was so large that more room had to be added, and still the Conference had not collected enough on the $20,000 proposition to erect buildings. At the meeting of the trustees in 1856 it was decided to erect a wing to the west end of the old building. This was completed within a year, and still everything was filled. The next two years were very prosperous. In May, 1859, a wing to the east end was begun, but before this was finished there were so many pupils that a good many had to board in private families.[3] By May, 1860, the Confer-

---
1. Journal of Greensboro Female College, 1846-1885, p. 676.
2. Ibid, pp. 40-48; North Carolina Teacher, March, 1886; Miss Dora Duty Jones; President Dred Peacock; Tomb-stone at Greensboro; Dr. Jones, Centennial of Methodism in North Carolina, p. 166.
3. Deems' Annals of Southern Methodism, 1857, p. 175; Dr. Jones, Centennial of Methodism in North Carolina, p. 167; Day Book of Greensboro Female College, 1855-1863.

ence had placed to the credit of the trustees sufficient bonds to confirm the $20,000 proposition. Of these bonds only $11,300 were ever collected; and thirty-one daughters of ministers received instruction, six of whom graduated, at a cost of $13,912. By 1861 the east wing could be used; and the capacity of the whole building was sufficient to accommodate one hundred and seventy-five boarders. From 1860 to 1863 there were enrolled each year more than two hundred pupils; during the past eight and a half years there had been one hundred and eighteen graduates. The income was also fairly good. According to the report of 1863, the assets were enough to pay all the indebtedness. On the 9th of August, 1863, came the great fire that consumed everything, even the institution's life for ten years.[1]

Soon after the fire a movement was made to rebuild at the earliest possible date, and public sentiment was decidedly in favor of it. Dr. Jones was appointed agent to secure funds. The work was begun in 1864, but was delayed for a long time by the great depression that came when the Civil War had turned against the South. However, some few kept up hopes. At the first Conference after the war Rev. Charles Force Deems, D. D., was selected as financial agent. He moved to New York City about 1865, and it was hoped that he could secure money from some philanthropist of that wealthy city. However, this hope was never fully realized, though Mr. William Vanderbilt gave $5,000. A new board of trustees was appointed, and they secured a new charter in 1869. In 1871 the work was again taken up, and by the summer of 1873 the present college building was ready for occupancy. It had cost about $60,000; and the money had been obtained from many sources. The most liberal

---

1. Dr. Jones. Centennial of Methodism in North Carolina, pp. 168–169; Journal of Greensboro Female College, 1846–1885; Day Book of Greensboro Female College, 1855–1863.

givers were: James H. Davis, $10,000; W. T. Sutherlin, $5,000; Dr. Allen Gunn, $2,000; W. Turner, $2,000; I. M. F. and E. Garrett, $2,068.82. The saddest occurrence connected with the whole affair was the accidental death of Rev. William Barringer, which happened March 10th, 1873. He had been for years the institution's warmest friend and best adviser.[1]

On August 27th, 1873, the college again opened, after a period of inactivity of eleven years. Dr. Jones taught elsewhere most of this time. He carried on the college at Louisburg from January, 1866, to June, 1869, and at Warrenton from September, 1869, to June, 1873.[2] From 1863 to 1873 fifty-one young ladies graduated under him and in the same course of studies as at Greensboro Female College.[3] The new building was so much larger and better arranged than the old, that it seemed as if the institution had just begun its life. The following enrollment speaks for itself: 1873-74, one hundred and fifty-four; 1874-75, one hundred and forty-two; 1875-76, one hundred and thirty-two; 1876-77, one hundred and four; 1877-78, ninety-one; 1878-79, eighty-seven; 1879-80, seventy-three; 1880-81, one hundred and thirty-five; 1881-82, one hundred and forty-eight.[4]

The debt incurred in erecting the new building was hanging over the trustees, and the Conference was very slow to relieve them. A large part of this indebtedness was due to Rev. N. H. D. Wilson, D. D., and Col. Charles Shober. When all the funds had been consumed in the building and still it was not by any means finished, these men came to the relief of the committee and advanced money with which to complete the work. The

---

1. Dr. Jones, Centennial of Methodism in North Carolina, pp. 170-173; Day Book of Greensboro Female College, 1855-1863; Catalogue, 1873; Dr. Reid, the Alumni Quarterly of the University of North Carolina, January, 1895.
2. Dr. Jones' Journal at Louisburg and Warrenton; Catalogue, 1873.
3. Catalogues, 1892-1898.
4. Catalogues, 1873-1883.

debts to these liberal men and to others were not paid, nor arranged for. The first mortgage of $20,000 was held by the North Carolina Railroad, T. M. Holt, president. The railroad was urgent for its money, and the Conference could or would not pay it. The whole property was put up for sale June 5th, 1882. For some time everything seemed dark, but in the emergency a company of large-hearted men was formed for the purpose of buying the property and saving it to the church. The original incorporators of this company were: Henry Lilly, E. J. Lilly, J. S. Carr, J. H. Ferree, J. A. Odell, J. A. Gray, J. M. Winstead, L. W. Crawford and T. M. Jones. R. R. Gwyn, J. M. Odell and O. W. Carr soon came in. The officers of the company were: J. S. Carr, president; T. M. Jones, treasurer; J. A. Odell, secretary. They paid off the first mortgage of $20,000, and obtained the whole property in fee simple. Dr. Jones had claims against the old institution for $6,500, and was given in payment sixty-five shares of $100 each in the stock company.[1]

As soon as the company had organized and placed the institution on its feet, they offered to give it back to the North Carolina Conference, upon the condition that the company be relieved of any financial responsibility assumed in its purchase. This proposition was made November 18th, 1882, but the Conference refused to accept it.[2] The company had come in at a time of great need and bought the property to save the institution to the church. It seems that the church did not want it back, at any rate the responsibility of keeping its finances in shape. After it was found out that the Conference did not want it again, the company at once decided to bond

---

[1]. Dr. Jones, Centennial of Methodism in North Carolina, p. 174; Raleigh Christian Advocate, 1882, June 7, July 26; Catalogue, 1882–1883; Record of the Directors of Greensboro Female College.

[2]. Record of the Directors of Greensboro Female College.

the property to obtain funds for improvement. Then began the new era of the old college; and the management of the company has grown wiser and stronger each year to the present. Dr. Jones remained president until his death, June, 1890. The credit of the college had been restored and the patronage began to increase. The annual enrollment for 1882–1890 was from one hundred and fifty-two to two hundred and six.[1]

Dr. Benjamin Franklin Dixon assumed control in the summer of 1890, and held the position till June, 1893. He was born in Cleveland county, North Carolina, March 27th, 1846; in the war 1861–65; joined the South Carolina Conference in 1868; pastor at Sumter, South Carolina, Monroe and Shelly Circuit; physician at Kings Mountain 1874–84; superintendent of the Oxford Orphan Asylum 1884–90; physician at Kings Mountain from 1894 to the present.[2] The three years of his administration were quiet and prosperous.[3] He won a place in the hearts of his pupils that few are ever permitted to enjoy.

Rev. Frank L. Reid, D. D., became Dr. Dixon's successor. He came at a time when great ability was required. The State Normal and Industrial College for women had opened up at Greensboro, October, 1892. This was supported by the State and Peabody funds, and had one of the strongest faculties ever gathered together in North Carolina. For some time many thought that this institution would soon prove the ruin of Greensboro Female College. Such forebodings were false. Dr. Reid, one of the very ablest men of his day, was at the head; and he knew not failure. Though he was the guide but little more than a year, still that time is very precious in the history of the college. He brought new

---

1. Catalogues, 1882–1890; Record of Greensboro Female College.
2. Legislature and Government of North Carolina, 1897, pp. 18–19.
3. Catalogues, 1890–1893.

life and hopes to the faculty and students; he purchased the first real chemical equipment the institution ever had, at a cost of $600; he erected the president's residence; he increased the scope of instruction and made and confirmed friends here and there.[1] He was born in Rockingham county, North Carolina, June 16th, 1851; student at Trinity College 1866–70, where he graduated with A. B. degree; principal of the Kernersville High School fall of 1870; joined the North Carolina Conference, December, 1870; pastor of the Madison Circuit 1870–73; pastor at Louisburg 1873–77; president of Louisburg Female College 1877–78; co-editor, with Rev. W. S. Black, D. D., of the *Raleigh Chritian Advocate* 1878–84; editor of same 1884–93; died September 24th, 1894.[2]

On the 2nd of October, 1894, Rev. W. C. Norman, then of Wilmington, was elected his successor. He had too much devotion for the ministry, and did not accept. On the 31st of the same month Dred Peacock, A. B., A. M., became president, and he still guides affairs. He was born in Wilson county, North Carolina, April 12th, 1864; student in Wilson Collegiate Seminary, Trinity College 1883–87, where he graduated with A. B.; principal of the Lexington Female Seminary 1887–88; professor of Latin and Science in Greensboro Female College 1888–94;[3] given A. M. in 1890 and Litt. D. in 1897 by Trinity College. His administration has been active in the way of improvements. When he assumed control the library had only a few hundred books. Now it contains five thousand well selected volumes, many of which are very rare and valuable. Mrs. Dred Peacock

---

1. Catalogues, 1893–1895.
2. Catalogue of Trinity College, 1897, p. 111; Manuscript sketch in the possession of the writer; Catalogues, 1893–1898; The News and Observer, September 25th, 1894; Record of the Directors of Greensboro Female College.
3. The News and Observer, November 1, 1894; President Peacock; Catalogues, 1888–1898; Greensboro Record, November, 1894.

in December, 1894, gave $1,000 toward an endowment for this. The directors at their private expense had a room fixed up in handsome style and arrangement. The old books were placed in the new quarters in January, 1895. There were few then, but now everything looks changed. There have been hundreds of gifts to this, of various kinds and amounts. The North Carolina collection has about fifteen hundred different titles, and is easily one of the very largest and most valuable in existence. The courses of studies have been intensified, and the work has became much more rigid. Written examinations have been introduced for entrance into any class. Though the system of instruction has been made far deeper and more rigid, still the patronage for 1897-98 is larger than it has been during the past seven years.[1]

The list of distinguished alumnae is too long to be given in this sketch. From 1848 to 1863 there were one hundred and ninety-one graduates; under Dr. Jones at Kittrell, Louisburg and Warrenton, 1863–73, fifty-one; from 1873 to 1897, four hundred and twenty-eight.[2] These are found all over the South, and some in the North and West. Wherever found, they are still loyal friends; many of the pupils of the past are the patrons of to-day. They remember their *alma mater* with little gifts of money and books now and then, and send their daughters as precious ones occasionally.

The gifts to the institution have been many, though none of them large. Among those not already mentioned is that of Dr. Siddell, who in 1883 gave $3,000. In this connection the great services of the members of the stock company should be mentioned. They have given their money and some of their time and attention

---
1. Catalogues, 1895–1898; Record of Greensboro Female College; President Peacock.
2. Catalogues, 1892–1898.

for the sake of the education of the young women of the land. They have made it possible for the college to offer fine courses of instruction at fair terms. Mr. J. A. Odell deserves special mention for his kind interest and liberality. Since the formation of the company he has been the institution's true adviser and warm friend. His gifts to the college and the Methodist Church mark him as liberal; his devotion to duty and all things noble make him exemplary.

The male members of the faculty have been: Rev. Solomon Lea, A. M., Anc. Lang., 1846–48; Rev. Bennett T. Blake, Mental and Moral Sci., 1846–48; William C. Doub, A. M., Math., Nat. Sci., 1847, 1851–53, 1861–68, 1873–78; Rev. James Jamison, Anc. Lang., Nat. Sci., 1848–50; Rev. A. M. Shipp, A. M., Math., French, 1848–50; Rev. F. X. Foster, A. M., 1849–51; Francis Cochen, Music, part of spring 1850; Rev. C. F. Deems, A. M., Anc. Lang., Phys. Sci., 1850–54; Rev. A. S. Andrews, Evidences of Christ., spring 1851; Andrew G. Kern, Music, 1851–53; Rev. Turner M. Jones, A. M., Math., Anc. Lang., 1853–54, Anc. Lang., Nat. Sci., 1854–63, Mental and Moral Sci., 1873–90; Theodore F. Wolle, Music, 1853–59; Ernest Jouanne, French, 1853–55; William K. Blake, A. M., Math., Anc. Lang., 1854–56; W. C. A. Frerichs, Drawing, Painting, 1855–62; Eugene P. Raillard, French, 1855–56; Samuel Lander, A. M., Math., Anc. Lang., author of an Arithmetic, 1857–59; W. F. Alderman, A. M., Math., Anc. Lang., 1859–93; F. J. Hahr, Music, Fine Arts, 1873–77; H. E. Rosenstack, Music, 1877–78; A. H. Bach, Music, 1879–80;[1] R. Fasolt, Music, 1886–88; Dred Peacock, A. M., Latin, Nat. Sci., 1888–94; Walter P. Sullivan, Music, 1888–90; B. F. Dixon, Mental and Moral Philos., 1890–93; Rev. J. D. Arnold, A. B., Math., Metaphysics,

---
1. Catalogues, 1846–1880; Journal of Greensboro Female College, 1846–1885.

1893-95; J. W. Parker, Music, 1894-; Charles L. Raper, A. B., Latin, Sci., 1894-98.[1]

The lady members have been so many and have held in some cases for such a short period, that the full list will not be given. They have done work equally as able as the men, and their names should be handed down in history as well as in tradition. In this connection space will not permit the mention of them all. However, the writer would name some of the leading and most consecrated of those who have been associated with him for the past four years: Lillian Long, English, History, 1893-; Minnie H. Moore, Mathematics, 1894-; Bettie Armfield, Business Department, 1890-; Louisa M. Batson, Music, 1892-96; Alta B. Cozart, A. B., Elocution, 1894-; Anne M. Sneed, Music, 1894-; Annie M. Page, French, German, 1895-; Ava L. Fleming, Latin, English, 1895-; Catharine F. Heiskell, Drawing, Painting, 1895-; Clara B. Orr, Music, 1896-98; Clara Puryear, A. B., A. M., English, 1897-.[2]

The present course of studies in the regular departments is: Freshman—English Grammar (Baskervill and Sewell), Exercises in Composition, Lockwood's Lessons in English, Selections from American Literature, Hawthorne's Tanglewood Tales, American History (Montgomery), The Beginner's Latin Book (Collar and Daniell, Viri Romae (D'Ooge), Keetel's Elementary French Grammar, French Conversation, Super's Reader, German Lessons (Collar-Eysenbach), Conversation and Dictation, German Grammar (Joynes-Meissner), Grimm's Maerchen, Complete Geography (Frye), Zoology (Burnet), Sutton and Kimbrough's Higher Arithmetic; Sophomore—Hill's Foundations of Rhetoric, Irving's Sketch-Book, Longfellow's Evangeline, and

---

1. Catalogues, 1880-1898.
2. Catalogues, 1892-1898.

Courtship of Miles Standish, Whittier's Snow-Bound and other poems, Lowell's Vision of Sir Launfal, parallel work in biography, Composition Work, Meiklejon's History of English Literature, Dickens' Christmas Carol and Cricket on the Hearth, Tennyson's Enoch Arden and other poems, Scott's Lady of the Lake and Lay of the Last Minstrel, History of England (Montgomery), Cæsar's Gallic War (Allen and Greenough), six books, Latin Grammar (Bennett), Latin Composition (Bennett), first twenty-two lessons, Elementary French Grammar finished, Super's Reader finished, Keetel's Complete Grammar, L'Abbe Constantin, German Grammar, Wilhelm Tell (Schiller), Historische Erzaehlungen, Conversation and Dictation, Minna Von Barnhelm, Die Journalisten, Physical Geography (Hinman), Physiology and Hygiene (Hutchison), Wentworth's Elements of Algebra, supplemented by Wentworth and Hill's Exercises in Algebra; Junior—From Milton to Tennyson (Syle), Pancoast's Introduction to English Literature, Composition Work, Rolfe's edition of Merchant of Venice, As You Like It, Twelfth Night, and Julius Cæsar, General History (Myers), Cicero's Conspiracy of Catiline. (Allen and Greenough), four orations, Latin Grammar, Latin Composition, (Bennett), History of Rome (Creighton), Vergil's Aeneid (Harper and Miller), four books, Roman Mythology, French Grammar, Le Petit Chose (Daudet), Le Cid (Corneille), Hernani (Victor Hugo), German Grammar (Whitney), Readings from the Lyric Poetry of Goethe and Heine, other German authors, Chemistry (Williams' New), Laboratory Manual (Williams), Wenthworth's New Plane and Solid Geometry; Senior—Tennyson's Arthurian Poems, selections from English Prose Classics, Rolfe's edition of Hamlet and Much Ado About Nothing, Theme Work, Rolfe's edition of Macbeth, King Lear, Othello and Henry IV., History of North Carolina, Horace, Odes (Smith and Greenough), four books, Roman Literature (as much as in Bender), Tacitus, the Agricola and Germania (Hopkins), Roman Constitution (Tighe), L'Ami Fritz (Erckmann-Chatrian), L'Athalie (Racine), La Litterature Francaise (Berlitz), Merope (Voltaire), Contes Choisies (Daudet), Un Mariage d'Amour (Halevy), Litterature Francaise, German Grammar (Whitney), Faust, Part I., Reading at Sight, Conversation and Dictation, Principles of Physics (Gage), Elementary Geology (Tarr), Wentworth's Plane and Spherical Trigonometry, Psychology (Steele), Ethics (Steele), Civil Government (Finger).[1]

### CHOWAN BAPTIST FEMALE INSTITUTE.

Murfreesboro has been the centre of a large Baptist community for a long time, and the Baptists here, as elsewhere, have always been active in the way of education. In 1848 the Chowan and Portsmouth Associations decided to establish a school for the higher education of young women. G. C. Moore, G. M. Thompson. S. Z. Wheeler, W. B. Mitchell, A. Z. Askew, T. Hume, J. Prince, and others of these associations, formed a company, purchased land and erected a house in the town of Murfreesboro, at a cost of $1,225. The school was opened in October, 1848, with Rev. A. McDowell, D. D., principal. He remained at its head for a short while only. Rev. M. R. Forey became the second principal, and held the position until August, 1853. The prosperity under him was great. It soon became necessary to have more room. A large brick building was erected in 1852. Rev. William Hooper, D. D., LL. D., was president from 1853 to 1862. Then Mr. McDowell, the

---

1. Catalogue, 1897-1898.

first principal, returned and served until his death in 1881. John B. Brewer, A. M., was president 1881–96; Rev. W. O. Petty, 1896–97; John C. Scarborough, A. B., ex-superintendent of Public Instruction of North Carolina, 1897.[1]

During these forty-nine years of its existence it has never closed. In this time it has sent out about three hundred graduates; and these have been from many of the Southern States. For a long time it has had a faculty of about ten members, and has given instruction in a course of studies about the same as that of Salem Female Academy, St. Mary's and Greensboro Female College. It has all the time been under the influence of the Baptist Church. The property now belongs to some of the members of the Chowan and West Chowan Associations, and is worth more than $50,000.[2]

### OXFORD FEMALE SEMINARY.

This school opened in the town of Oxford in 1851, and was known for some time as Oxford Female College. At the Baptist State Convention of 1849 the following report was made: "The necessity of establishing a Female College for the State, in which suitable testimonials of a high grade of scholarship will be awarded, is seriously entertained by many of our brethren and is an object worthy of their united and zealous efforts." The Convention of 1850 was assured by the town of Oxford of at least $10,000, if the college would be located there. By the same convention the school was located and trustees were appointed. Elder J. J. Jones was selected as agent. He

---

1. Some of these points are given also by Smith in his History of Education in North Carolina, pp. 121–122; Catalogues, 1887–1897; Points gotten up by Rev. M. T. Plyler; Letters from Presidents Petty and Scarborough; North Carolina Teacher, January, 1889.

2. Catalogues, 1887–1897; Letters from Presidents Petty and Scarborough; Biblical Recorder, December 5, 1897.

secured a charter in March, 1851. Rev. Samuel Wait, D. D., was elected president in April, 1851; and the school began July 21st of the same year. In June, 1852, the financial report showed a debt of $9,001.42. The trustees then employed four agents in succession, but they did not obtain enough money to pay their own salaries. Dr. Wait took the field in 1857, but met with no better success. The college was in a bad condition; it had no money and less credit. At this emergency Mr. J. H. Mills made the trustees an offer of $5,000 for the whole property. This proposition was accepted; and the school became a private institution, which it has been ever since.[1]

Mr. J. H. Mills ran the college until January, 1861, when a part was sold to L. R. Mills; and from then until 1868 it was kept up by Mills and Company. Mr. J. H. Phillips, Rev. R. H. Marsh, Dr. R. H. Lewis and others had charge of it until 1880. Then F. P. Hobgood, A. M., purchased the property. He has had a flourishing school ever since under the name of Oxford Female Seminary.[2]

The property is now worth about $20,000. The faculty consists of ten members; and the average annual enrollment under him has been one hundred and twenty, coming from the Carolinas and Virginia. The course of studies is about the same as those of the female colleges already given. The terms are in some subjects higher and in others lower than in many of the female schools of the State: preparatory English, $30.00; collegiate English, $40.00; Latin and French, each, $5.00; Drawing, $30.00; Painting, $40.00; Elocution in Class, $20.00; Elocution in Class, and one private lesson a week additional, $35.00; Needle-work, $15.00; Instru-

---

[1]. Biblical Recorder, April 7, 1859; Catalogue, 1861.
[2]. Catalogue, 1861; Letters from President Hobgood.

mental Music, from the professor, $45.00; Instrumental Music, from the assistant, $40.00; Voice, $40.00; Use of Piano, 1½ hours per day, $5.00.[1]

Prof. Hobgood has been in the educational work so long and has performed such valuable services, that he deserves more than a mere passing notice. He was born in Granville county, North Carolina, 1847; student at Horner School; graduated at Wake Forest College in 1868; teacher in Oxford Female College 1868–69; principal of the Reidsville High School 1869–71; teacher in the Raleigh Baptist Female Seminary 1871; president of the same 1871–80;[2] president of Oxford Female Seminary from 1881 to the present; president of the North Carolina Teachers' Assembly 1894.[3]

### OAK RIDGE INSTITUTE.

This institution is now North Carolina's largest and best training school. It goes back to 1850 for its beginning. During that year Dr. John Saunders, Jesse Benbow, Allen Lowrey, James B. Clark, Samuel Donnell, Daniel Pegram, Robert Bell, Wyatt Bowman, T. J. Benbow, and other citizens of the northwestern corner of Guilford county, decided to have a high school in that community. They chose a site fifteen miles from Greensboro and erected a building sixty feet long and one story high. John M. Davis, a graduate of Emory and Henry College, Virginia, became the first principal. He was a fine scholar and teacher, and the school was soon filled to its greatest capacity. Rev. D. R. Bruton had charge in 1857. After him, Mr. T. Whittington and a Mr. Pickett kept it up till the Civil War. From 1861 to 1866

---

1. Catalogues, 1892–1897; Letters from President Hobgood.
2. Dowd's Prominent Living North Carolinians, pp. 214–215; Biblical Recorder, December 8, 1897.
3. The North Carolinian, May 21, 1896; The News and Observer, August 21, 1897.

it was closed. The building was burned in 1866, but was replaced in a short while. Mr. O. C. Hamilton ran it 1866-69; Pendleton King 1869-71; Rev. Gideon D. Hines, one session of 1871; W. S. Crouse 1872-75. In the fall of 1875 J. Allen Holt, A. M., assumed control and the school entered upon its new and great career.[1]

When Prof. Holt began in 1875 there were but two small rooms, one 14x24, the other 26x24. He began work with great earnestness, and was full of correct educational ideas. There were forty pupils under him the first year, and fifty the next. From this small beginning it has grown until it has had for some time an annual enrollment of two hundred and fifty. In the spring of 1879 Martin H. Holt, his brother, came in as associate principal, and they together have builded a great structure, one of the most remarkable high schools in the whole country. As their patronage has increased they have multiplied the faculty, equipment and buildings. In 1884 the chapel was built at a cost of $8,000. In 1891 the Holt Hall was erected at a cost of about $12,000; and the same year the institution was incorporated with a capital stock of $51,600 and with power to grant diplomas. The course of studies is high and extensive for training schools in the South. Students who complete the regular literary course enter the Sophomore and Junior classes of the best colleges and the University of the State.[2] The expenses for tuition per session of nineteen weeks are: Literary department, $25.00; Commercial department, $25.00; Shorthand and Typewriting, $25.00; Telegraphy, $25.00; Primary department, $15.00; Surveying, $10.00; incidental fee, $1.00; graduation fee, $5.00; library fee (to members of the societies nothing), $3.50.[3]

---

1. Oak Leaf, September, 1884; Catalogues, 1882-1895.
2. Ibid.
3. Catalogue, 1897-1898.

The educational work of J. Allen and Martin H. Holt has been distinguished for devotion and ability. They themselves have become well known throughout the Carolinas and Virginia, from which States the most of their students have come; and Oak Ridge Institute is known far and wide through the South and Southwest. They have opened their courses to the rich and poor alike, to girls as well as boys. They have worked from the standpoint of training and culture; and though their school has not been denominational, still it has been Christian-like. They charge good terms and have made money, still have given numberless charities.[1]

### HORNER SCHOOL.

There is much in common between this and Bingham School. Both have been famous classical institutions. They have never attempted to have large numbers. They have charged high prices and given extensive classical courses; and have cared only for a few. A part of the history of this school was given under Horner and Graves at Hillsboro. As has been stated, the school was begun by James Hunter Horner, M. A., LL. D., in Oxford, in 1851. Mr. Horner ran the school as sole principal until 1870, when R. H. Graves, A. M., came in as co-principal. Horner and Graves kept it up at Oxford until 1874, when they moved to Hillsboro. In 1876 Mr. Horner went back to Oxford; and he was sole principal from this until his death in 1892. Then his sons, Jerome C. Horner, A. M., and Rev. Junius M. Horner, B. A., B. D., took charge and have kept it up since.[2]

The military feature was first introduced in 1864, and again after the war in 1875. It still adheres to this sys-

---

[1]. The writer has been a pupil and a teacher in the Institute, and has had a personal acquaintance for eleven years.
[2]. Catalogues, 1867, 1887-1898; Letters from Principals J. C. and J. M. Horner.

tem. There were seventy-five pupils each year before the war, and there have been about one hundred and ten since. From its founding more than three thousand students have received instruction at this fountain head, and most of these were under the care of Mr. James Hunter Horner. He was a conspicuous educator for forty-one years, and justly ranks among the immortals of our educational history. His school had such a reputation for good honest scholarship and training, that pupils came from New York, Pennsylvania, Illinois, Iowa, Maryland, Virgina, the Carolinas, Georgia, Florida, Alabama, Mississippi, Texas, Tennessee, Kentucky, West Virginia, and other States. Many of these have taken high positions in the various avocations. George. T. Winston, LL. D., president of the University of Texas, Rev. Wilber F. Tillet, D. D., dean of the Theological Department of Vanderbilt University, Judges George Brown and R. W. Winston, of the North Carolina Superior Court, W. W. Fuller, New York, are illustrations. The school has had other fine talent in its teaching force besides the principals. Among the teachers have been A. F. Redd, Porter Paisley, J. A. Fishburne, W. R. Webb, and Thomas J. Drewry.[1]

For some time the faculty has been composed of six members. These are in every case well trained. The instructors for 1897–1898 are: J. C. Horner, A. M., Latin, Mathematics; C. J. Moore, B. S. (V. M. I.), Mathematics, Natural Science; J. M. Horner, B. A., B. D., (Johns Hopkins, General Theological Seminary), Greek, English Grammar; W. T. Shannonhouse, B. A. (University of Virginia), Latin, Mathematics; Miss Nina Horner, Music; S. D. Booth, M. D., and S. H. Cannady, M. D., surgeons.[2] The course of studies in

---
1. Catalogue, 1890–1891, historical sketch; Letters from Principals J. C. and J. M. Horner; The News and Observer, August 21, 1897.
2. Catalogue, 1897–1898.

Latin, Mathematics, Greek, English, Geography, History, Science, is high enough to prepare boys for entrance into any American college. The buildings were enlarged in 1880 and again in 1890, so that eighty boarding and fifty day pupils can be well cared for. The expenses per year amount to $272.00.[1]

### CATAWBA COLLEGE.

This institution belongs to the German Reformed Church of North Carolina. Some points of the early history of this church have already been given. It has had a gradual growth throughout the nineteenth century. In 1889 it had a pastoral charge in Guilford, East Rowan, Catawba, Concord, Central Rowan, Lower Davidson, Hickory, West Rowan, Lincoln, Upper Davidson, St. Paul's Mission, Lincoln Mission, Mt. Tabor Mission and Thomasville. To serve these charges there were fifteen ministers.[2] The ministers of the church have always advocated education, but the circumstances of the members have been such that in many cases these views have not been well carried out. In addition to Catawba College, Claremont College at Hickory, Pilgrim's Academy, Arnold Academy, Hedricks Grove Academy, all in Davidson county, Mt. Hope Academy in Guilford, and Faith Academy in Rowan, belong in part or entirely to this church.[3]

As early as 1828 the Classis of North Carolina was organized, and with this was begun a fund known as the Loretz Beneficiary Fund. From the money of this fund a good many young men were sent North for their education. It was a long distance to go and the conveniences of traveling were few. Soon the plan of establishing a

---
1. Catalogue, 1897–1898; Letters from Principals J. C. and J. M. Horner.
2. Proceedings of the Classis of North Carolina, 1889.
3. Letter from President Clapp.

college in North Carolina was proposed. This idea was approved, and by 1851 they had opened Catawba College. Newton, the county seat of Catawba county, was chosen as the best site. Revs. G. H. Crawford, George W. Welker, Jeremiah Ingold, each gave for the buildings $100 out of their salaries, which were only $300 a year. This great generosity caused many others to give; and the buildings were soon erected. This was the first institution of the kind in Western North Carolina and its influence soon spread far and wide. However, financial troubles came in a short while, and the college curriculum and faculty were displaced by a high school equipment; and this condition continued until 1860, when about $25,000 on an endowment fund were secured. The Civil War destroyed this and closed the halls of the high school.[1]

A Rev. Mr. Albert, from Pennsylvania, was the first president. He served one term only, and was followed by H. H. Smith, of New Hampshire, the father of Hon. Hoke Smith, of Atlanta, Georgia. Mr. Smith held the position for four years. A Mr. Smythe, from Maine, was principal 1856–59. Rev. A. S. Vaughn, of Pennsylvania, brought back the college curriculum and raised the $25,000 endowment 1859–60. In 1865 Rev. J. C. Clapp, D. D., reorganized the school under the name of Catawba High School. In 1866 Major Sidney M. Finger came in with him, and remained as teacher of Mathematics and Latin until 1874. From 1874 to the summer of 1885 Mr. Clapp ran it as sole principal. At this date the charter and name of Catawba College were resumed.[2] Dr. Clapp was then elected president, and he still occupies the position. He has been connected with

---

[1]. Church Corinthian. June, 1897; Catalogues, 1890–1897; Letter from President Clapp.

[2]. Letter from President Clapp; Catalogues, 1890–1897; North Carolina State Normal Magazine, June, 1897, p. 102.

the institution so long, that he deserves more than a mere mention. He was born at Clapp's Mill, Guilford county, September 5th, 1832; student under Rev. George W. Welker, D. D., and at Catawba; at Amherst College 1853–57, where he graduated; connected with Catawba College the most of the time since 1859.[1]

The college now has a small endowment fund, about $11,000, a library of fifteen hundred volumes, and a faculty of twelve members. It offers courses almost equal to those of Davidson, Wake Forest and Trinity; A. B. and B. S. degrees are granted to women as well as to men. The annual enrollment for the past seven years has been from one hundred and forty to one hundred and ninety-two. The leading teachers since 1890 have been: Rev. J. C. Clapp, D. D., Mental and Moral Philosophy, Aesthetics, Political Economy, 1890– ; Rev. J. A. Foil, A. M., Ph. D., Mathematics, Natural Science, 1890– ; W. H. Thompson, A. B., Latin, English, 1890–95; W. W. Troup, A. M., Greek, German, History, 1890–92; C. H. Mebane, A. B., present superintendent of Public Instruction of North Carolina, Greek, German, History, 1893–96; I. S. Leiby, German, 1895– ; Rev. P. M. Trexler, D. D., Greek, History, 1897–.[2]

### WEAVERVILLE COLLEGE.

This institution is located in the town of Weaverville, eight miles northwest of Asheville. It was chartered as a college by the legislature of 1872–1873.[3] The property belongs to the Western North Carolina Conference of the Methodist Episcopal Church, South; and the Conference now makes an annual assessment of $1,500 for its support.[4] The college is the outgrowth of the Ma-

---

1. Letter from President Clapp.
2. Catalogues, 1890–1898.
3. Catalogues, 1890–1897.
4. Minutes of the Western North Carolina Conference, 1897, p. 34.

sonic and Sons of Temperance High School, established in 1852. Rev. J. A. Reagan, M. D., was the first principal, and held the position until 1858. Under him the school had an annual enrollment of one hundred pupils. J. H. Colfee was principal 1858–1862, when the doors were closed by the war. A. J. McAlpin and a Mr. Lewis were the principals at different times from 1866 to 1872. At this time the property was given to the Methodist Church and the institution became a college.[1]

Rev. J. A. Reagan, A. M., M. D., was elected the first president of the college. During 1872–1873 the old building was burned, and the school was carried on for a time in the church. By 1875 a new building was ready; and this served for all purposes until 1894, when a still larger and more convenient one was erected. In 1875 Dr. Reagan resigned and Rev. J. S. Kennedy, A. M., D. D., became president. Dr. Kennedy held the presidency for three years; Rev. W. C. McCarthy, A. M., 1878–80; E. M. Goolsby, M. A., 1880–83; Rev. D. Atkins, A. M., D. D., 1883–87; Rev. S. B. Traywick, 1887–88; Rev. J. F. Austin, 1888–89; M. A. Yost, A. M., 1889–.[2] Dr. Reagan has had the longest connection, either as principal, president or professor, of any one in its whole history. He was its real founder and has been its best friend.

Since 1890 the matriculates each year have numbered from one hundred and fifty-five to two hundred and thirty-five. The courses, which lead to A. B. and B. S. degrees, are about the same as those of Guilford, Catawba and Elon, and are open to both sexes. There is also a preparatory department connected with the college. The terms are very low, tuition in the college course for session of eighteen weeks being only $18.00. The faculty

---

1. Letter from Dr. J. A. Reagan.
2. Ibid; Catalogues, 1890–1897.

has always been small. For a long time there were only two teachers besides the president; and during the past six years there have been five with the president. Since 1891 they have been: M. A. Yost, A. M., Ancient and Modern Languages; J. J. Reagan, A. M., Mathematics; J. E. Rheim, A. M., Mental, Moral and Natural Sciences; Mrs. N. B. McDowell, A. M., English, Elocution and preparatory department; Mrs. M. A. Yost, A. M., Music and Art.[1]

### NORTH CAROLINA COLLEGE.

This institution belongs to the Evangelical Lutheran Synod of North Carolina. It is located at Mt. Pleasant, Cabarrus county, nine miles from Concord. It was first opened in 1855 under the name of the Western Carolina Male Academy, and received a charter as North Carolina College January 21st, 1859. Rev. William Gerehard was principal 1855–58; Rev. D. H. Bittle, D. D., president 1858–61, when the college was closed on account of the war. During the period 1861–1867 a private school was kept up most of the time. Since that time the presidents have been: Rev. C. F. Bansemer, D. D., 1867–69; Rev. L. A. Bikle, A. M., acting president, 1869–70; Rev. L. A. Bikle, A. M., 1870–75; Rev. J. B. Davis, D. D., 1875–77; Rev. L. A. Bikle, D. D., 1877–82; Rev. G. D. Bernheim, D. D., 1882–83; Rev. G. F. Shaeffer, 1884–86; Rev. J. G. Schaid, 1887–89; Rev. J. D. Shirey, D. D., 1889–96; Rev. M. G. G. Scherer, A. M., 1896.[2]

The prime movers in the establishment were Revs. J. A. Linn, W. G. Harter and Samuel Rothrock, C. Melchoe, Mathias Barrier, C. A. Heilig and John Shimpoch. Early in its history three buildings were erected,

---

1. Catalogues, 1891–1897.
2. Ibid, 1871–1872, 1892–1897; Letter from President Scherer.

and later another, and they all have a valuation of $15,000. The Synod does not make any annual appropriation, though its members have given $15,000 as an endowment. In addition to this institution, the Lutheran Church has in this State Mount Amoena Female Seminary, Lenoir College, Concordia College at Conover, and several academies. The annual enrollment for some time has been from seventy-five to one hundred. The courses lead to A. B. and B. S. degrees, and they are as high as those of Catawba and most of the other colleges in the State. However, only four or five teachers have been in the faculty at any one time, and they have to do the preparatory work also. The expenses per year are from $85.00 to $137.00. The library has thirty-five hundred volumes. The faculty for the past few years has been: Rev. J. D. Shirey, A. M., Mental and Moral Philosophy; H. T. J. Ludwig, A. M., Ph. D., Mathematics, Astronomy, Physics; E. B. Setzler, A. M., Ancient Languages; Rev. J. H. C. Fisher, A. M., M. A. Boger, A. B., and Rev. P. H. E. Derrick, A. M., principals of the preparatory department; Rev. M. G. G. Scherer, A. M., Mental and Moral Philosophy.[1]

### DAVENPORT COLLEGE.

This school was run as a girls' college from its beginning in 1857 until 1893. At that time it was made coeducational. As early as 1850 the Presbyterians of Caldwell county agitated the movement of establishing a female school at Lenoir. The Presbytery of Concord went so far as to obtain a $10,000 subscription for the building. This plan was never realized by the Presbyterians, and they soon located their school at Statesville. In 1853 the Methodist took up the matter. At the

---

1. Letter from President Scherer; Catalogues, 1892-1897.

Centre Camp Meeting, October, 1855, Rev. Henry Hill Durant presented the subject in strong terms, and a subscription of $12,000 was made. The most liberal givers were: Col. William Davenport, $2,000 at first and later another $1,000; Col. James C. Harper, $1,310; Capt. W. A. Lenoir, $1,200; James Harper, $1,000; Col. E. W. Jones, $750; Uriah Cloyd, $600. With this money they erected a brick structure, at a cost of $9,800, purchased sixteen acres of land and furniture. In 1857 the stockholders offered the whole property to the South Carolina Conference. The Conference accepted the offer, appointed trustees, and elected Rev. H. M. Mood, A. M., president.[1]

Mr. Mood began to make preparations for the opening. He asked the trustees to erect a boarding house. This they agreed to do, and another subscription of $3,000 was taken up. In July, 1858, the school was opened under the name of Davenport Female College. During the first year only fifty-six pupils matriculated. However, Mr. Mood's administration of four years was very successful. He resigned in 1862 and Rev. R. N. Price, of the Holston Conference, succeeded him. Mr. Price remained but one year, and was followed by Rev. A. G. Stacy. When Stoneman's army came toward the close of the war, Mr. Stacy took his school to Shelby, North Carolina. The Federal soldiers occupied the buildings for two days, pillaged and despoiled the library and furniture, and left little but the naked buildings. In 1865 the school was again organized under the temporary charge of Rev. George H. Round. By the Conference of the same year Rev. Samuel A. Weber was elected president, but he resigned in a short while. Rev. Joseph R. Griffith had charge 1866–67, and Rev. Samuel Lander,

---

1. Manuscript of Mr. J. R. Wilson, Lenoir; President W. M. Roby, Centennial of Methodism in North Carolina, pp. 193–200.

A. M., 1867–70. Mr. Lander's term of office was very successful and the college became prosperous. However, when the General Conference of 1870 transferred that section of the State from the South Carolina to the North Carolina Conference, he thought it best to retire. Most of the patronage had been from South Carolina, and it seemed very probable that this change would diminish the numbers greatly.[1]

In December, 1870, Rev. W. M. Robey, D. D., was elected president. When he took hold the buildings needed repairs, and the trustees sent out an agent to collect funds. Only $1,300 were secured, and $625 of this were used in paying the agent's expenses. The college now belonged to the North Carolina Conference and expected the Conference to support it. In this expectation it was much disappointed. Mr. Robey struggled on as best he could, but toward the close of his administration he had but one boarding pupil. In February, 1877, the buildings were burned, and Mr. Robey retired. The trustees at once began to collect money with which to erect a new building. About $3,000 were subscribed in Caldwell county, and the building was begun. In 1881 Rev. George H. Round was elected president, but owing to the unfinished condition of the building he resigned in 1882. Mr. W. H. Sanborn in 1884 leased the property for fifteen years, and ran a fairly successful school until 1889. At that time he was asked to give back the property to the trustees. In June of that year John D. Minick, A. M., became president, and he has kept the school up to the present. By the Conference of 1889 $1,000 were appropriated to repair the building, of which about $625 were collected and expended. Under the present administration there have been five teachers

---

1. President W. M. Robey, Centennial of Methodism in North Carolina, pp. 201-202; Manuscript of Mr. J. R. Wilson.

and about eighty pupils. Since the war the patronage has been for the most part local. However, the institution has had a considerable influence on that section, and throughout its trials and successes it has had an interesting history.[1]

### LOUISBURG FEMALE COLLEGE.

This institution is located in the town of Louisburg. It was chartered in 1857. However, it had been running as a small school since 1845. Mr. A. H. Ray was in charge from 1845 to 1856. His building was small until the present commodious one was erected in 1855–1857. Mr. J. P. Nelson was president 1857–58; Columbus Andrews, 1858–61; James Southgate, 1861–65. It was closed by the war, and was not reopened until Dr. T. M. Jones removed Greensboro Female College to the building in January, 1866. Dr. Jones had about two hundred boarding pupils, the largest number the institution has ever had. In June, 1869, he went to Warrenton. Rev. F. L. Reid, D. D., was president 1877–78. From this until 1889 the college was closed, and a high school was run in the building. Among the teachers of this period of high school work were W. B. Doub and B. W. Ray. Mr. S. D. Bagley reopened it as a college in 1889 and kept it for five years. Rev. J. A. Green was president 1894–1896, and Mathew S. Davis from 1896 to the present. It has been run under the care of the Methodist Church, though the church has given nothing to its support. For some time the property has in theory belonged to a stock company of Louisburg. Mr. Washington Duke is the real owner by virtue of money loaned by him to the school. It had gone down very much

---

1. Catalogues, 1872–1873, 1893–1897; Manuscript of Mr. J. R. Wilson; Journal of the North Carolina Conference, 1889, p. 37; Dowd's Prominent Living North Carolinians, pp. 192–194.

when Mr. Green was in charge, but during the past year under Mr. Davis and his daughter the patronage has again increased. The faculty for the past nine years has been composed of about seven teachers.[1]

### STATESVILLE FEMALE COLLEGE.

This institution was established by the Concord Presbytery in 1857. As to who were the first principals the writer has not found out. Rev. J. M. M. Caldwell took charge some time during the war and ran it till he came to Greensboro in 1868. From 1868 to 1872 Rev. E. F. Rockwell, A. M., D. D., was president. Mrs. Elizabeth N. Grant and Miss Margaret E. Mitchell, daughters of Prof. Elisha Mitchell, of the University of North Carolina, were in charge from 1873 to 1884; and it was during this time that the school won its reputation. In 1885 Miss Fannie Everitt assumed control and maintained its reputation, but she retired in 1894. From that till 1896 it was closed. In the fall of 1896 John B. Burwell, A. M., became president. The college has again begun to manifest life and influence. The property is now worth $30,000. He has a faculty of nine teachers, and has offered a course of studies best suited to the training of girls at very low terms. He has had one of the largest experiences in female education of any living North Carolinian. He was co-principal of the Charlotte Female Institute for ten years and principal of Peace Institute for eighteen.[2]

### RUTHERFORD COLLEGE.

This institution is unique among the schools of North Carolina. It has been the college of one man, Rev.

---

[1]. Letter from President M. S. Davis; Catalogues, 1893-1897; Dr. Jones' Journal; Manuscript sketch of Dr. Reid.
[2]. Letter from Mr. S. C. Caldwell, Tallahassee, Florida; Semi-Centennial catalogue of Davidson College, p. 15; Letter from President J. B. Burwell; Catalogues, 1896-1898; Dowd's Prominent Living North Carolinians, pp. 212-213; North Carolina Teacher, May, 1885.

Robert L. Abernethy, D. D. It was begun as a private school in 1854, and so it has remained to the present. Mr. John Rutherford gave six hundred acres of forest land, ten miles east of Morganton, in 1853; and on this Mr. Abernethy opened his school. In 1858 it was chartered as Rutherford Academy. In 1861 its name was changed to Rutherford Seminary and power was given to grant degrees. It continued under this name until 1870, when it was made a college. The first building was a double log cabin. Soon this was replaced by a larger structure. From its beginning to 1890 the institution was very flourishing. At that time the building was destroyed by fire, and since troubles have come thick and fast. This fire, the debt incurred in erecting the present building and the death of the great founder soon afterwards, have almost taken away the very existence of the school. William E. Abernethy, A. M., assumed the presidency upon the death of his father. Several times during the past seven years it seemed that Rutherford College would be no longer except in memory.[1]

Dr. R. L. Abernethy was its head for about forty years; and though he did not maintain a school of much scholarship, still he made himself one of the greatest characters in our whole educational history. He was born in Lincoln county, North Carolina, April 3rd, 1822; educated himself; a member of the South Carolina Conference; given A. M. by Trinity College 1880, and D. D. by Alfred University, New York; died November 28th, 1894. During his term of office about four thousand students matriculated, of whom as many as fifteen hundred paid no tuition. He made money, but he gave it away, and died poor. His whole life had been wrapped up in his school, still he had to leave this $1,500 in debt.[2]

---

1. Catalogues, 1874, 1884, 1892, 1893-1897.
2. Catalogue, 1892-1893, 1895-1896; Dowd's Prominent Living North Carolinians, pp 207-209; Letter from President W. E. Abernethy.

## MOUNT AMOENA FEMALE SEMINARY.

The idea of having a college for women was discussed by the Synod of the Lutheran Church as early as 1860. Even before this date Rev. George F. Schaeffer and Mrs. D. H. Bittle had a high school for girls in Mt. Pleasant. The war interfered with the plan, and nothing was done toward founding the college until 1868. At the Synod of that year Rev. G. D. Bernheim, D. D., who had been conducting a school in Mt. Pleasant, offered to turn over his property to the church. The Synod accepted the offer and appointed Dr. Bernheim financial agent. He soon secured enough money to pay off the indebtedness on the buildings. When the property was given over to the Synod it was worth about $3,500; since that improvements have given it a value of $5,000.[1]

Dr. Bernheim remained agent but one year. Rev. D. I. Dreher followed him in 1869 and served till his death in 1870. W. A. Barrier was principal 1870-72; Misses H. V. and M. Ribble, 1872-74; Rev. P. A. Strobel, 1874-75; L. H. Rothrock, 1875-82; Rev. G. F. Schaeffer, 1882-84; Rev. J. A. Linn, 1884-92; Rev. C. L. T. Fisher, 1892-97; Rev. H. N. Miller, Ph. D., 1897.[2] These principals have been assisted by from eight to ten teachers. They have offered about the usual courses for girls in North Carolina schools of this kind, and do not charge but $150 per year for board and tuition in all subjects. Their patronage has been from several Southern States, though in the main from the Carolinas; and for the past few years the annual enrollment has been one hundred.[3]

---

1. Letter from Rev. J. H. C. Fisher; the Mount Amoenian. September-October, 1897.
2. Letters from Revs. J. H. C. Fisher and H. N. Miller; the Mount Amoenian, September-October, 1897.
3. Catalogues, 1894-1897; letter from Mr. Fisher.

## PEACE INSTITUTE.

This school was opened at Raleigh in 1872. It is claimed by some that it had its beginning at Hillsboro in 1837. It is true that Rev. Robert Burwell, D. D., began a school for girls at Hillsboro at that early date, and that he taught there until 1857, when he went to Charlotte and established the Charlotte Female Institute. It is also true that after teaching in Charlotte for fifteen years, ten of which he had been associated with his son, Capt. John B. Burwell, he moved to Raleigh in 1872, and that he and his son became the first principals of Peace Institute. It is better, however, to place the date of the beginning of this school in 1872, and to mention the teaching of the Burwells elsewhere in its proper place, as has been done.[1]

It was the original intention that this be a school of the Presbyterian Church. Rev. Joseph M. Atkinson, D. D., pastor of the Presbyterian Church of Raleigh, was a strong advocate of this idea. Mr. William Peace, of Raleigh, offered to give $10,000, and others gave smaller amounts. The institution was incorporated in 1857, and the building was begun. The war came and put an end to the enterprise for the time. The building, which was only partly finished, was used by the Confederates as a hospital for three years; and after the war the Federals used it for a freedman's bureau. Then the money subscribed could not be collected and for some time it seemed as if the whole affair would fall through. However, a new subscription was taken and the property was mortgaged to secure money with which to complete the building. This was finished and ready for occupancy by 1872; and it was constructed of brick,

---

1. Letters from Principal Dinwiddie, and Capt. J. B. Burwell; the North Carolina University Magazine, February, 1894.

four stories high, and contained parlors, library, music rooms, recitation rooms, an art studio, fifty-seven bedrooms. The buildings and grounds were worth about $60,000. In 1872 the property was leased to Rev. Robert Burwell, D. D., and Capt. John B. Burwell, A. M. In September of that year the first term was begun. So that from its beginning it has been run as a private institution.[1]

The Burwells had had fine success at Charlotte, and soon the institute became prosperous. They secured a fine faculty, among whom were S. J. Stevens of Mathematics and Natural Sciences and A. Bauman of Music. They enrolled during the year 1872–1873 one hundred and four pupils, and from that on the number increased each year. They entered into the work as a private affair, to educate as well as possible and to make as much money as they could. In 1875 Rev. Robert Burwell retired as co-principal and Capt. John B. Burwell was sole principal until 1889. At that time he sold his interest to James Dinwiddie, A. M., and retired to his country home. During his administration the institution won a high place and its patronage came from the whole South.[2]

Prof. Dinwiddie has had a long and valuable experience in school work. He graduated at Hampden-Sidney College 1858 and at the University of Virginia 1861; professor of Mathematics in the South Western Presbyterian University for ten years; professor of the same in the University of Tennessee; founder of Central Female Institute, Gordonsville, Virginia. During his management of Peace Institute there has been an average annual enrollment of one hundred and sixty-six. He has nine teachers in the literary department, two in Art and

---

[1]. Our Living and Our Dead. Vol. III., pp. 313–316; Letters from Capt. J. B. Burwell; The North Carolina University Magazine, February, 1894; The North Carolina Journal of Education, August, 1875.

[2]. Ibid.

six in Music. The advertised courses are as high as those of any of the female schools of the State. The expenses for half year are: board, English tuition and Latin $100; washing $7.50; medical fee $5.00; Greek, French or German, each $10.00; Music $25.00-$35.00; Art $20.00-$25.00; Elocution $10.00-$20.00; subjects in the Business Course, each $15.00-$20.00.[1]

### CLAREMONT COLLEGE.

This school for women was established at Hickory in 1880. While a good many of its builders were of the German Reformed Church, still it is under an independent board of trustees and is run as a non-sectarian institution. The property is valued at $30,000; and this was purchased for the most part by H. W. Robinson, W. P. Reinhardt, A. Shuford, R. B. Davis, J. G. Hall, M. L. McCorkle, and Dr. Ingold. They have offered extensive collegiate courses, upon the completion of which an A. B., L. B., or S. B. degree is given. There is also a preparatory department. The expenses per term in the college courses amount to $75.00, German, French, Music or Art being extra and at a cost of $20.00 each. The faculty for some time has been composed of nine teachers; and the annual enrollment has been from one hundred to one hundred and fifty. The presidents have been: Rev. A. S. Vaughn, Mrs. V. R. Bonney, A. C. Hottenstein, W. H. Sanborn, Rev. J. L. Murphy and S. P. Hatton.[2]

### LITTLETON FEMALE COLLEGE.

Very little has been found out about this school. It seems to have had very little history. The writer has

---

[1] Letter from Principal Dinwiddie; Catalogues, 1893-1897; The North Carolina University Magazine, February, 1894.

[2] Letter from President Hatton; Catalogues, 1896-1898.

again and again written to President Rhodes for information, but with one exception he has shown his supreme indifference. He is either ashamed of the record he has made for his school or has a queer idea of common courtesy. The institution was first chartered in 1883 under the name of Central Female Institute. Under this name it ran for about four years. Rev. J. M. Rhodes, A. M., was its principal. He then ran the Henderson Female College for a short while. After this he came back to Littleton and established the Littleton Female College; and since then he has been the president and for the most part the owner. He has erected a good building, and has given some of the stock to the North Carolina Conference. However, the school still remains largely under his control. For some time he has had a faculty of nine teachers, all ladies, and has secured a patronage of from seventy-five to one hundred and six pupils. His advertised courses are about as high as those of most of the girls' schools already considered. His expenses per term are: board, washing, fuel, lights and tuition in English course and languages, $75.00; Instrumental Music $20.00; Voice $20.00; Art. each subject from $5.00 to $20.00.[1]

## ST. MARY'S COLLEGE.

This is the only Catholic college south of Maryland, except the one at Mobile, Alabama. In 1876 Rev. Fr. Herman Wolf and some Benedictine brothers came to Gaston county from St. Vincent Abbey in Pennsylvania. They located at Belmont, eleven miles southwest of Charlotte, and at once began to work. By 1878 these Benedictine Fathers at the solicitation of Cardinal Gibbons

---

1. The North Carolina Teacher, May, 1895; Catalogues, 1890-1898; Catalogue of Henderson Female College, 1888; Journal of the North Carolina Conference. 1897. pp. 45-46.

began the erection of a college building. In 1881 the first graduate was sent out, Hugh McHugh; and from 1882 to 1896 eighty-nine more have gone forth. There is a monastery connected with the college, and this was raised to an abbey by Pope Leo XIII. in 1885. At the same time Rev. Leo Haid was elected first abbot, and since then St. Mary's College has been under his personal supervision.[1]

The buildings and church are now worth about $140,000. Some of this was obtained from donations, but a large part came from tuition and board. On April 1st, 1886, the institution received a charter with all the privileges of a North Carolina college or university. The courses now offered are: preparatory, commercial, classical and divinity. There have been for some time fourteen teachers; and these are all priests or clergymen in Holy orders. The annual enrollment for the past four years has been almost one hundred. While the college was established for the training of Catholic young men in the South, still all denominations can enter and take the college courses. The institution has no endowment fund, hence expenses are high.[2]

### ELON COLLEGE.

This institution belongs to the Christian Church. It was opened September 2nd, 1890, and is located on the North Carolina Railroad, five miles west of Burlington. While it is a young institution and belongs to a church that is by no means large, still it has had a rapid and sure growth. A few points of the history of this church will help explain the circumstances of the college. The church goes back to the Baltimore Confer-

---

[1]. J. S. Bassett's A North Carolina Monastery, Magazine of American History, 1898, XXIX.; Letter from Vice-President F. Bernard, O. S. B.; Gastonia Gazette, April 8, 1897.
[2]. Ibid; Catalogues, 1894-1897.

ence of the Methodist Episcopal Church in 1792 for its origin. At that meeting Rev. James O'Kelly revolted against the tyranny of the Bishop; and he and about thirty other members sent in their resignation. In 1793 Mr. O'Kelly and several others who had withdrawn from the Conference held a convention in Manakin Town, North Carolina. At this place they organized under the name of Republican Methodists. The next year this opposition party held their meeting at Lebanon Church, Surry county, Virginia, and it was here that the name Christian was first assumed.[1]

In the beginning of this century there was a similar revolt against the tyranny of the Synods and Conventions of the Presbyterians and Baptists. These revolters also assumed the name of Christians. From that time on they have grown, though slowly. The church now has in the whole of the United States about 130,000 members, of whom the South has 25,000, 1,550 ministers, ten colleges and several high schools. In 1818 the first regular convention was held at Holy Neck, Virginia, and in 1819 this convention was named the Eastern Virginia Conference. The North Carolina and Virginia Conference was organized a little later. This church has thoroughly believed in education, and that too of both sexes alike. Among its best schools in the North are: Union Christian College, Marion, Indiana; Antioch College, Yellow Springs, Ohio; Starkey Seminary, Eddytown, New York. The three leading ones in the South have been: Graham Institute, founded in 1852; Suffolk Collegiate Institute, 1872; and Elon College.[2]

Elon College is the outgrowth of Graham Institute. This was established at Graham in 1852. It was carried

---

1. Hurley's Christians Not Disciples, pp. 9-36; The Christian Annual and Almanac, 1896; The Centennial Christian Sun, December 6, 1894.

2. Hurley's Christians Not Disciples, pp. 9-86; The Christian Annual and Almanac, 1892-1896; Christian Sun, December 6, 1894.

on with much success by Revs. J. R. Holt, A. G. Anderson, Job Swift, Mr. Archibald Ray, Rev. W. H. Doherty and Col. T. H. Brame, to 1861. During the war the school was closed and the property sold. Rev. W. S. Long, A. M., reopened the school in 1865, and soon afterwards purchased the property. Rev. D. A. Long, D. D., LL. D., bought it in 1875. In 1880 it was chartered as Graham Normal College. In 1883 Dr. D. A. Long became president of Antioch College, and Rev. W. S. Long, A. M., D. D., again became principal. He kept up the institution as a private affair until June 10th, 1887, when the property was leased to the Convention of the Christian Church, South. At a General Convention of the church in 1888 it was decided to choose another location and to erect larger buildings. The site was chosen in 1888, and a charter secured March 11th, 1889. The first brick was laid May 20th, 1889, and by August 1st, 1890 the buildings were finished.[1]

The college exercises began September 2nd, 1890. Dr. W. S. Long was elected the first president, and he held this position with much success until June, 1894. Rev. W. W. Staley, A. M., D. D., became his successor; and is still president in name, though in reality the administration is carried on by Rev. J. O. Atkinson. The courses offered lead to Ph. B., A. B., and A. M. degrees; and they are high enough to admit students into the Senior class at the University of the State. These are open to young women as well as men. The faculty has been composed of from seven to ten members. The male members have been: Rev. W. S. Long, A. M., D. D., Moral Philosophy, Biblical Instruction and Social Sciences, 1890–94; Rev. J. U. Newman, A. M., Ph. D., Greek, Mathematics, 1890– ; Rev. J. O. Atkinson, A. M.,

---

1. Catalogue of Graham Normal College, 1883–1884; Catalogues, 1890–1898; The North Carolina Teacher, September, 1887.

Latin, Moral Science, 1890–; E. L. Moffitt, A. M., English, French, German, 1890–95; S. A. Holleman, Ph. B., preparatory department 1890–94, Mathematics, 1894–; R. G. Kendrick, A. M., adjunct of Latin and German, 1892; Herbert Scholz, A. B., adjunct of English and Political Science, 1892; J. M. Bandy, A. M., Mathematics, 1893; W. P. Lawrence, Ph. B., English, 1894–; Rev. W. C. Wicker, M. A., Natural Science, preparatory department, 1897.[1]

### LENOIR COLLEGE.

This school was opened at Hickory September 1st, 1891, and for one year was known as Highland College. There had been an academy on the same site for some time, and the college used the old building for a short while. Col. Walter W. Lenoir gave the site and grounds near by, and the college assumed his name. In 1892 the trustees erected a large brick structure, two stories high, 100x125 feet. On January 4th of the same year the institution was incorporated and granted the usual powers of North Carolina colleges. Rev. R. A. Yoder, A. M., became the first president, and he still serves in this capacity.[2]

He has placed around himself a faculty of from five to nine teachers. The institution offers primary, preparatory, collegiate, theological and music departments, and grants A. B. and B. S. degrees. The annual number of matriculates for the seven years of its existence has been from one hundred and three to one hundred and seventy, and these have been of both sexes. The principal teachers have been: Rev. R. A. Yoder, A. M., Psychology, Logic; Rev. J. C. Moser, D. D., Latin; Rev.

---

1. Catalogues, 1890–1898.
2. The Educator, Hickory, February, 1898; Letter from President Yoder; Catalogues, 1892–1897.

A. L. Crouse, A. M., German, Theology; Rev. W. P. Cline, Ph. B., Science, History; Rev. J. P. Miller, A. B., Greek, English; Rev. R. L. Fritz, A. M., Mathematics. Taken as a whole it is one of the finest institutions of learning in Western North Carolina. It is under the management of the Tennessee Synod of the Evangelical Lutheran Church, and is distinctly a Christian college.[1]

### ELIZABETH COLLEGE.

This is the only real college for women in North Carolina. Whether it can succeed with such extensive courses can not yet be said. It opened in October, 1897, and is located in Charlotte. It was established and built for the most part by the Lutheran Church. It has a plant worth $75,000. The city of Charlotte gave the site and $10,000 on the building. The building is one of the finest and best adapted in the whole State. The original contract for the naked structure called for $48,790; and this did not include the engine, dynamo and stained glass windows. The college courses lead to A. B., B. S., and B. L. degrees; and for those who can not stand the entrance examinations to the Freshman class there is a preparatory department. The advertised courses are as high as those of the best boys' colleges in the State.[2]

The faculty have all had fine training, in most cases having been University students: Rev. C. B. King, A. M., president, Moral Philosophy; Rev. C. L. T. Fischer, A. M., vice-president, Greek; Julia E. Painter, Ph. D., English; Rev. R. L. Fritz, A. M., Mathematics, Astronomy; A. W. Fogle, A. M., Ancient Languages; D. F. Culler, A. M., German, French, Italian, Spanish; Edwin B. Setzler, A. M., Natural and Political Sciences;

---

1. The Educator, Hickory, February, 1893; Letter from President Yoder; Catalogues, 1892-1897.
2. Catalogue, 1897-1898; Charlotte Observer, May 20, 1897.

Julia L. Abbott, Ph. D., History, Intellectual Sciences; Erie Caldwell, Elocution, Physical Culture; W. M. Montgomery, commercial department; C. Aldyth Cline, preparatory department; Friedrich Carl E. Cranz, M. Ruth McLinn, and Blanche L. Rueckert, Music; Bettie V. Alexander, Art.[1]

### THE BAPTIST FEMALE UNIVERSITY.

This is located at Raleigh. It is the intention of the church to make it the equal of Wake Forest College. Work has been going on for the past three years, still it is by no means ready to open. Thirty-three thousand dollars have been spent on the building, and $15,000 or $20,000 more will be required to finish it. Rev. O. L. Stringfield is the financial agent, and he is pushing the work as rapidly as possible. The last Baptist Convention at Oxford pledged $5,004. The people of Raleigh are now taking up the matter, and plans are being matured by which the city can furnish the money necessary for its completion.[2]

1. Catalogue, 1897-1898; Charlotte Observer, May 20, 1897.
2. Circular of the Agent; the News and Observer, December 19, 1897, and January 26, 1898.

NOTE.—This pamphlet is made up of reprints taken at each issue of THE COLLEGE MESSAGE. There has been no opportunity to make corrections. Some of the errors are due to the author as writer and proof-reader; and some can be laid to the printer. The whole work was written in the spare time of five busy months and many a time the proof had to be read in a hurry. Circumstances, over which the author has no control, have necessitated that the last chapter (conclusions) be left off.                                                 C. L. R.

www.ingramcontent.com/pod-product-compliance
Lightning Source LLC
Chambersburg PA
CBHW031729230426
43669CB00007B/301